FROM BULLETS TO BALLOTS

FROM BULLETS TO BALLOTS

Violent Muslim Movements in Transition

David L. Phillips

Transaction Publishers
New Brunswick (U.S.A.) and London (U.K.)

Copyright © 2009 by Transaction Publishers, New Brunswick, New Jersey.

All rights reserved under International and Pan-American Copyright Conventions. No part of this book may be reproduced or transmitted in any form or by any means, electronic or mechanical, including photocopy, recording, or any information storage and retrieval system, without prior permission in writing from the publisher. All inquiries should be addressed to Transaction Publishers, Rutgers—The State University of New Jersey, 35 Berrue Circle, Piscataway, New Jersey 08854-8042. www.transactionpub.com

This book is printed on acid-free paper that meets the American National Standard for Permanence of Paper for Printed Library Materials.

Library of Congress Catalog Number: 2008012709
ISBN: 978-1-4128-0795-1
Printed in the United States of America

Library of Congress Cataloging-in-Publication Data

Phillips, David L.
    From bullets to ballots : violent Muslim movements in transition /
    David L. Phillips.
        p. cm.
    Includes bibliographical references and index.
    ISBN 978-1-4128-0795-1 (alk. paper)
    1. Islamic countries—Politics and government—21st century. 2. Political participation—Islamic countries. 3. Democratization—Islamic countries. 4. Radicals—Islamic countries. 5. Islamic fundamentalism—Political aspects. 6. Nonviolence—Islamic countries. 7. Political parties—Islamic countries. 8. Islam and politics. I. Title.

JQ1852.A91P443 2008
322.4'2091767—dc22   2008012709

To my beloved daughters Tara and Maya:
May all parents discover what it means to leave the world
a better place than they found it.

Contents

Foreword

This book by David Phillips is an important resource for understanding the transformation of violent movements into political parties or social organizations. His topic is one in which I have personal experience. For many decades, I was a figure in East Timor's national liberation struggle and now am a public servant of my people.

Just as my generation was consumed by the fight against colonialism, countering religious extremism will be the defining struggle of the twenty-first century. Violence in God's name is more than perplexing. Indiscriminate targeting of civilians is abhorrent. The resulting cycle of deadly violence is all the more intense when secular leaders fear the imposition of religious law. Religious extremists not only want the mantle of power in their own country. They also envision a worldwide revolution based on religious doctrine.

In his writing, Phillips brings to bear several decades of work on behalf of international social justice. He recognizes the legitimacy of resistance by oppressed peoples; appreciates and understands the frustration that arises when social and economic development is constrained; and understands the anger that results from the denial of political rights. *From Bullets to Ballots* is, however, unique in focusing on Muslim movements that become radicalized when their aspirations for human fulfillment are denied.

This book offers a critique of U.S. policy that, since 9/11, has been dominated by a national security paradigm rather than a coherent approach to international relations aimed at addressing popular grievances that are the root cause of conflict. More than analysis, *From Bullets to Ballots* is prescriptive. It proposes practical remedies that go beyond confrontation and coercion to include an agenda for international cooperation that can help win the battle of ideas so that tolerance, pluralism and an open-society may prevail.

We are indebted to David Phillips for his thought provoking assessment and his comprehensive recommendations on the way forward.

Diplomats, humanists and students will all be enriched by the thoughtful content of these pages.

José Ramos-Horta
Dili, East Timor (January 2008)

Mr. Ramos-Horta received of the Nobel Prize for Peace in 1996 and currently serves as President of East Timor.

Introduction

Terror and sensational violence are not new. They have always been a part of conflict. In the thirteenth century, Mongol hordes swept across Asia massacring civilians, using prisoners as human shields, and stacking the skulls of their victims in huge pyramids. Many perished during the Crusades and the European wars of religion. The Nazi death camps, Cambodia's killing fields, Bosnia's ethnic cleansing, and Rwanda's slaughter of ethnic Tutsis are more recent examples. Saddam Hussein's chemical weapons attacks against the Kurds and America's nuclear strikes on Hiroshima and Nagasaki were also state-sponsored acts of terror deliberately targeting innocent civilians.

During the twentieth century, terror morphed into a tactic of non-state liberation movements struggling against colonialism and occupation. Some employed random and indiscriminate violence. Others, like the African National Congress (ANC) and the Irish Republican Army (IRA), used violence in order to force repressive regimes to the negotiating table. With the onset of political engagement, these groups abandoned ideology opting to pursue a pragmatic political path. The ANC's Nelson Mandela explained, "It was only when all else had failed, when all channels of peaceful protest had been barred to us, that the decision was made to embark on violent forms of political struggle. Formation of the military wing was purely a defensive action against the violence of apartheid. We expressed the hope that a climate conducive to a negotiated settlement would be created soon, so there would no longer be need for armed struggle."[1]

The definition of terror and the tactics used by terror groups are always evolving. Today's greatest challenge is terror committed in God's name by groups that use the Holy Qur'an to justify violence. *From Bullets to Ballots* considers extremist Muslim movements abandoning violence at different stages and pursuing their goals through political processes. Some have successfully made the transition. Others are in mid-stream. Some have tried but backtracked, splintered, or simply abandoned ef-

1

forts to partake in politics. *From Bullets to Ballots* offers case studies of the Muslim Brotherhood of Egypt, Hamas, Hezbollah, the Kurdistan Workers Party, the Free Aceh Movement, and the Jammu and Kashmir Liberation Front, considers the historical and national context of these movements and offers a multi-national, multi-region view that includes but is not limited to the Middle East. Each organization's origin, structure, and leadership are assessed. Financing, operations, and their communications strategies are examined. *From Bullets to Ballots* evaluates each organization's commitment to elections and acceptance of the responsibility that comes with governance. The link between political participation and ideological trends is discussed. The role of patrons and international actors is evaluated. Each chapter concludes with recommendations aimed at facilitating the group's transition from violence to politics.

I have selected these groups because they are undergoing internal debates on the efficacy of political participation. Profiles are detailed, but the book's format does not permit a comprehensive approach. Other violent Muslim movements, such as Jemaah Islamiyah in Southeast Asia, are not included. Their leaders are not yet debating a transition to politics. Al Qaeda is also omitted. Al Qaeda and its ilk will never change. They have no political agenda, just a fanatical hatred that drives them to murder so-called non-believers as well as Muslims who do not subscribe to their brand of Sunni Islam. Such groups must be defeated and their leaders eliminated.

The September 11 attacks established terror as the defining issue of our times. A shocked world looked to the United States for wisdom and leadership. President George W. Bush focused on a traditional security response, affirming that the war on terror could not be won on the defensive. He promulgated a Doctrine of Preemption that maintained America's right to attack potential foes before they could attack the United States.[2] According to Bush, "We must take the battle to the enemy, disrupt his plans, and confront the worst threats before they emerge. In the world we have entered, the only path to safety is the oath of action. And this nation will act."[3] "For as long as whole regions of the world simmer in resentment and tyranny, violence will gather. It is the policy of the United States to seek and support the growth of democratic movements and institutions in every nation and every culture, with the ultimate goal of ending tyranny in the world."[4] America's military response was predictable, but military action alone has proved ineffective in meeting the challenge of shadowy groups with no territory or nation to defend.

While it is important to be steely-eyed when confronting terror, draining the swamp must be based on a deeper understanding of the disenfranchisement that gives rise to despair and the conditions that delude individuals into believing that sensational violence serves their cause. *From Bullets to Ballots* considers a range of responses to Muslim extremists who scorn liberalism, reject the political path and instead pursue pathological violence to advance their goals.

The book begins from the premise that democracy is essential to the realization of U.S. foreign policy and global interests. Democracies do not fight wars against each other, nor do they engage in terrorism or produce refugees. They also make more reliable allies and better trading partners. Democracy has proven to be the best system of governance to realize universal human aspirations for freedom and to support human development. Decades of experience with democracy assistance has yielded some guiding principles. They proceed from the recognition that America's role in democracy assistance should always be to stand behind, not in front of democracy movements. The United States must avoid arrogance and tread softly. Leaving a heavy footprint alienates allies, foments further violence and undermines local initiative.

Thus the United States missed a golden opportunity after 9/11. Backed by sympathy for Al Qaeda's victims, America's action against the Taliban was supported as legally and morally justified by Muslims and others worldwide. They welcomed America's pledge to democratize and rebuild Afghanistan, but the Bush administration's failure to expend the required resources gave rise to doubt about the sincerity of America's commitment.

The debacle in Iraq made matters worse. Attacking Iraq was seen by the Muslim world as part of an imperial strategy to control the country's oil wealth and occupy "Muslim lands."[6] Using democracy to justify the U.S. occupation convinced detractors that democracy promotion was merely a Trojan horse for toppling governments hostile to U.S. interests. Instead of catalyzing democracy and human development in the Middle East, the Iraq War had the unintended consequence of bolstering radical Islam and emboldening America's enemies. It helped inspire a new generation of "holy warriors" from the Maghreb and countries such as Yemen, Sudan, and Somalia who flocked to Iraq for armed struggle against the United States.

The United States further compounded problems by neglecting the Israeli-Palestinian peace process.[7] As Mahmoud Labadi explains, "Western carelessness and inability to settle this painful conflict and alleviate the suffering of the Palestinians casts Western governments as accomplices in the eyes of Arabs and Muslims. Such an attitude generates feelings of victimization and fury, and creates fertile ground for extremism. It also constitutes a source of religious fundamentalism and Muslim extremism."[8] The spiral of anti-Americanism continued because the Muslim world is convinced that the United States is not serious about Middle East peace.

Distrust of the United States has been exacerbated by America's support for corrupt, tyrannical and, in the eyes of devout Muslims, impious regimes. Bush criticized the Egyptian and Saudi rulers but then turned a blind eye when they locked up pro-democracy advocates and closed independent media. For all Bush's talk about democracy, Muslims wonder why he ignores the tyranny of their leaders. Many concluded that the United States cares much more about its narrow definition of America's national interest than it does for lofty ideals of human rights and democracy.

Watching extremist and violence-prone groups such as Hamas in Palestine or Hezbollah in Lebanon causes even the most enthusiastic pro-democracy advocate to ask: Which groups can be influenced and what is the most effective way of going about it? Has the Bush administration's approach to democracy promotion unleashed forces that increase the likelihood of conflict? Do violent groups participate in elections because they genuinely embrace democracy or are they using the ballot to gain power and advance their fanatical views?

Today extremism is on the rise. Its proponents promote their violent agenda by highlighting the hypocrisy of U.S. policies. To recruit, they capitalize on the intellectual and cultural isolation of Muslims as well as the waste of human resources in the Muslim world where education is scarce and poverty widespread. To compel sacrifice, they appeal to the injured pride of Muslims arising from contradictions between Islam's glorious past and today's woeful development deficits. For centuries—and to this day—embittered Muslims resent Western imperialism, colonialism, and their perceived inferiority to the West.

From Bullets to Ballots offers a global template with a combination of strategies aimed at transforming groups from violence to politics. For each group, a different balance between confrontation, coercion, and cooperation is required. Policy options must be nimble in response to ever-changing conditions. I, too, had to be flexible in writing this manuscript. In more than one instance I rewrote sections that were overtaken by dramatic events such as the Israel-Lebanon War or the spiral of deadly violence between Hamas and Fatah in Palestine.

Though recommendations are primarily offered to U.S. policymakers, *From Bullets to Ballots* should also be of interest to diplomats from other countries, representatives of international organizations, scholars and students. It draws on my experience working for twenty years on democratization and conflict prevention in the Middle East, the Balkans, the Caucasus, and South Asia. I hope this book informs a more effective approach to addressing the rise of violent Muslim movements. It will take generations to restore goodwill and overcome recent mistakes. Revitalizing the democracy agenda—and getting it right—must be a priority for future U.S. administrations.

David L. Phillips
New York City
March 1, 2008

Notes

1. Nelson Mandela. "The Sacred Warrior." *Time Magazine*. December 31, 1999. p. 124.
2. Adopted on September 20, 2002.
3. George W. Bush, remarks made at the United States Military Academy, West Point, New York, June 1, 2002.
4. Inauguration Speech by President George W. Bush. January 21, 2005.
5. Lincoln A. Mitchell and David L. Phillips. "Enhancing Democracy Assistance." The National Committee on American Foreign Policy, the Atlantic Council of the United States and the Arnold A. Saltzman Institute of War and Peace Studies at Columbia University. January 2008.
6. Dan Murphy. *The Christian Science Monitor*. "Al-Qaeda and the West: it's about policies."
7. The State of Israel official position is that the Territories are "Disputed" territories, rather than "Occupied" because: (1) the Territories were part of the British Mandate, (2) the Arab states rejected the 1947 partition plan, (3) no attempt was made to establish a Palestinian state between 1949 and 1967, (4) the Geneva Conventions relating to occupied territories applies only to sovereign territories captured from a signatory to the conventions, and (5) Israel took control of the Territories as a result of a *defensive war*.
   In general, the Israeli Supreme Court of Justice has held that Israel holds the Territories in "Belligerent Occupation," thereby limiting the application of the IV Geneva Convention, to the extend adopted by the Israeli government on an humanitarian basis, rather than a legal obligation. The International Community, with the limited exception of the United States in some cases, but including the International Court of Justice, position is that the Territories are "Occupied" territories because: (1) they were captured by force of arms and against the will of their population, (2) the residents in those areas were stateless, and (3) Israel has

put the Territories under military rather than civilian administration, creating *de facto* state of occupation.

8.   Mahmoud Labadi. "Democratization of the Middle East." *Palestine Times*. February 6, 2007. p. 7.

1

The Muslim Brotherhood of Egypt

The *Al Salam,* an aged Egyptian passenger ferry, left Saudi Arabia on February 3, 2006. When it sank in the Red Sea a little after midnight, more than 1,000 passengers drowned in the dark waters. It took hours before the Egyptian navy launched a search-and-rescue operation. As news surfaced about the accident, family members flocked to the Egyptian seaside port of Hurghada. Desperate for news, they wandered between the dock, the morgue, and a local hospital. While the Muslim Brotherhood rushed to the port offering water, food, and comfort, President Hosni Mubarak dispatched riot police to quell the restive crowd. Mubarak belatedly offered $5,000 to each family and pledged an investigation. Many Egyptians accused Mubarak's government of being insensitive, incompetent, and corrupt.

History

The Society of Muslim Brothers was founded by Hassan Al Banna in the Suez Canal city of Ismailia in 1928. Inspired by the Prophet's teachings, the Brotherhood today has two million active "Brotherhood followers" (*Ikhwani*) and three million supporters among Egypt's population of 74 million.[1] Though it has not been allowed to register as a political party, legislators sympathetic to the Brotherhood represent the largest opposition group in parliament. The Muslim Brotherhood is more than a national phenomenon in Egypt. It has morphed into a worldwide movement with franchises in about seventy countries.

Egypt's Royal Palace initially tolerated the Brotherhood, using it as a check on the popular Wafd Party. In the 1940s, Al Banna created the "Special Apparatus" a paramilitary wing to fight against British rule (*al-nizam al-khas*). It gained popularity by dispatching fighting units against the British in the Suez Canal Zone in the late 1940s and early 1950s. Al Banna declared that the organization would use all necessary means—including violence—to establish Islamic rule, the Brotherhood

7

quickly fell out of favor. It was banned in 1948 after it had assassinated the prime minister and, in February 1949, Al Banna himself was gunned down by Egyptian government agents.

The Palace miscalculated in assassinating Al Banna. It mistakenly thought that his death would depress the movement's popularity. Instead tens of thousands of grieving mourners flocked to Al Banna's funeral. His murder fueled even more fervor, zealotry, and widespread support for the Brotherhood.

The decision to get rid of Al Banna was ill-conceived. The Palace failed to gauge the evolution of Al Banna's views away from violence and extremism. Foregoing the direct exercise of political power, Al Banna increasingly understood the need to avoid confrontation by emphasizing incremental rather than radical change and dedicating the movement to providing social services. Despite intermittent acts of violence, such as the assassination of Egypt's prime minister and some other officials, Al Banna made the strategic decision by the time of his death to embrace mainstream political Islam and steer the Brotherhood towards the political center.

The Brotherhood collaborated with the Free Officers in the 1952 coup with Anwar Sadat serving as a liaison between the Free Officers and the Brotherhood. They celebrated together when Gamal Abdel Nasser toppled King Farouq in 1952. However, it grew wary of Nasser when he quickly took steps to consolidate power by abolishing the monarchy, the constitution, and political parties. Nasser successfully tapped into feelings of nationalism prevalent in Egypt and other countries in the Non-Aligned Movement. Rejecting foreign control and ownership of Egypt's national assets, he championed the poor and disenfranchised members of society. Though Nasser's pan-Arabism instilled nationalistic pride among Egyptians, his secularism did not reflect the Islamic identity of many Egyptians. Not only did his secular rule rile the Brotherhood, it also triggered the emergence of even more hostile, violent, and radically neo-fundamentalist groups committed to imposing Shari'a as the law of the land.

By 1954, the Brotherhood had rejected Nasser and organized a series of massive street protests. A Brother tried to assassinate Nasser. When Nasser uncovered a broader assassination plot hatched by Brothers in the armed forces, he immediately banned the Brotherhood and arrested 20,000 of its members in nationwide security sweeps.

No event, however, accelerated Islamic extremism in Egypt more than the humiliating defeat of its armed forces by Israel in the Six Day War of June 1967. Egypt's air force was almost entirely destroyed. Caught in flight from the battlefield, its mechanized divisions littered the roadsides of the Sinai Peninsula. Egypt suffered not only from lost pride. It also surrendered large swaths of territory to Israel in the Sinai and the Gaza Strip.

On the so-called Arab street, the defeat of Egypt and its allies was widely viewed as punishment for the corruption of the ruling elites and retribution for deserting Allah. Repudiating Nasser's secular Arab nationalism, Egyptian columnists pilloried the government. Many Egyptians dealt with the defeat by seeking refuge in spiritual life and finding community in the Brotherhood. Ashamed and embarrassed, they rejected Nasser's self-proclaimed role as a leader of the Arab world and the Non-Aligned Movement. When Nasser died in 1970, he was succeeded by Vice President Anwar Sadat.

Sadat cultivated an image of piety taking the title of "believer-president" and insisting that he be called by his first name—Muhammad. He assumed the practice of beginning all of his public remarks with the Islamic incantation "In the name of God." He also made a habit of ending his public presentations with quotations from the Qur'an. Nasser reached out to clerics and religious scholars. His strategy was to co-opt the Brotherhood by giving it access to state controlled media and permitting its message to be disseminated in neighborhood mosques. To foster goodwill, he even amended the constitution in 1971 establishing the principles of Shari'a as a main source of legislation.

Sadat's place in history will forever be defined by his 1977 trip to Jerusalem and his willingness to make peace with Israel at Camp David two years later. Determined to normalize relations with the United States and Israel, he believed leftists and their supporters in the Soviet Union were Egypt's real enemy. As reward for Egypt's commitment to peace with Israel, the United States agreed to provide a large assistance package valued at $2 billion annually. U.S. aid included development assistance, weapons transfers, and extensive cooperation between the Egyptian and American militaries.

Though Sadat was heralded worldwide for his vision and leadership, the Brotherhood condemned him for bowing to Israel. Sadat originally supported the Brotherhood as a counterweight to the leftists and communists, but they turned against him. After Camp David, the Brotherhood called him a stooge of the United States and organized mass demonstrations across the country to protest the accord. Sadat cracked down, targeting both the Brotherhood and more fanatical neo-fundamentalist organizations. One such group was Islamic Jihad. It had been founded by Ayman Al Zawahiri who vowed to assassinate Sadat. After spending years in jail, he would emerge as Osama bin Laden's right-hand man.

Egyptian army soldiers who were disciples of Islamic Jihad broke ranks during a military parade on October 6, 1981. They charged the colorfully festooned presidential viewing stand killing Sadat in a hail of gunfire. Hosni Mubarak, who was at Sadat's side during the melee, assumed the presidency and remains in power to this day.

Ideology

Originally defined by Hassan Al Banna, the Brotherhood's ideology focused on the creation of an Islamic order in Egypt (*al-nizam al-islami*). The Brotherhood believes that all facets of the human experience should be ruled by the will of God as described in the Qur'an and enshrined in Shari'a. "Islam is the solution" is the Brotherhood's slogan. Two crossed swords over the Qur'an is its symbol.

The Brotherhood's pamphlet, called *The Initiative*, spells out the organization's goals:

> [The Brotherhood is] working to establish God's law as we believe it to be the real effective way out of all sufferings and problems. The mission could be achieved through building the Muslim individual, Muslim family, Muslim government, and the Muslim state that leads Islamic countries, gathers all Muslims, regains Islamic glory, gives lost Muslim land back to its owners and carries the flag of the call of God, thus making the world happy via the teachings and right of Islam."[2]

Al Banna believed that Egypt had become morally decadent. He criticized scholars at Cairo's Al Azhar University, the center of worldwide Sunni scholarship, for straying from strict interpretation of the Prophet's teachings. Al Banna maintained that official corruption was rooted in Al Azhar's failure to teach Egyptians how to be good Muslims and adhere to Islamic discipline. He lamented the extent to which Egyptians were subservient to foreign ideas and criticized the community of clerics (Ulama) for being influenced by the British.[3]

Not only did Al Banna object to external imperialism (*al-isti'mar al-khariji*). He also condemned the domestic imperialism (*al-isti'mar al-dakhili*) of elite Egyptians whom he believed had become tools of Western ideology by helping foreign powers to exploit the country. According to Al Banna, establishing Shari'a was part and parcel of the broader goal of replacing foreign values with Islamic beliefs. The Brotherhood equated secularism with weakness. Only the creation of a Muslim order could ensure the spiritual and material welfare of society.

"It is the nature of Islam to dominate not be dominated; to impose its law on all nations and to extend its power to the entire planet," Al Banna wrote.[4] Al Banna also articulated the Brotherhood's slogan: "God is our objective, the Qur'an is our constitution, the prophet is our Leader, struggle is our way, and death for the sake of God is our highest aspiration."[5] "God permits us "he wrote" to defend ourselves if you rise against us and stand in the path of our message."[6]

Al Banna wanted to restore the caliphate to Cairo. Though Al Banna espoused an incremental approach, his ultimate goal was to see Shari'a codified through officially enforced rules thereby establishing the basis for an Islamic state (*Dawla Muslima*). To this end, Al Banna emphasized the creation of a Muslim order focused on ensuring the welfare of society. His Islamist populism was well received by Egyptians in the lower echelons of society.

Egypt's parliament was initially criticized by Al Banna as a puppet of the British, allowing the plunder of Egypt by outside powers. However, his position on constitutionalism and parliamentary democracy evolved over the years. Persuaded that democratic institutions could function under the guidance of Islamic legislation, Al Banna eventually likened democratic debate to the Islamic process of consultation (*Shura*). Under Al Banna's leadership, the Brotherhood agreed to foreswear violence and accept constitutional rule in exchange for a role in the political process. Its strategy relied on elections as a vehicle for popularizing Islamic beliefs and spreading the word of God. The Brotherhood also saw its political involvement as a bulwark against the Wafd Party and its godless communist allies.

Though the Brotherhood participated in parliamentary elections of 1941, it soon grew disenchanted with the political process. Scorning politicians for using them and condemning Egypt's political elite for betraying the national trust, a more radical ideology gradually emerged. The Brotherhood's Special Apparatus targeted British interests, political rivals, and the leadership of minority groups especially Christian Copts.[7]

Sayyid Qutb mentored the Brotherhood's radicalization. Arrested in Nasser's sweeps, Qutb wrote *Signposts on the Road* (*Ma'alim fi al-tariq*) while in jail. Published in 1964, *Signposts* was the seminal literary work articulating radical Islam. It is now considered the founding manifesto of jihadism.[8]

Though Qutb believed that Egypt had been overtaken by pagan ignorance (*Jahiliyya*), he rejected the heresy of constitutional democracy embracing instead the all encompassing power of God: "To declare divinity for God alone…means a full revolt against human rulership in all its shapes and forms, systems, and arrangements. It means destroying the kingdom of man to establish the Kingdom of God on earth…the wresting of power from the hands of its human usurpers to return it to God alone; the supremacy of divine law alone and the cancellation of human laws."[9] He lamented the woeful state of Egypt's secular society: "Everything around us is Jahiliyya: people's perceptions and beliefs, habits and customs, the sources of their culture, arts and literature, and their laws and legislation."[10] Qutb's radical treatise also argued that unjust Arab rulers were infidels who should be eliminated for betraying their people and faith.

In 1966, Nasser tried to silence Qutb by ordering his public execution. Killing him, however, only broadened the appeal of his ideas. By the time of his death, Qutb's writings had given focus to an increasingly radical segment of disenfranchised and impoverished Egyptians.

Structure

The Muslim Brotherhood of Egypt is a hierarchical and secretive body led by a Supreme Guide (*al-murshid al-'amm*). He is assisted by the 13-member Guidance Bureau that formulates policies, manages activities, and selects leadership. A Shura (consultative) Council functions as a consultative assembly. Though clerics do not run the organization, all leaders share the goal of Islamicizing Egypt.

Despite its hierarchical nature, the Brotherhood has decentralized operations with 7,000 branch offices working at the municipal, district, and neighborhood levels. To fill the gap caused by government incompetence and corruption, the Brotherhood maintains a network of private voluntary organizations affiliated with neighborhood mosques and run by local clerics. Not only does the Brotherhood operate health clinics, schools, and sports clubs in service of Egypt's poor and needy, it also assists businesses by providing credit through its informal banking system.

By penetrating Egypt's twenty-two professional syndicates, which have 3.5 million members, the Brotherhood has been able to expand its membership and access influential segments of Egyptian society.[11] It also uses the syndicates to deliver services thereby endearing the organization to its constituents. For example, the Brotherhood worked through Egypt's Doctor's Association to provide shelter and supplies to earthquake victims in October 1992. In response to its efficient relief effort, the interior minister asked: "What is going on here? Do we have a 'state within a state'?"[12]

The Brotherhood's media activities are restricted just as all independent media is restricted in Egypt. In March 2006, *Arab Horizons* (*Afaq-Arabiya*), a Brotherhood-affiliated newspaper, was closed and charges filed against its editor in chief for reporting instances of fraud in the 2005 elections. Pressures have also been brought to bear on other publications, such as the *Daily Star of Egypt*, which are sympathetic to the Brotherhood.[13]

Absent any formal Brotherhood television, radio or print media, the organization relies on the Web to disseminate its message and provide updates on current developments. The "Muslim Brotherhood Movement Homepage" highlights the organization's ideological and religious orientation. It states that the Brotherhood is devoted to following the Salaf (righteous predacessors), establishing the Sunna, and increasing the Imam (leader of the mosque or community of believers) by concentrating on purity of heart. It also has a section on building the Caliphate as a union between Muslim states. The *Ikhwan* website concentrates more on news and current affairs. It includes a section on "MB in the news" and "MB in the press." Reports highlight juridical proceedings involving Brothers. The site is interactive, asking viewers to post comments. It also conducts public opinion polls on such topics as "Should the MB and the United States engage in dialogue?" In addition, dozens of chat rooms are orchestrated by Brotherhood loyalists. Members of the Brotherhood youth movement also have their own blogs posting opinions and responding to events of special interest to the younger generation as well as the movement as a whole.

Financing

The Brotherhood embraces the Islamic principle of charity (*Zakat*) that requires Muslims to alleviate the suffering of others. As a result, its primary financing comes from alms collected by local clerics and from contributions from professionals associated with various unions and syndicates.

The Brotherhood also receives considerable support from international sources. Most contributors are wealthy Salafi businessmen from Saudi Arabia and other Gulf States where Sunni Arabs predominate. Some revenue is also derived from international affiliates. The U.S. chapter of the Brotherhood, which operates mosques, schools, and youth camps, requires its members to contribute 3 percent of their annual income. Though most of these dues support local projects and cultural activities, some revenue flows back to operations in Egypt.

U.S. authorities keep a close watch on Brotherhood revenues out of concern that money is being laundered to finance terrorist activities. Though no terrorist finance charges have been filed against the U.S. chapter, in 2001 the Justice Department identified Youssef Nada, a Brotherhood member, and his Swiss-based investment group as a terrorist financier.[14] Nada's Al Taqwa Investment Group was charged as a co-conspirator in the 1998 bombings of the U.S. embassies in Kenya and Tanzania. In 2001, Swiss police detained two senior members of the Brotherhood's international branch alleging they were involved in financing Al Qaeda and, in 2003, the U.S. Attorney in Alexandria accused Soliman Biheiri, a Brotherhood businessman from Virginia, of raising funds for terror groups.

Leadership

Despite its appearance as a coherent and disciplined organization, a growing rift has emerged between the Brotherhood's older generation (*Mamun al-Hudaybi*) that dominates the Guidance Bureau and the so-called middle generation. Prominent in the campus and student movements of the 1970s, members of the middle generation became professionals in the 1980s and leaders of the syndicate movement.

Assuming prominent positions in the Political Bureau, they grew increasingly resentful of the older generation for isolating the Brotherhood from contemporary developments and objected to the organization's obsession with discipline, autocracy, and ideologically rigidity. They also complained about the lack of democratic decision-making. The middle generation is committed to making the organization more mainstream and influential.

What most distinguishes the middle generation is its pragmatic agenda and its focus on working within the political process to establish the Brotherhood as a legal political party that would be required to clarify its position on Shari'a law, women's rights, and plans for invigorating Egypt's sluggish economy. Prominent figures include Abdel Moneim Abul Fotouh, from the Cairo University Student Union, Essam El Eryan, assistant secretary of the Doctor's Syndicate, Ibrahim El Zaafarani, secretary general of the Alexandria chapter of the Doctor's Syndicate, and Mohammed Habib, a professor at Assiut University.

During the 1990s, the Political Bureau and Guidance Council feuded over the Brotherhood's tactics and political strategy. The internal dispute worsened in 1996 when the Guidance Council failed to consult with the Political Bureau on the appointment of seventy-six-year-old Mustafa Mashhur to replace Hamid Abu Nasr as the Supreme Guide. In 1995, the behind-the-scenes power struggle emerged in full view when the middle generation broke ranks, announcing plans to form the Center Party (Wasat).

Wasat was envisioned as a "civic platform based on the Islamic faith, which believes in pluralism and the alternation of power."[15] Demonstrating its commitment to diversity and a more modern approach, 19 women and three Copts were among its 93 founders. Committed to organizational transparency, Wasat believed that Shari'a can help advance its goals of modernity if it is subject to independent interpretation (*Ijihad*) by open-minded and democratically elected figures. It published a detailed political program and encouraged public debate on its plan for reforming Egypt's moribund economy.

Achieving legal recognition was Wasat's central objective. However, the government refused to grant it status as a political party fearing that Wasat was really a front organization of the Brotherhood. Their efforts stymied, Wasat established the Egyptian Society for Culture and Dialogue as a private association dedicated to political mobilization.

Over the objections of the middle generation, Mohammed Mahdi Akef was elected Supreme Guide by the Guidance Bureau in January 2004. Akef has a long history of struggle against the Egyptian government. Originally sentenced to death for plotting the assassination of Nasser in 1954, Akef spent twenty years in prison before joining the Labor Party as a member of parliament from 1987 to 1990.

Akef is well known for his fiery rhetoric. He led demonstrations against the American occupation of Iraq asserting that, "The Muslim Brotherhood movement condemns all bombings in independent Arab and Muslim countries. But the bombings in Palestine and Iraq are a [religious] obligation. This is because they are occupied countries and the occupier must be expelled in every way possible. The Muslim Brotherhood supports martyrdom operations in Palestine and Iraq in order to expel the Zionists and the Americans."[16] He also proclaimed, "If the gates of jihad in Palestine open before the Brotherhood, we will not hesitate a single moment and we will be with them on the battlefield."[17]

Despite the tough talk, the Brotherhood's mainstream faction (Umar Al Tilimsani) renounced violence and adopted a strategy of incremental change. During a rally at Cairo's Al Fateh Mosque in March 2005, Brothers chanted: "Islam is coming. The Qur'an will rule. No extremism. No terrorism."[18]

Elections

Hassan Hodeibi became Supreme Guide in 1950. He refuted Qutb's call for jihad against non-believers. Hodeibi was a judge who embraced the goal of establishing an Islamic state through peaceful means. Analyzing the compatibility of Islam and democracy, Hodeibi concluded that Islam and democracy were not contradictory so long as democracy did not impose Western values on Islamic societies. To be sure, Hodeibi envisioned democratic institutions functioning under the guidance of Islamic legislation. His willingness to work within the existing political system to achieve the Brotherhood's goals represented a rejection of the militancy espoused by Qutb and an endorsement of the more moderate views of Al Banna.

When the Brotherhood paramilitary wing led by Abdl Fatah El Saudi rejected Hodeibi rancorous debate erupted within the Brotherhood. On one side was the older generation of Brothers who like Qutb viewed democracy as heresy and insisted that only the Qur'an could serve as Egypt's constitution. Mustafa Mashhour, the Supreme Guide who died in November 2002 presented this view asserting, "Islam is creed and state, book and sword, and a way of life."[19] Younger Brothers and technocrats insisted that the first order of business should be to establish an Islamic society and then focus on revising laws and legislation. Though factions differed on the sequence of events, there was no debate about the ultimate goal of Islamicizing Egypt.

Mubarak maintains that the Brotherhood's desire to participate in elections is a Trojan horse for imposing extremism on Egyptians. Mubarak embraces a secular ideology that precludes the use of religion in policy formulation. He often expresses concern that Shari'a would be used to impose religious authoritarianism by enforcing Islamic jurisprudence (*Fiqh*) and the Islamic interpretation of criminal law (*Hudud*).

The Brotherhood's decision to participate in electoral politics would prove pivotal. As Gamal Al Banna, the brother of the movement's founder, asserted: "The real test of the Brotherhood is to let it enter politics. They will be in a different situation when they confront the necessities of ruling, and there are only two possible outcomes. They will have to compromise or fail."[20] According to Ibrahim Hodeibi, whose grandfather and great grandfather ran the Brotherhood: "Revolutions don't really lead to democracies, just look at Iran. The Brotherhood really wants a democracy in Egypt, and it is willing to wait to make that happen peacefully."[21]

Opponents of the Brotherhood's decision to engage in politics pointed out that Egypt's political pluralism was a farce. Opposition parties functioned, but they had little influence. Moreover, opposition parties were so weak their existence merely gave the impression that the ruling party's claim that Egypt was democratic. The National Democratic Party (NDP) controlled the People's Assembly (*Majlis al-Sha'ab*), the Consultative Council (*Majlis al-Shura*), and local councils. With the NDP's tight grip on power, the parliament was little more than a rubber stamp for the government's policies.

The internal debate proved moot. The government persistently refused to grant the Brotherhood permission to function as a legal political party. To exercise political power, the Brotherhood infiltrated the trade union movement in the 1980s. It also sought a voice in the political process by presenting parliamentary candidates who were loyal to the Brotherhood but were otherwise affiliated with legally established parties.

Brotherhood candidates stood for election as part of the Wafd Party in 1984, which won 58 seats in the 454-member parliament. In 1987, the Brotherhood formed an alliance with labor groups and the coalition won 56 seats. In the labor bloc, 36 parliamentarians were members of the Brotherhood. The Brotherhood boasted that it could marshal a quarter of the votes in the NDP-dominated parliament on any Islamic issue.

In 1992, Mubarak launched an offensive to root out the country's underground militant Islamic cells. Scores were arrested. Swift military justice was rendered before tribunals. University campuses were raided. The Egyptian Human Rights Association reported widespread torture by Egyptian state security forces. Mubarak renewed emergency laws that allow the police to detain persons for 45-day renewable periods without informing them of their crime or pressing charges. The campaign of harassment and intimidation intensified before the 1995 parliamentary elections. About 50 people were killed, 900 injured, and 1,000 Brothers were arrested in nationwide security sweeps.

Though the 1995 elections were widely criticized as fraudulent, Mubarak paid little note and took steps to ensure that he would win a fourth term as president in 1999. As expected, he was re-elected—with an overwhelming 93.8 percent of the vote. Mubarak's landslide victory exacerbated the growing sense of cynicism among Egyptians. It also galvanized the opposition, including members of the Brotherhood.

Mubarak tried to placate his critics by pledging electoral reform for parliamentary elections in 2000. He changed the rules so that candidates could run as individuals and not only on a party slate. All told, more than 4,000 candidates from twelve legal parties competed for 444 seats. Though it was still banned, the Brotherhood fielded 180 candidates running in their individual capacity.

International and domestic observers criticized the elections as neither free nor fair. The government banned opposition campaign rallies under a law promulgated after Sadat's assassination that restricted political gatherings as a threat to "national unity." It outlawed the Islamic-backed Labor Party and imposed restrictions on independent media. During the run up to the election, the authorities arrested 500 members of the Brotherhood. Scores were tried in military courts.[22] On Election Day, voters were prevented from reaching the polling stations by roadblocks and riot police deployed in Brotherhood strongholds.

Despite the government's efforts, the NDP received only 85.5 percent of the vote as opposed to 1995 when it won 97 percent. Sixty-five percent of incumbents fell victim to a protest vote and lost their bid for reelection.

The Brotherhood's message resonated even more strongly during the parliamentary elections of 2005. It blamed the NDP for "the economic crisis that has not only led to the suffering of all Egyptians, but the technological and educational backwardness of the nation, and the marginalization of Egypt's pivotal role in the regional and international front."[23] Its call to Islam also inspired many voters: "If Islam were applied, no one would be hungry. Islam is a religion of construction. Islam is a religion of investment. Islam is a religion of development. If Islam were applied, Iraq could not have been invaded, Israel could not occupy Jerusalem, and aggression could not have been used to humiliate Muslims everywhere."[24]

Many skeptical voters asked why they should vote if the NDP's victory was a foregone conclusion. Only 25 percent of those eligible actually went to the polls. Capitalizing on widespread voter apathy, the Brotherhood won 88 seats compared with 17 in 2000. A quarter of those who voted for the Brotherhood did so, not because they were Brotherhood enthusiasts, but to protest official corruption and Egypt's woeful economic conditions.

Today three million Egyptians are unemployed. Thirty-five percent live below the poverty line and the average per capita GDP is $1,470.[25] Young people have scant educational opportunity and, as a result, only 57.7 percent of Egyptians are literate.[26] The Brotherhood was able to successfully enlarge its ranks by appealing to the pervasive sense of injustice felt by many Egyptians. Islamists have gained popularity not only because of their religious appeal but because they claim to represent the interests of the poor and hopeless.

The Brotherhood was also able to broaden its grass-roots appeal by highlighting its victimization at the hands of Egypt's security services. Mubarak increasingly used Egypt's extensive portfolio of anti-terror legislation to narrow the space for democratic participation. Egypt's Emergency Law is the major flash-point for discontent. The Emergency Law limits political freedom and expression. It also allows the government to detain citizens indefinitely without charge. Under the Law, more than 30,000 Islamists have been arrested since Sadat's assassination. Today, about 15,000 arrested under Emergency Law provisions languish in detention without charges.[27]

Freedom of assembly is further curtailed via laws stipulating that private associations cannot be involved in any sort of political activity. The Law on Political Rights restricts the activities of journalists and independent media by giving the government arbitrary authority to close newspapers. It also establishes as a punishable offense the publication of "false" information that influences election results. Even Internet bloggers have been targeted and arrested.

When Egyptians demonstrated against the extension of the Emergency Law, convenings were forcefully disbanded and protesters arrested. Not only did the government maintain an extensive network of spies and informants, it also sponsored vigilante groups to suppress popular protests and intimidate opposition groups. Targeting militants in hotbed areas of Upper Egypt, the government launched a brutal counter-insurgency suspending due process and trying suspects in military courts.

In March 2004, the Brotherhood published a manifesto identifying thirteen reform items. It called for an end to martial law, the establishment of a genuine multi-party system, and the rule of law. Its economic program recommended respect for private property, shrinking the government bureaucracy, and downsizing the public sector.

Mohammed Mahdi Akef, head of the Brotherhood's Guidance Bureau, maintained: "Though no group has been so enormously harmed by the regime like the Muslim Brotherhood [and] no one has sacrificed like we have, we are not resorting to confrontation or violence. We want love and peace."[28] Akef was much less conciliatory a year later describing Mubarak's government as "corrupt and expired."[29] Akef asserted that political stagnation "has led to the spread of corruption to all government and public institutions; it has led to a suffocating economic crisis."[30]

The Brotherhood entered into a strategic alliance with the Egyptian Movement for Change (*Al-Haraka al-Masriyya min ajli 'l-Taghyir*), more commonly know as "Enough" (*Kifaya*). Kifaya was born as a protest movement in 2003 but did not fully emerge until two years later.

During the Cairo Spring of 2005, Kifaya organized mass anti-government demonstrations demanding an end to rule by Mubarak, his family, and henchmen. The Brotherhood joined forces with the Labor Party and the Islamic Socialist Party to swell the ranks of demonstrators. Kifaya also incorporated the Internet into its mobilization strategy organizing spontaneous "lightning" demonstrations.

Despite the outward appearance of unity in Kifaya, dissension surfaced during the rallies when Brothers started chanting religious slogans. There was no love lost between the groups. The relationship between the Brotherhood and Kifaya was always one of convenience. Though the Wafd Party did not support legalizing the Brotherhood as a political party, it did recognize that its interests would be served by allowing Islamists to organize politically. Like other groups in the adhoc coalition, the Brotherhood maintained a watchful eye only participating when its interests were served.

In addition to internal dissention, Kifaya suffered from a lack of focus. Kifaya was essentially a protest movement. Rather than offer a constructive alternative, it targeted Mubarak and rejected the status quo.[31] Kifaya also failed to be inclusive. It was dominated by civil society groups such as Youth for Change, Doctors for Change, Writers for Change, Journalists for Change, and Lawyers for Change whose members came largely from the middle class and urban elite. Egypt's working class and unemployed were not extensively involved.

The decision to exclude Ayman Nour's Tomorrow Party (*Al Ghad*) further exacerbated divisions within Kifaya. After revoking Nour's parliamentary immunity, the government convicted him of fraud for forging signatures on his party's license application. Though Nour insisted that the charges were fabricated, his appeal was rejected in December 2005 and he was sent to jail for a five-year term. Nour was the most recognizable figure in the opposition, which made his absence from Kifaya all the more striking.

In February 2005, Mubarak went on the offensive. He surprised his opponents by proposing to revise article 76 of the constitution allowing multiparty elections for president.[32] The amendment was initially welcomed by opposition leaders who hoped it would enable a more representative government. However, their enthusiasm waned as the

NDP-dominated parliament debated the proposal and imposed conditions on the eligibility of candidates. It finally agreed on conditions requiring eligible candidates to represent parties with at least 5 percent of seats in the assembly, forbidding the formation of religiously based parties, and requiring a super-majority in the assembly, shura council, and local councils.

The Brotherhood claimed that such conditions made it impossible for any serious candidate to contest Mubarak for the presidency. In May 2005, it organized 17 simultaneous rallies across the country involving about 70,000 people. Some other opposition parties joined. Efforts to form a united front failed. Secular and leftist parties did not show up. At the same time, a rapprochement was taking place between Mubarak and the Brotherhood during the run up to the 2005 parliamentary elections. Instead of rounding up Brotherhood activists, as it did before previous elections, the government actually released some Brothers from jail. For the first time ever, *Al Ahram*, the main state-owned newspaper, published an interview with the Brotherhood's Supreme Guide.

The constitutional amendment passed. Independent election observers claimed that only 5 percent of eligible voters participated. However, official results indicated that 53.6 percent of 32 million eligible voters participated and 82.8 percent of voters supported the constitutional amendment. When Egyptians took to the streets, NDP vigilantes attacked, beating and humiliating women in their ranks. The government arrested prominent opponents such as Mahmoud Ezzat, the Brotherhood's secretary general. When the vote for president was held September 7, 2005, Mubarak won handily with 88 percent of votes cast.

Mubarak wanted the Brotherhood to make some gains in parliamentary elections two months later. He calculated that its strong showing would squeeze the secular opposition parties and alarm Bush administration officials enough so that they would walk-back their push for democracy. The Brotherhood performed better than anticipated in the first round leading the government to crack down in the second and third rounds. Nonetheless, Brotherhood loyalists emerged as the big winners of parliamentary elections in November 2005 winning 88 of 454 seats. The 2005 election revealed the broad populist appeal of the Brotherhood's agenda. It exposed the NDP to be much weaker than suspected. The outcome also highlighted weaknesses of the opposition as the Wafd, Nasserists, Tagammu', and the Tomorrow Party failed to form a united bloc (*Kutla*).

When judges demanded electoral reform and the rule of law, Mubarak launched a wholesale assault on Egypt's judiciary.[33] Egypt's judges have always demonstrated a streak of independence. For example, judges who refused to submit to Gamal Abdel Nasser's executive authority were fired in, what became known as the "Judge's Massacre." Those refusing to join the ruling party were dismissed en masse in 1969.

In 2005, Mahmoud Mekky and Hesham Bastawisi, were especially outspoken. The prominent jurists accused the government of rigging presidential and parliamentary elections citing numerous irregularities including document forgery and the use of riot police to block voter access to polling places. In response, the government pressed charges even as Bastawisi lay in hospital recovering from a heart attack. It also lifted immunity protections for seven other judges, members of the prestigious Judges Club, who staged a sit-in demanding greater independence of the judiciary. Claiming to represent almost all of Egypt's 9,000 judges across the country, the Judge's Club chafed under government controls. It demanded full judicial independence including control of judges' salaries. When the sentence was handed down for Mekki and Bastawisi, ten thousand troops ringed the High Court to prevent demonstrators from showing support.

During the campaign, Mubarak pledged to replace the emergency law and institute political reforms such as amending the constitution, empowering parliament, relaxing laws governing political parties, and allowing greater freedom of expression. Upon winning the election, however, Mubarak recanted on promises for reform.

Following the Dhahab and Taba terror attacks in April 2006, Egypt renewed the Emergency Detention Law that allowed the government to hold citizens indefinitely without charge. The government claimed the law was needed to fight terrorism but Mubarak's critics insisted that it was really intended to shield the government from criticism.

Mubarak's decision to postpone local elections for two years was widely seen as an effort to impede the Brotherhood's ascendancy. It was expected that the Brotherhood would emerge from local elections with control of many local councils, which would put it in a position to broaden its popular base even further by delivering support to schools, hospitals, and other social services. Mubarak defended the postponement of local elections, claimed that his decision was solely intended to allow time for enhanced local self-rule by implementing decentralization.

Amendments to 34 articles in the constitution of 1971 were proposed by Mubarak on December 26, 2006. He heralded the amendments as implementation of his reform commitments. The amendments were anything but. They banned the formation of political parties based on religion, gender, or ethnicity; allowed only licensed political parties to nominate presidential candidates; and limited the role of election monitors. Mubarak also sought to lay the ground for a new anti-terrorism law by clarifying presidential emergency powers. The only positive amendments were modest measures to enhance parliamentary oversight of the cabinet and budgeting process.

Egyptians increasingly believed that Mubarak was manipulating the political process in order to position his son, Gamal Mubarak, for the presidency in 2011. Opposition parties were also concerned that Gamal would be promoted to secretary general of the NDP and end up serving as president for life. They demanded terms limits as well as shortened terms in office for the president.[34]

Fearing the Brotherhood's political ascendancy, the legislature adopted measures further restricting the formation and activities of religious political parties. Article 5 of the constitution stipulated "political activity of political parties shall not be based on any religious background or foundation."[35] The Brotherhood specifically objected to Mubarak's proposed reform of Article 76 in the constitution limiting presidential candidacies to legal parties.

Mubarak showed no tolerance for dissent when protesters objected to his position on the Israel-Lebanon war of 2006. He intensified his campaign against Egypt's democratic movement by cracking down on independent media. Bloggers were tracked down and arrested. Legislation was passed making it a punishable offense to "affront the president of the republic"—or insult parliament, public agencies, the armed forces, the judiciary or "the general public interest."[36]

Mubarak's crackdown dashed hopes that the Brotherhood would be allowed to function as a legal political party. It discredited members of the middle generation who advocated an incremental approach. Mubarak's advisers warned that legalizing the Brotherhood as a political party would be a repeat of Algeria's mistake allowing the Islamic Salvation Front. When the Front swept the first round of elections in 1990, the Algerian government suspended the second ballot and banned the Front. The move polarized Algerians and led to civil war.

Escalation

The Brotherhood's rejection of terrorism sets it apart from neo-fundamentalist groups that, inspired by Qutb, embrace the use of force to immediately establish Shari'a. Over decades, these neo-fundamentalist groups undertook a spate of attacks and kidnappings.

In 1974, the Islamic Liberation Party stormed the National Military Academy. Repentance and Flight (*Al-Takfir wa al-Hijra*) revised conditions for declaring an apostate in order to justify attacks on government officials as well as their supporters in the media and civil society. It was responsible for assassinating the minister for religious affairs in 1977.

Founded in 1978, the Struggle and Crusade (*Al-Jihad*) launched a campaign to harass Christians and Copts. The Popular Islamic Movement supported a version of Saudi Arabia's religious police insisting on modest clothing and a ban on alcohol. In the mid-1980s, *Samawiyya* attacked video clubs that they claimed were disseminating indecent material. Saved from Hellfire (*Al-Najun min al-nar*) murdered two former Interior Ministers and a liberal magazine editor in 1987.

Gama'a Islamiya was founded by Sheik Omar Abdel Rahman who is now serving a life-sentence for his role in the 1993 World Trade Center bombing and his plans to blow up other landmarks in New York City including the United Nations. In 1997, Gama'a Islamiya attacked and shot to death 58 foreign tourists visiting the ancient ruins of Luxor.

Today Mubarak's most rabid detractors are Bedouins residing in the northeast near Egypt's border with Gaza. The Bedouin economy is a shambles. Just 8 percent of those aged twenty to thirty have full-time employment and 92 percent who have jobs depend on seasonal employment such as farming that pays no more than $2 each day. Heavily influenced by Wahhabism, Bedouin women have entirely abandoned their traditional dress for more conservative clothes prevalent in the Gulf States.

The radical Bedouin cell called Tawhid and Jihad was responsible for a series of suicide attacks in Taba, Sharm el Sheik, and Dhahab between 2004 and 2006.[37] The attackers claimed that they were motivated by a desire to harm Egyptian interests in reprisal for Egypt's peace treaty with Israel and its support for Middle East peace. However, the primary victims were Egyptians from Cairo who do seasonal work in the tourism industry in towns along the Gulf of Aqaba.

A Brotherhood official denounced the targeting of foreigners, "These are criminal acts that contradict Islamic teachings. Violence only leads to insecurity."[38] Condemning Bedouin suicide attacks further earned the rancor of Egyptian neo-fundamentalists professing kinship with Al Qaeda.[39]

Several of Osama bin Laden's chief deputies, including Ayman Al Zawahiri, were originally members of the Brotherhood who broke away because they felt there was no room within the organization for their militant views. In his 1991 book, *The Bitter Harvest*, Zawahiri condemned the Brotherhood for foregoing violence and, instead, emphasizing social programs and political activities.

The Brotherhood pointed out that the founding of Al Qaeda outside of its ranks was proof of its intolerance for violence. Though six of the 22 of the "Most Wanted Men" identified by the FBI after 9/11 were Egyptian, the Brotherhood immediately distanced itself from the terror attacks against the United States. It even went so far as to endorse the extradition of bin Laden to the United States if the Bush administration furnished proof of his involvement.[40]

The middle generation makes a strong case against violence and for entering politics. It argues that the Brotherhood prevented radicalism by appealing to the demand of Egyptians for social justice: "When the path is blocked even to those presenting the most moderate vision, then the only alternative is extremism and violence."[41] The Brotherhood also made the point that if it were allowed to become a legal political party, its transition to politics could serve as a model for moderating fanatical groups across the Middle East.

However, the Brotherhood is increasingly under pressure from devout Egyptians who sympathize with groups that turn to violence because government restrictions do not permit political participation by religious organizations. The Brotherhood is hedging its bets. Though it called the Dhahab attack a "cowardly act," it also expressed sympathy with the perpetrators. A Brotherhood spokesman indicated that the attacks were a "reaction to injustice" of Mubarak's regime.[42]

While intensifying the government's campaign against neo-fundamentalist groups, Mubarak adopted conciliatory policies towards the Brotherhood lest more radical groups emerge to take its place. Mubarak's state-sponsored religiosity tolerates clerics who demand a stricter interpretation of Islam. His government provides resources to Al Azhar University. It also sponsors religious newspapers and television programs while banning books and films with un-Islamic messages. Playing to popular opinion, it even tolerates anti-American websites and the distribution of cassette tapes with anti-American propaganda. Mubarak's efforts to co-opt Islamic leaders mirror the approach of his predecessors. For example, Nasser established Muslim schools and sponsored the Qur'an radio station. In 1971, Sadat authorized Article 2 of the constitution. Mubarak's dual approach to the Brotherhood tolerates its political activities and social mobilization, while simultaneously increasing pressure.

The Brotherhood has its critics. Many Egyptians believe that the organization is more concerned with gaining power than with salvation in the hereafter. They claim that the Brotherhood's economic program, which embraces free trade and globalization, is a misguided effort to enlist the loyalties of Egypt's underclass especially its impoverished youth.

Egyptian Copts, who represent 10 percent of the population, are especially concerned. Copts and secular Egyptians look around and see a growing number of Egyptians devoted to Islam. A majority of women, especially young women and girls, are veiled. Many men point with pride to the colored calluses on their foreheads that are caused by their heads hitting the floor during daily prayers. According to a leading newspaper editor, "[The Brotherhood] once relied upon secrecy, underground organizations and a militia until they decided to ride the wave of democracy to reach power.... Once they do, they will adopt dictatorship, fascism, Nazism. They will say they are God's deputies, God's in-laws, God's friends, God's spokesman, and whoever opposes them, differs with them or becomes their enemy will become the enemy of God."[43]

In July 2005, the Brotherhood sought to address its critics by inviting them to a conference designed to develop a consensus reform agenda. According to the Brotherhood, the conference sought to forge an alliance committed "to exercise peaceful pressure on the regime through legal and constitutional means to make it respond to democratic change."[44] The conference demanded that the government end the state of emergency and close the state security courts. It called for independence of the judiciary and greater respect for human rights, as well as electoral reform, new regulations on the formation of political parties, and the peaceful rotation of power.

By reaching out to secular parties, the Brotherhood was also sending a strong message to the United States. It wanted to convey that the organization is not a fanatical, violence-prone Islamist group. Rather, the Brotherhood wanted to be seen by the United States as a national movement and a credible alternative to Mubarak.

International Actors

United States

The 2002 Pew Global Attitudes Project determined that only 6 percent of Egyptians viewed the United States favorably.[45] Negative perceptions are largely a result of America's unmitigated support for Mubarak to the tune of $2 billion each year. The Bush administration has tried to reach out to ordinary Egyptians. In his 2006 State of the Union speech, Bush called on Egypt to "show the way toward democracy in the Middle East."[46] Secretary of State Condoleezza Rice echoed the message stating, "The day must come when the rule of law replaces emergency decrees and when the independent judiciary replaces arbitrary justice.[47] Some Members of the U.S. Congress have demanded a reevaluation of America's generous aid package citing contradictions between Bush's call for greater democracy in the Arab world and Mubarak's crackdown against dissent. An Egyptian Foreign Ministry spokesman responded, "Egypt totally rejects any interference in its internal affairs or any value judgment on internal issues."[48]

Two years later, Bush finished an eight-day trip to the Middle East with a visit to Sharm El Sheik and a meeting with Mubarak. Gone were the public references to human rights and democracy. Having committed to an Israeli-Palestinian accord by the end of his presidency, Bush spoke only about regional security and the peace process. Needing Arab support for his diplomatic initiative, Bush was handcuffed by the contradictions of his Middle East policy. Freedom and liberty faded in importance when compared to the need for support from autocratic leaders to Middle East peace.

Mubarak and Bush had an uneasy relationship from the beginning. To placate his domestic critics, Mubarak never missed a chance to create the appearance of distance between himself and the Bush administration. He opposed the U.S. occupation of Iraq and strongly condemned America's abuse of prisoners at Abu Ghraib. His criticism was a far cry from Egypt's strong support for the U.S.-led coalition that opposed Iraq's occupation of Kuwait in 1991 when Egypt was one of the first and largest Arab countries to commit troops to the multinational force.[49]

Going further, the Brotherhood supported the Iraqi insurgency as a legitimate protest against occupation. Some Brothers went so far as to publicly endorse the kidnapping and beheading of foreigners in Iraq. The Brotherhood accused the United States of cynically supporting democracy only when the outcome serves America's interests. Akef called America a "Satan" whose "attempt to take over the world is not new. What is new is that it appears with such a grim face, without morals, without principles, without law. American tyranny is well known."[50]

The United States officially refuses contact with the Brotherhood.[51] According to Rice, "We have not engaged the Muslim Brotherhood … and we will not."[52] Leaders of the Brotherhood believe that the Bush administration is unable to distinguish between Islamist militants who use violence to advance their political goals and broad-based popularly supported Islamic movements whose message of human development and social justice resonates across Egyptian society. There have, however, been an increasing number of unofficial contacts between low-level U.S. officials and Brotherhood members at conferences and other events.

Israel

No issue galvanizes hatred of the United States in the Arab and Muslim World more than America's unflinching support for Israel. According to a Brotherhood spokesman, "U.S. support to tyrannical regimes is one reason for the hatred expressed towards the United States. But the most important reason is its total bias towards the Zionist entity and U.S. aggression in Iraq and Afghanistan."[53]

Ties between the Brotherhood and Hamas run deep. Hamas was once the Brotherhood's Palestinian branch. The Brotherhood inspired Sheikh Ahmed Yassin, Hamas' founder as well as other radical Palestinian groups, such as Islamic Jihad. Like Hamas, the Brotherhood denies Israel's right to exist and calls on Arab and Islamic governments to arm the Palestinians. It believes Israel is an aggressor nation occupying Muslim holy lands and, therefore, condones Hamas' suicide bombings in Israel as legitimate resistance. Egyptians condemn Israel's collective punishment in Gaza. They are also angered by Mubarak's efforts to pressure Gazans, which many condemn as complicity with Israel.

The Brotherhood expressed support for Hamas when it tunneled into Israel killing Israeli soldiers and capturing Cpl. Galid Shalit in July 2006. It also endorsed Hezbollah's cross-border raid into Northern Israel a few weeks later. According to the Brotherhood, "Hezbollah, with its modest military capabilities relative to the capabilities of organized state armies, was able to achieve what several Arab governments did not do while they were satisfied to remain silent about the slaughter of our brothers in Palestine."[54] Accusing "Arab and Muslims [of] impotence while Israel massacres the unarmed Palestinian people," it has called on Arab and Muslim countries to sever ties with governments that recognize Israel.[55]

Egypt was one of the first Arab countries to normalize relations with Israel. However, Mubarak found himself increasingly marginalized as violence escalated between Fatah and Hamas. Egyptian armored units at the Rafah crossing were responsible for sealing Egypt's border with Gaza. Mubarak had grown accustomed to criticism for failing to prevent the transfer of rockets and munitions from Egypt to Gaza. He looked ineffectual when Hamas blew up the border gate in January 2008 and thousands of Palestinians streamed into Egypt on a shopping spree. Mubarak's response: Decry violence and factionalism while inviting Palestinian leaders to a meeting that he knew Fatah would not attend.

Iran

Tehran severed diplomatic relations with Cairo after Egypt made peace with Israel in 1981. Relations were already tense because Egypt provided asylum for the Shah Reza Pahlavi in 1979. Egypt's support for Iraq in the Iran-Iraq War (1980-88) as well as Iran's harboring violent Islamists convicted in Egyptian courts exacerbated tensions. Mubarak believes that Iran is trying to undermine Egypt's position as a regional leader by supporting Hamas and Hezbollah. Fearing that Iran might develop a "Shiite bomb," he has joined with the United States and other Sunni Arab states in efforts to curb Iran's enrichment program. Iran also objects to Egypt's close military cooperation and economic ties with the United States. The rivalry extends to religious affairs; Al Azhar University in Egypt is the center of Sunni scholarship while Qum in Iran is the center of Shi'a studies. Despite sectarian differences, neo-fundamentalist groups in Egypt and Iranian hardliners have found common cause in their hatred of the United States and their desire to drive America from the region.

The Way Forward

Egypt needs to balance its stability requirements with the need for a long-term and meaningful reform process. The government cannot use the security threat posed by terror groups as a pretext for abrogating reforms. Mubarak's failure to implement meaningful political and electoral reforms has radicalized the opposition and exacerbated extremism within the Brotherhood as well as Egyptian society as a whole.

To prove that it is serious about civil liberties, the government must lift the Emergency Law. It should also replace Law 10 [1914] and Law 14 [1923] restricting the right to assembly and public demonstrations as a first step towards allowing greater freedom of expression. Mubarak should publicly condemn attacks against peaceful pro-democracy demonstrators by members of the security services and restrict their use of truncheons, stun guns, rubber and live ammunition. Law enforcement agents need training on international norms governing the use of force, as well as on human rights.

Egypt's main problem is the concentration of power in the presidency and the co-mingling of powers between the NDP and the state. Constitutional reform is the best way to end the government's monopoly of power. To this end, Mubarak should implement reforms that he promised in 2005. Meaningful checks and balances on presidential authority can be accomplished by redistributing power within the executive branch from the president to the prime minister and the cabinet. Revising Article 77 of the constitution by introducing term limits and shortening terms for the president would pave the way for a more credible rule after Hosni Mubarak.

Consistent with the need for greater balance between the legislative and executive branches, the powers of parliament should be expanded in order to enhance its role in oversight and accountability. Empowering parliament would invigorate civil society, help limit corruption, and create legal conditions for a more robust judiciary. It would also help to increase the representation of women in parliament. So would constitutional reform emphasizing decentralization and measures strengthening local authorities.

To enable more representative government, the government needs to allow more open and straightforward procedures for licensing political parties. Political pluralism would also be served by getting rid of the Political Parties Committee and lifting restrictions on the formation, registration, and operation of opposition parties. Free and fair elections can be achieved if the Interior Ministry stopped obstructing national and international election monitors. Via the Egyptian Judges Club, the judiciary should be mandated to supervise the entire electoral management process from voter registration to vote counting. The Independent Commission for the Supervision of the Presidential Elections should be eliminated and its onerous requirement that elections be conducted over a 24-hour period, which makes it impossible for judges to act as nationwide election observers, amended. Complementing an independent and empowered electoral commission, international election monitors should also be allowed to register and operate without constraints.

Amending Article 76 of the constitution would reduce the threshold of support for candidates in the assembly, shura council, and local councils.

No meaningful electoral reform can be achieved, however, without addressing the role of the Brotherhood in politics. This is not without risks. Allowing the Brotherhood to function as a political party could create conditions for Islamic identity to supplant national identity. The Brotherhood might also exert its own form of authoritarianism by imposing Shari'a law on secularists and Christian Copts. Once in power, the

Brotherhood could cancel Egypt's accord with Israel, which would have a chilling affect on U.S.-Egyptian relations, and lead to a reduction in the $2 billion in foreign aid provided anually by the United States.

There are also serious risks associated with obstructing the Brotherhood's participation in politics. Absent political recourse, the Brotherhood might be tempted to join forces with more militant neo-fundamentalist groups.

A step-by-step process should be adopted allowing the organization greater participation in political life. Confidence building could start with the release of Brothers in administrative detention. When the government initiates direct discussions with the Brotherhood on its political activities, it should focus initially on the legalization of the Brotherhood as an association. Once the Brotherhood pledges to abide by the constitution and proves its commitment to act in accordance with international standards of civil and political rights, discussions could continue regarding the terms under which the Brotherhood would be allowed to register as a political party and participate in future parliamentary and presidential elections.

Finding a path for the Brotherhood to enter politics would make Egypt the undisputed leader of democracy in the Arab world. The Brotherhood's entry into politics would also test the notion that legalizing a non-violent Islamist party can help moderate more fanatical Islamist groups by luring them into the political system.

In addition, it is also important to open the political space for civil society. Relaxing pressure on trade unions and professional associations would allow NGOs and civil society institutions to become more engaged in the political process. Removing security agents and spies from college campuses would encourage their political participation free from fear.

A more robust role for civil society would also have a positive effect on Egypt's economy. Targeted investment and job creation activities in Upper Egypt would help eliminate conditions that radicalize the Bedouin population. In Cairo and other major urban centers, anti-corruption watchdog groups should be strengthened. Transparency coupled with reforms would create conditions for the government to work with the private sector in order to address Egypt's economic and development requirements. Newspapers and other media outlets sympathetic to the Brotherhood should be able to report without restrictions. An independent media is essential to hold the government.

In Egypt and througout the Arab world illiteracy, access, and education quality are pervasive obstacles to human development. Such problems are compounded by the lack of infrastructure and technology necessary for information and communications technology (ICT). The Egyptian government can remedy these problems by getting serious about educational reform and increase investment in public education. More investment would not only enhance educational quality. It would also mitigate the need for alternative education through madrassas. While the government should not control educational curriculum, standards are necessary. Emphasizing teaching of math and science in primary and secondary schools would cultivates critical thinking that acts as a bulwark against intolerance.

The United States can encourage Egypt's democratic development by publicly affirming its support for democracy, the rule of law and electoral reform. However, the United States must be careful to offer advice rather than rely exclusively on public pressure. Egypt's democratization will backfire if it appears to be a concession to the United States rather than an organic process engaging Egyptians of all faiths and from across the country's political spectrum.

Notes

1.   Jailan Halawi. *Al-Ahram Weekly*. 18-24 August 2005.
2.   Michael Slackman. "With No Status as a Party, Egyptian Group Wields Power." *The New York Times*. August 16, 2005.
3.   Great Britain occupied Egypt in 1882.
4.   Neil MacFarquhar. *The New York Times*. "Egyptian Group Patiently Pursues Dream of an Islamic State." January 20, 2002. p. 3.
5.   Nazih N. Ayubi. *Political Islam: Religion and Politics in the Arab World*. Routledge Press. p. 132. 1991.
6.   Richard P. Mitchell. *The Rise of the Muslim Brotherhood*. Oxford University Press. p. 319. 1993.
7.   Carrie Rosefsky Wickham. *Mobilizing Islam: Religion, Activism, and Political Change in Egypt*. Columbia University Press. p. 113. 2002.
8.   James Traub. "Islamic Democrats?" *International Movement for a Just World*. June 4, 2007.
9.   Nazih N. Ayubi. *Political Islam: Religion and Politics in the Arab World*. Routledge Press. p. 140. 1991.
10.   Nazih N. Ayubi. *Political Islam: Religion and Politics in the Arab World*. Routledge Press. p. 139. 1991.
11.   1995 Figures.
12.   Carrie Rosefsky Wickham. *Mobilizing Islam: Religion, Activism, and Political Change in Egypt*. Columbia University Press. p. 203. 2002.
13.   Mirat e-Nagger. Knight Ridder News Service. *The San Diego Union-Tribune*. March 10, 2006.
14.   *Al-Sharq-al-Awsat*. November 11, 2004.
15.   Carrie Rosefsky Wickham. *Mobilizing Islam: Religion, Activism, and Political Change in Egypt*. Columbia University Press. p. 218. 2002.
16.   *Al-Arabi* (Egypt). January 18, 2004.

17.   *Al-Sabil* (Jordan). January 20, 2004.
18.   Nadia Abou El-Magd. "Egypt arrests dozens of banned Islamic group members." *Associated Press*. March 27, 2005.
19.   *The Times* (London). Mustafa Mashhour. December 31, 2002.
20.   Neil MacFarquhar. "Will Politics and Success at the Polls Tame Egypt's Muslim Brotherhood?" *The New York Times*. December 8, 2005. p. A18.
21.   Dan Murphy. "Cairo is open to political reform, but won't include Islamic group." *Christian Science Monitor.* June 7, 2005. p. 1.
22.   Harvey Morris. Alexandria's Muslim Brotherhood offers a sister and a Christian in elections." *Financial Times*. September 16, 2000. p. 8.
23.   Jailan Halawi. *Al-Ahram Weekly*. 18-24 August 2005.
24.   Neil MacFarquhar. "Will Politics and Success at the Polls Tame Egypt's Muslim Brotherhood?" *The New York Times*. December 8, 2005. p. A18.
25.   *CIA World Fact book* 2003.
26.   Frank Viviano. "Terrorists put heat on secular states." *The San Francisco Chronicle*. October 14, 2001. p. A1.
27.   *Ibid*.
28.   Salah Nasrawi. "Egypt opposition leader opposes election plan." *Associated Press*. May 15, 2005.
29.   *Ibid*.
30.   *Agence France Presse*. Egypt's Muslim brotherhood slams corruption. November 6, 2003.
31.   "Reforming Egypt: In Search of a Strategy." *The International Crisis Group*. October 4, 2005.
32.   February 26, 2005.
33.   Law No. 153 (1999).
34.   Michelle Dunne. "Time to Pursue Democracy in Egypt." *Carnegie Endowment for International Peace*. 2007.
35.   James Traub. "Islamist Democracy?" *International Movement for a Just World*. June 4, 2007.
36.   "The Crackdown in Cairo." *The Washington Post* (editorial). July 19, 2006.
37.   Brian Murphy. "Islam's 'civil war' strikes deep." *Associated Press*. May 12, 2005.
38.   Brian Murphy. "Islam's civil war strikes deep." *Associated Press*. May 14, 2005.
39.   Brian Murphy. "Islam's 'civil war' strikes deep." *Associated Press*. May 12, 2005.
40.   Scott MacLeod. Is al-Qaeda in Sinai?" *Time Magazine*. October 18, 2004.
41.   Neil MacFarquhar. *The New York Times*. "Egyptian Group Patiently Pursues Dream of an Islamic State." January 20, 2002. p. 3.
42.   Brian Murphy. "Islam's 'civil war' strikes deep." *Associated Press*. May 12, 2005.
43.   Adel Hamouda, editor of Al Fagr quoted by Neil MacFarquhar. "Will Politics and Success at the Polls Tame Egypt's Muslim Brotherhood?" *The New York Times*. December 8, 2005. p. A18.
44.   Salah Nasrawi. "Muslim Brotherhood launches national campaign to remove Mubarak peacefully." *Associated Press*. June 30, 2005.
45.   Lisa Anderson. Egypt's cultural shift reflects Islam's pull." *Chicago Tribune*. March 21, 2004.
46.   State of the Union Speech. January, 23, 2006.
47.   James Traub. "Islamist Democracy?" *International Movement for a Just World*. June 4, 2007.

48.   Statement by Egypt's Foreign Ministry. May 19, 2006.

49.   During the Gulf War, Egypt was an indispensable ally. It committed 36,000 troops to the battle. The United States rewarded Egypt by writing-off $7 billion of its debt.

50.   *Nahdhat Misr* (Egypt). January 21, 2004.

51.   *Agence France Presse*. "Egypt's Muslim Brotherhood says Bush has missed the point." November 7, 2003.

52.   James Traub. "Islamist Democracy?" *International Movement for a Just World*. June 4, 2007.

53.   *Agence France Presse*. "Egypt's Muslim Brotherhood says Bush has missed the point." November 7, 2003.

54.   Statement posted on the Muslim Brotherhood web site, July 13, 2006.

55.   *Agence France Presse*. Egypt's Muslim Brothers urge Arab governments to supply arms to the Palestinians." October 25, 2001.

2

Hezbollah

A yellow Mercedes truck lumbered into the south parking lot of the United States Marine compound near Beirut International Airport. It circled slowly before accelerating through a barbed wire fence and crashing into the Marine sentry, stopping against a sandbag bunker. The truck's deadly cargo, equivalent to 12,000 pounds of explosives, detonated, demolishing the front end of the four-story Marine barracks and killing 240 Americans—part of the multinational peacekeeping force for Lebanon. In another part of the city, fifty-six French paratroopers were killed in a separate attack. With its coordinated suicide strikes of October 23, 1982, Hezbollah exploded onto the scene as one of the world's deadliest terrorist organizations.

History

Hezbollah means the "Party of God" after a verse in the Qur'an: "Lo! The Party of God, they are victorious."[1] Hezbollah was founded in 1983 with the goal of restoring Lebanon's sovereignty and ridding the country of foreign forces. Hezbollah's goal is to expand its influence with Lebanese Shi'a, consolidate control of southern Lebanon, and ultimately take over or be in a position to veto decisions of the Lebanese government. Since the outbreak of the Second Intifada in 2000, the Party (*Hizb*) wrapped itself in the struggle of Palestinians for self-determination, expanding ties with Hamas and Islamic Jihad. Hezbollah maintains that Palestine is occupied Muslim land and that the State of Israel should be destroyed.

Hezbollah's power base is with Lebanon's downtrodden Shi'a minority. Of Lebanon's 4.5 million people, about 40 percent are Christians and, of that number, about half are Maronites. Of the balance, about 50 percent are Shi'a Muslims, 40 percent are Sunni Muslims, and 10 percent are Druze.[2] Governance is based on the principle of power sharing between ethnic and religious groups (*Mithaq al-watani*).

The 1943 National Pact, which allocated political and bureaucratic positions based on population percentage, gave the Maronites a leading role in Lebanese affairs. Many non-Maronites questioned the validity of the 1932 census upon which the power-sharing formula is based. Inter-communal tensions turned violent with the outbreak of Lebanon's civil war (1973-1990), which took a disproportionate toll on the country's Shi'a.[3] Many were uprooted by Maronite-Palestinian fighting in 1976. One quarter million more were dislocated to Beirut's southern suburbs when Israel invaded southern Lebanon in 1978 and later undertook full-scale operations (1982-85).[4]

The balance between Lebanon's communities was also disrupted by the influx of Palestinian refugees beginning in 1949. About 100,000 Palestinians fled to southern Lebanon when Israel was founded. Tens of thousands more streamed into Lebanon as a result of Jordan's civil war in 1970. The Palestinian Liberation Organization (PLO) set up its headquarters in southern Lebanon. After the 1969 Cairo Accord of the Arab League sanctioned the PLO, it intensified military operations, ignoring the Lebanese government's authority and establishing a virtual state within a state.[5] Disaffected with the government's ability to deliver development and social justice, scores of young Shi'a joined Palestinian organizations and found common cause with the PLO.

Beginning in 1978, Israeli military strikes against the PLO in southern Lebanon helped create conditions that gave rise to Hezbollah. By the spring of 1982, Hezbollah had taken root and, "to maintain the balance of terror," rained Katyusha rockets on towns such as Kiryat-Shmona and Naharia as well as farming villages in northern Israel.[6] In response, Israel's Defense Minister Ariel Sharon led Israeli forces into Lebanon to expel the PLO and secure a friendly government. Israeli Defense Forces (IDF) encircled Beirut and besieged PLO positions north of the city.

U.S. President Ronald Reagan appointed Philip C. Habib as Special Envoy and tasked him with negotiating a cessation of hostilities. A seasoned diplomat, Habib successfully brokered an agreement allowing PLO fighters and Syrian troops in Beirut to withdraw under the protection of an international force of 1,200 American, French and Italian troops. As Yasser Arafat and the PLO leadership fled to Tunis, multinational forces were ordered back to their amphibious troop carriers. Heralded as a big success, the entire deployment lasted only sixteen days.

Just as it seemed that Lebanon had been stabilized, President-elect Bashir Gemayel was assassinated. With deadly conflict escalating,

Christian Phalangist militias composing the South Lebanon Army moved behind Israeli lines to attack the refugee camps of Sabra and Shatilla. More than 800 Palestinian and Lebanese civilians were slaughtered. Enraged Palestinians and Lebanese Shi'a promised reprisals.

By 1985, Israel established a security zone in southern Lebanon to prevent cross-border guerilla attacks. The security zone ranged from 27 km (about 18 miles) to 4 km (1.7 miles). Hezbollah objected, maintaining that the Israeli presence inside Lebanon was illegal and illegitimate. About 1,500 Israeli troops and 2,500 allied militias with the South Lebanon Army were involved in regular skirmishes with Hezbollah fighters. Hezbollah also attacked Israeli interests around the world. In March 1992, a suicide bomber struck the Israeli embassy in Buenos Aires killing 38. Nearly two years later, Hezbollah's affiliate, Islamic Jihad, bombed a Jewish cultural center in Buenos Aires killing 95 people. Hezbollah was also responsible for two suicide bombings on Jewish targets in London.

Hezbollah simultaneously intensified operations against Israeli troops in the southern security zone. Israel launched "Operation Grapes of Wrath" in 1996. When an artillery bombardment killed 105 refugees at a UN camp in the village of Qana, Hezbollah accused Israel of deliberately targeting civilians and stepped up its attacks. By 2000, about 900 Israeli soldiers had died in clashes with Hezbollah. With world support turning against Israel, popular support among Israelis for the occupation of Southern Lebanon also waned. Israel unilaterally withdrew from the security zone on May 25, 2000.

Its withdrawal, however, did not bring peace. United Nations Security Council resolution 425 (2000) established the so-called Blue Line demarcating the withdrawal of Israeli troops, separating southern Lebanon from Israel and the Golan Heights, and establishing Israel's 70-mile border with Syria. But it failed to address ownership of the Shaba'a Farms, a postage stamp-size territory of 15.6 square miles on Mount Hermon and along the western edge of the Golan. Though the original deed to Shaba'a Farms was issued by the Republic of Lebanon, border problems were compounded by lack of documentation from the French-British mandate period and adjustments made by the IDF. Israel claimed that it had fully satisfied its international obligations, but the UN demarcation left ambiguous whether 425 required Israel to vacate the Shaba'a Farms. A water dispute over the Hasbani River and Wazzani Springs also fueled tensions.

Hezbollah argued that Israel continued to occupy Lebanese territory and refused to disarm claiming its weapons were needed to liberate the

Shaba'a Farms. Iran and Syria also used Shaba'a Farms as a pretext for sponsoring Hezbollah's attacks against Israel and for sustaining the presence of foreign troops in Lebanon.

Leadership

Musa Al Sadr established the Legions of Lebanese Resistance or Amal ("Hope") as a political party representing different denominations in 1974. By demanding equal rights for Lebanon's deprived Shi'a, Amal gained especially strong support among Shi'a professionals and members of the middle class. After Sadr's death in Libya, Hussein Al Husseini headed Amal. He gave way to Nabih Berri who transformed the organization into a purely Shi'a militia practicing banditry and a lavish patronage network involving Amal's commercial benefactors and the Shi'a clerical establishment.

Over time, however, many Shi'a grew disaffected with Amal. Though Berri insisted that he was an antagonist of Israel's, Amal's rank–and–file was upset by Berri's decision not to oppose Israel's 1982 invasion of southern Lebanon, which drove out the PLO. Amal's secular ideology was anathema to young Shi'a devotees committed to "strive in the path of God"—the literal meaning of jihad.

Hezbollah was created in 1982 during the Israeli invasion, but its existence was not formally announced until three years later on the anniversary of the Sabra and Shatilla massacres. Hezbollah capitalized on Lebanon's sectarian frictions to recruit supporters among Shi'a yearning for equal treatment from the state. Moreover, the absence of a central authority during the civil war created a vacuum, which was filled by Hezbollah. In conception, Hezbollah defined itself as the mirror opposite to Amal.

Born in 1960, Hassan Nasrallah is the son a grocer from Bezourieh, a poor Lebanese village near the Israeli border. Known for his fiery rhetoric, Nasrallah wears a black turban signifying that he is a direct descendant of the Prophet Mohammed *(Sayyed)*. He and other young Shi'a clerics went to Najaf for studies at the Imam Ali Shrine but fled Iraq in 1978 to avoid arrest by Saddam's Mukhabarat (intelligence agencies). After fleeing Iraq, Nasrallah returned to Lebanon and joined Amal. Spurned by Musa Al Sadr, he rejected the clerical establishment. Nasrallah castigated Amal's accommodation of Israel after the 1982 invasion and its ties with Syria. After a falling out between Nasrallah's supporters and Amal, which resulted in vicious bloodletting between Shi'a factions, Nasrallah joined Hezbollah where he served as finance and military chief under Sheikh Subhi Al Tufayli.

Al Tufayli was replaced by Sheikh Al Musawi who was loyal to Ayatollah Khomeini and Iran's hard-line interior minister. Al Musawi was behind the taking of Western hostages. When two Israeli attack helicopters fired missiles at a convoy killing Al Musawi, his wife and six-year-old son on February 16, 1992, Nasrallah succeeded him as Hezbollah's secretary general.[7]

Nasrallah's son, Hadi, was also killed by the IDF. However, Nasrallah was unconcerned about assassination. He proclaimed, "We are a people who love martyrdom."[8] Nasrallah became a hero throughout the Arab world for his resistance against Israel. He also proved to be a tough negotiator. In 2004, he secured the release of 429 prisoners and the handover of 59 bodies of Hezbollah fighters in exchange for a single Israeli businessman and the remains of three Israeli soldiers.

Mohammed Hussein Fadlallah is Hezbollah's spiritual leader upon whom devotees worldwide rely for guidance (*Marja'iyya*). Reflecting the rivalry between Iran and Syria for influence in Lebanon at the time, as well as feuding between Persian and Arab religious leaders, Fadlallah criticized Iranian clerics for trying to establish the Iranian city of Qum as the center for Shi'a learning as opposed to Najaf, site of the Holy Imam Ali Shrine. Ayatollah Khomeini snubbed Fadlallah. In turn, Fadlallah refused his successor, Ayatollah Khamenei, any title other than Supreme Leader (*Rahbar*). Fadlallah believes that he, not Khamenei, is the model for emulation (*Marja' al-taqlid*).

As Hezbollah became more and more a proxy of Iran, Fadlallah took steps to establish his own power base by emphasizing financial and operational independence from the Party. He cultivated his own cadre of followers who gave alms rivaling contributions to Hezbollah.[9] As a measure of Hezbollah's unhappiness with Fadlallah's independence, Hezbollah rank-and-file sprayed graffiti on Fadlallah's home in the Beka'a reading: "Traitor and blasphemist."

Fadlallah and Nasrallah share the goal of justice for Shi'a. However, Fadlallah openly embraces democracy as a vehicle for establishing Shi'a power in Lebanon. He also supports Lebanon's confessional system that awards positions based on population percentages. Fadlallah accepts secular definitions of the rule of law. Yet, at the same time, he criticizes constitutional democracy as a Western construct alien to the Arab world. Fadlallah also sends mixed messages on the appropriate use of violence. He condemns suicide terrorism, while condoning violence under certain conditions.

Fadlallah is adamant that Hezbollah should not become just another militia engaged in indiscriminate violence. To this end, he denounces random violence instead emphasizing guerilla activities that are global in scope. He claimed, "I did not know about the bombing of the American Marines in Beirut until after it happened."[10] He also criticized the 1993 World Trade Center bombing, "There is no justification for such actions in a country where Muslims have freedom to practice their faith. The people in the World Trade Center had no link to politics; we had no right to hurt them. We condemn all similar murders of innocent people in public places."[11] Fadlallah was the first Islamic figure to speak out about September 11.[12] He endorsed dialogue "especially with one's enemies"[13]

Despite some conciliatory statements, Fadlallah's Arabic language sermons typically convey a more militant approach. "We are proceeding toward a battle with vice at its roots and the first root of vice is America." While distancing himself from Khomeini, he also referred to him as "Our leader [who] has repeatedly stressed that America is the cause of all catastrophes and the source of all malice." Fadlallah promised, "We will turn Lebanon into a graveyard for American schemes."[14]

Despite their differences, Nasrallah and Fadlallah are united in their hatred of the United States, which they both refer to as the world's leading terrorist state. In addition, both are committed to the destruction of Israel, although Fadlallah hedges by indicating that Israel could exist if it accepts a just peace with Palestinians. Both are staunch champions of Lebanon's sovereignty and have a deep disdain for Saudi Arabia's royal family, which they accuse of pouring money into Lebanon to support Sunni sects and their pro-Western protégés. Nasrallah and Fadlallah also share tactics. Both supported Hezbollah's decision to participate in parliamentary elections. They also supported the release of the last Western hostages in 1992.

Some of the world's most notorious terrorists are associated with Hezbollah. Imad Mugniyah was the most infamous. Mugniyah commanded Islamic Jihad, which the U.S. Office of Counterterrorism called the clandestine branch of Hezbollah. An original member of Force 17, Arafat's personal guard, Mugniyah joined Fadlallah's security detail when Arafat left for Tunis.

Mugniyah was behind much of the hostage-taking in Lebanon. It is believed that he personally tortured and killed William Buckley, the CIA Station Chief in Beirut. He engineered the 1988 murder of Lt. Col. William Richard Higgins, a Marine on peacekeeping duty in Lebanon. Mugniyah also inspired freelance hostage taking cells, such as the Revolutionary Justice Organization and the Organization of the Oppressed on Earth, which held Terry Waite, and other Western hostages the last of whom was released in 1992.

Involved in hijacking and murder, Mugniyah was indicted by U.S. courts for masterminding the hijacking of TWA Flight 847 in 1985 and the execution of U.S. Navy diver Robert Stethem, whose body was dumped from the cockpit onto the tarmac of Beirut International Airport. Hezbollah's Shura Council denies the existence of an external security wing and publicly disavows actions by Mugniyah, who report-edly changed his appearance several times using plastic surgery. A car bomb exploded in Damascus killing Mugniyah in early 2008. No one claimed responsibility.

Structure

Hezbollah is a hierarchical organization that emphasizes discipline and secrecy. The Party is a coalition of Shi'a clerics, each with their own constituents and loyalties to Iranian personalities. The Shura Council is led by Nasrallah and includes seventeen clerics. It is responsible for overall administration as well as executive, legislative, judicial, political, and military affairs. Until 1993, Iranian officials served on the Shura.

The General Secretariat is made up of an executive committee com-prising district heads (i.e., Beirut, the southern suburbs, the South, and Beka'a), as well as five people appointed by the Shura Council. The Politburo, which includes fifteen members, coordinates the activities of Party committees (i.e., Enforcement Recruitment and Propaganda, Holy Reconstruction, Security, and the Combat Committee, which includes the Islamic Resistance responsible for suicide attacks and the Islamic Holy War, which is engaged in more conventional military operations against Israeli forces). As a Lebanese journalist noted, "Hezbollah thrives on perpetual conflict."[15] It includes at least 1,000 full-time experienced fighters and up to 10,000 reservists. Militias are local men with family ties and jobs who are totally integrated into Lebanese society.[16]

Though Hezbollah acts at a community level, it is a far-flung multi-national organization with a worldwide presence. Hezbollah maintains a network of terrorist cells and training camps in Asia, Europe, and in South America where it uses the triple frontier of Brazil, Argentina, and Paraguay as a base of operations. Deep in the Amazon rainforest, it runs weekend terror-training seminars. South American operations are financed by smuggling, narcotics, and the sale of contraband such as bootleg software and CDs. Funds are also raised through extortion and money laundering.

Clerics sympathetic to Hezbollah also encourage believers to provide funds. According to Nasrallah, "We can all contribute money.... We must not treat this matter lightly. All the institutions, committees, parties, private and collective initiatives throughout the Muslim world must be spurred on to collect money...and to bring that money to Palestine.... If we cannot give them arms, we can give them the money to buy them."[17]

Ideology

Hezbollah was inspired by the Iranian Revolution of 1979. Its founders were dedicated to the establishment of an "all-encompassing Islamic state based on Shari'a law including Lebanon."[18] They maintained, "We do not constitute an organization and closed party in Lebanon nor are we a tight political cadre. We are a community (*Umma*) linked to the Muslims of the whole world by the doctrinal and religious connection to Islam."[19] Its founders believed that, "The divine state of justice realized on this earth will not remain confined within [Lebanon's] geographic borders. Dawn will lead to the appearance of the Mahdi, who will create the state of Islam on earth."[20] The Mahdi is the twelfth Imam and a direct descendant of Ali bin Abi Talib, the cousin and son-in-law of the Prophet who mysteriously disappeared and, it is believed, will manifest himself again on earth to establish justice. Shi'a believe that the hidden Imam will appear on Judgment Day.

Hezbollah's ideology is rooted in the cult of martyrdom, which dates back to 680 AD when Ali was betrayed and murdered in Karbala: "Hezbollah's strength resided in its ability to harness a hundred grievances to one sublime purpose, and to persuade its downtrodden adherents of their own hidden strength—the strength of sacrifice."[21] Hezbollah "transformed an exemplary act of suffering and sacrifice into an inspiring model for revolution and action [including suicide attacks]."[22] According to Deputy Secretary General Sheikh Naim Qasim, "We do not call them suicide operations because suicide comes out of a loss of hope in life, while martyrdom is a love of life."[23]

Released in February 1985, Hezbollah's open letter to "The Downtrodden in Lebanon and in the World" described a struggle between the oppressor (*Mustakbirun*) and the oppressed (*Mustad'ifin*). It endorsed the use of violence against the enemies of Islam. Fadlallah insists: "We're not advocating violence because we like to kill people. When other people impose violence, when they occupy my country, I have to use violence to fight violence."[24] According to Fadlallah, "The Qur'an says to us, if you have a choice, use nonviolence for it will transform your enemies into friends. But if your fate and freedom are at stake, if someone occupies your country and you cannot end that occupation through nonviolent means, then occupation is violence done to you.... Islamists do not resort to violence unless they are denied political freedom."[25] The letter blamed Israel and its patron, the United States, for Lebanon's problems—and the world's ills.

According to Nasrallah, "In our opinion, the Jewish state is an illegitimate and illegal state and will remain so in the eyes of the Arab and Muslim people even if it exists for 50, 100, or 200 years."[26] Invoking United Nations Security Council Resolution 425 that called for Israel's unconditional withdrawal from Lebanese territory, Nasrallah insisted, "The Mujahadin from Hezbollah are exercising their right to fight an occupying force ... if the Israelis withdraw from all Lebanese territory, then [Hezbollah] will cease all action."[27] According to Nasrallah: "If we searched the entire world for a person more cowardly, despicable, weak, and feeble in psyche, mind, ideology and religion, we would not find anyone like the Jew."[28] A member of the Shura Council intoned "[The Jews] can go back to Germany or wherever they came from [after we] finish off the entire cancerous Zionist project."[29]

Its message resonated with Lebanese Shi'a who believe that by their miserable lot in life is exacerbated by Israel's presence—and America's unflinching support. Hezbollah draws no distinction between civilians and members of Israel's security services because "in occupied Palestine there is no difference between a soldier and a civilian, for they are all invaders, occupiers, and usurpers of the land."[30] Symbolized by its flag, a yellow banner with a raised fist and AK-47, Hezbollah is committed to perpetual jihad. "[Israel] is an illegal state," asserts Nasrallah. "It is a cancerous entity and the root of all the crises and wars. We can not acknowledge the existence of a state called Israel, not even far in the future, as some people have tried to suggest."[31] Nasrallah pledged to "Liberate the whole of Palestine from the sea to the river."[32]

Hezbollah's promise to establish an Islamic state resonated with Lebanon's devout and downtrodden Shi'a. Over the years, Hezbollah moderated its extremist views as it entered politics and needed to satisfy an increasingly multifaceted constituency. Consolidating its grassroots support, Hezbollah maintained that it was merely a social service organization and political party. It made the strategic decision to accept the

1989 Taif Accord that ended Lebanon's civil war and institutionalized sectarian power sharing. However, its acceptance should not be misunderstood as support for the principle of power sharing embodied in the accord. It was, moreover, based on the recognition that Lebanon could not become an Islamic state overnight and that Hezbollah's long-term interests could best be achieved by acceptance of the established rules.

During Lebanon's civil war, Hezbollah provided essential services to the country's Shi'a, including special assistance to the families of Hezbollah fighters "martyred" in combat. Food distribution centers gave rations to thousands of families including survivors of "martyr operations." To provide medical services, it created mobile infirmaries, dental clinics, and pharmacies. Among its four hospitals and 500 clinics, facilities in Nabatiya and the Beirut southern suburbs are state-of-the-art. Assistance included the set-up of agricultural cooperatives that provided seeds, fertilizers, and insecticides at subsidized rates. Between 1988 and 1991, it rebuilt more than 1,000 homes damaged during military actions. Reconstruction activities also involved the repair of water and utility systems. Hezbollah operates dozens of schools. At the Shared Witness School, a few minutes from the airport barracks where the bombing occurred in 1983, children of martyrs represent 25 percent of the student body.

The Party has developed an increasingly sophisticated communications network and public relations strategy. Its television station, the Beacon (*Al Manar*), is licensed by the Lebanese government and claims 15 million viewers each day. Al Manar produces 70 percent of its programming including talk shows, children's shows, and religious programs. Chairman Nayyef Krayyem states, "It's a political weapon, social weapon, and cultural weapon."[33]

Hezbollah also operates radio stations—Voice of Faith (*Sawt Al Imam*) and Voice of Struggle (*Sawt Al Nidal*). Its publications are *Al Ahed*, a weekly party mouthpiece, and *Al Bilad*, a monthly magazine. In addition, Hezbollah has four different websites in three different languages.

Elections

Hezbollah agonized over the decision whether to participate in Lebanon's 1992 parliamentary elections. Islamists within the organization rejected electoral participation maintaining that governance is not the right of the polity but only of God. They argued that no constitution transcends the Qur'an and no parliamentary democracy trumps Allah. Fadlallah responded, "Change does not happen only through revolution

… it could be achieved by penetrating democratic institutions to promote Islamic ideals."[34]

Nasrallah pointed out that Hezbollah's electoral participation would be a step towards toppling the secular government through peaceful means. He espoused the belief that participation in elections represented an acknowledgment that an Islamic state could be achieved at the ballot box. He believed that Lebanese society would be best served through the institutionalization of Islamic law (Shari'a) via an evolutionary rather than a revolutionary process.

In the elections of 1992, Hezbollah won eight of 128 seats. However, it refused to take a cabinet post out of concern that joining the government would require it to bear responsibility for its mistakes. Free from the responsibility of governing, Hezbollah constantly harangued Prime Minister Rafiq Hariri, charging him with political corruption and administrative inefficiency. It also criticized Hariri for failing to provide funds for development projects in Shi'a-populated parts of the country.[35]

Hezbollah had previously tried to stay above the fray and transcend trivial politics. Over the years, Nasrallah's measured leadership caused many Lebanese to view him as a national rather than a sectarian or pan-Islamic figure. Nasrallah explained Hezbollah's decision to expand its political role: "We felt that Lebanon today is at a crossroads and this requires that we be more active internally."[36]

The Party became deeply immersed in political deal-making drawing up its own lists in some districts and entering into coalition lists in others. In the next round of parliamentary elections, Hezbollah established a functional alliance with the Hariri family. It joined Walid Jumblat's Druse list in the east; formed a coalition with Maronite Christians and Michel Aoun in the north; and teamed up with Amal and the Progressive Socialist Party in the south. All told, Hezbollah fielded fourteen candidates across Lebanon. It performed well. With heavy turnout in Shi'a areas, the Hezbollah/Amal coalition won every seat in southern Lebanon on the border with Israel.

The United States welcomed Hezbollah's political participation. The Bush administration hoped it "would set off a virtuous cycle, as Hezbollah's continuing political success would depend on its ability to bring stability and prosperity to its Lebanese constituents instead of on its violent efforts against Israel and the United States."[37] It believed that a more open political system in Lebanon would place increasing disarmament pressures on Hezbollah. According to President George W. Bush: "[Though] we view Hezbollah as a terrorist organization, I would hope that Hezbollah would prove that they are not by laying down their arms and not threatening peace."[38]

It was significant that Bush called on Hezbollah to disarm itself rather than threaten the group with violence. It was also significant that U.S. officials described steps for Hezbollah's removal from the list of Foreign Terrorist Organizations (FTOs). According to the White House spokesman, "Organizations like Hezbollah have to choose. Either you're a terrorist organization or you're a political organization."[39]

Hezbollah struck a conciliatory tone after elections. Nasrallah indicated, "We are ready to talk about everything...without foreign interference."[40] Hezbollah also pursued a less confrontational regional policy. To avoid jeopardizing Israel's withdrawal from the Gaza Strip, Hezbollah scaled back support for radical Palestinian groups. Nasrallah also suggested that Hezbollah's military wing could be dismantled in the event of a comprehensive Middle East peace.

After Israel's withdrawal from southern Lebanon in 2000, some Shura members advocated less focus on the Palestinian cause and greater focus on Lebanese politics. They argued that Hezbollah could no longer use the issue of Israeli occupation to garner broad popular support. The Shura debated and ultimately agreed to accept a ministerial post in the new government. It reasoned that Hezbollah's presence in the parliament and government could be used as leverage to reduce pressures for Hezbollah to disarm.

In July 2000, UN Secretary General Kofi Annan and Nasrallah met in Beirut. Their meeting was heralded by the American Arab Anti-Discrimination Committee: "Hezbollah's status as a legitimate political movement and genuine liberation force is universally recognized outside of Israel."[41]

Despite the fact that Hezbollah dominates scores of city councils, it has failed to fully realize that "all politics are local." Unaffiliated Shi'a criticized Hezbollah for failing to participate in the debate over privatization and thereby allowing the marginalization of Shi'a workers in 2003. That same year, Shi'a taxi drivers in Beirut were angered when Hezbollah raised no objection to new government regulations requiring them to upgrade engine performance at considerable cost. Many Shi'a also criticized Hezbollah for failing to secure significant government funding for development projects in the Beka'a.

Financing

The Islamic Republic of Iran and Iranian charities were the primary sponsors of Hezbollah during the Party's early years. Estimates of Iran's financial contributions vary widely. On the upper end, the representative of a politically active Shi'a family in Lebanon asserts that Iran gave Hezbollah $20 billion between 1982 and 1992.[42]

Funds were not only used for guerilla activities but also to pay for social services such as schools, hospitals, and agricultural projects. Iran's Martyr's Foundation dispensed grants to families with relatives who died or were wounded.[43] Hezbollah used these funds to gain a foothold in the Shi'a community. It also earned favor with clerics by giving funds to local mosques that served as recruitment centers for its militia.[44]

Since 1992, Hezbollah has taken steps to become more financially self-sufficient. It owns various enterprises including a construction and engineering company employing Party members and the families of martyrs. Hezbollah's dominant position in the power and telecommunications sectors assures it reliable revenues from legitimate sources. Hezbollah also has significant stock market investments making it a stakeholder in Lebanon's economy.

Not all of Hezbollah's funds come from foreign contributions or domestic enterprises. To enhance its revenue, Hezbollah forged alliances with prosperous Shi'a clans in the Beka'a involved in heroin trafficking. Hezbollah is engaged in other illicit activities such as gunrunning and counterfeiting. It also supports its terror operations by dealing in diamonds mined in war zones such as in Liberia, Congo, and Sierra Leone.[45]

Escalation

In January 2001, Israel intercepted the *San Torini* that had embarked from Lebanon carrying arms bound for Palestinian groups. Later that year, Hezbollah members were arrested in Jordan for smuggling Katyusha rockets to Palestinians. In 2002, the *Karine A* embarked from Iran with a Hezbollah-trained crew before it was seized on its way to Gaza. In May 2003 the *Abu Hasan*, an Egyptian-flagged fishing boat, was boarded at sea and found to be carrying explosives bound for Gaza.

Even after 9/11, the United States remained far more concerned about threats from Iran than it was about Al Qaeda. In February 2002, Deputy National Security Adviser Stephen Hadley warned of Hezbollah "dormant cells" in the United States.[46] In 2003, Deputy Secretary of State Richard Armitage asserted, "Hezbollah may be the A team of terrorists," while "Al Qaeda is actually the B team." Armitage also warned that Hezbollah was an organization with "global reach."[47] Concerns were echoed by CIA head George Tenet: "I'll tell you that Hezbollah, as an organization with capability and worldwide presence, is Al Qaeda's equal, if not a far more capable organization [with] ongoing capability to launch terrorist attacks within the United States."[48]

On November 3, 2002, the United States classified Hezbollah as an FTO (foreign terrorist organization). The designation authorized immediate and unilateral sanctions against any third party that does not take steps to freeze Hezbollah's assets or extradite its personnel. The U.S. Office of Counterterrorism described Hezbollah as a "radical Shi'a group dedicated to the creation of an Iranian-style Islamic republic in Lebanon and removal of all non-Islamic influences from the area."[49] It maintained that Hezbollah and Islamic Jihad are the same organization.[50]

U.S. officials pressed European and other governments to declare Hezbollah an FTO in order to strangle its finances. Canada designated Hezbollah a terrorist organization in 2002. Given close ties between President Bush and Australia's Prime Minister John Howard, Canberra followed suit the following year. On March 8, 2005, the European Parliament voted 473 to eight to condemn Hezbollah terrorism. In response Nasrallah claimed, "We are a Lebanese Party that fought occupation forces on Lebanese territory. We have not carried out operations anywhere in the world."[51]

Shin Bet, Israel's security agency, concluded that Hezbollah provided weapons, funding, and guidance to 70-80 percent of Palestinian insurgent activities in the West Bank.[52] It maintained that Hezbollah operates terrorist organizations and cells within Israel; smuggled terrorists and collaborators into Israel using foreign and forged documents; and provided financial support and guerilla training to Palestinians organizations and groups. It also asserted that Hezbollah bombmakers trained Hamas in the use of land mines and improvised explosive devices (IEDs). In addition, "Hezbollah's Palestinian squads have conducted arms smuggling, recruitment, attempted suicide bombings, sniper and roadside shooting attacks, pre-operational surveillance of Israeli communities and army bases, and planned kidnapping of Israelis."[53]

Shin Bet also asserted correctly that Hezbollah was aggressively expanding its weapons stockpile to include large numbers of Katyusha rockets, Sagger and Strella anti-tank missiles, Fajr ground-to-ground rockets with a range of seventy km, and Stinger anti-aircraft missiles.[54] It speculated that Hezbollah's arms build up may be part of a deterrence strategy to dissuade Israel from taking military action against Lebanon or it could be part of a plan to use military action as a way of sabotaging prospects for an Arab-Israeli peace that excluded Syria.

On February 14, 2005, a white Mitsubishi van left Syria and traversed Hezbollah strongholds in the Beka'a on its way to Beirut. Parked outside the St. George Hotel, it exploded just as Rafik Hariri's motorcade was passing by. The blast damaged buildings blocks away killing scores including Hariri. The UN's assassination report implicated top Syrian intelligence officials including President Bashar Al Assad's brother, Maher, and his powerful brother-in-law, General Asef Shawkat. The Popular Front for the Liberation of Palestine; which has close ties with Syria as well as Hezbollah, was also believed to have participated in the operation.

Hundreds of thousands demonstrated in Beirut demanding an investigation into Hariri's assassination and the withdrawal of Syrian military and intelligence. The ensuing "Mercedes Revolution" was led by Sunni and Christian members of the upper and middle classes. The Christian opposition demanded that Hezbollah disarm. It argued that Lebanon is no longer occupied and, therefore, there is no need for private groups or parties to have weapons. On March 8, Hezbollah organized a counter-demonstration of almost one million people in Riad Al Sulh Square; Nasrallah praised Syria for its support and vowed to keep resisting until a comprehensive settlement was reached.

Syria crossed the line by assassinating Hariri. Despite their falling out over the Iraq War, the United States and France worked together to adopt UNSC Resolution 1559 on September 4, 2005. It called for the withdrawal of all foreign forces from Lebanon and the extension of Lebanese government sovereignty throughout the country. The resolution also condemned Syria's involvement and demanded full cooperation with the UN investigation.

Nasrallah rejected 1559 calling it a device to create chaos and justify foreign intervention.[55] He was especially concerned about Article 3, which called for "disbanding and disarmament of all the Lebanese and non-Lebanese militias."[56] Insisting that Hezbollah is a resistance movement not an armed militia, he rejected external pressure. Nasrallah argued that Hezbollah's weapons were needed to protect Lebanon from Israeli attacks. He warned his followers not to allow foreign powers to meddle in Lebanese politics. "[Resolution] 1559 constitutes foreign intervention, with the encouragement of Israel, which wants to get rid of our weapons and of the resistance so that it can do whatever it likes. But if anyone, no matter whom, even thinks about disarming the resistance, we will fight him like the martyrdom seekers of Karbala. Any such step is an Israeli act and any hand reaching for the resistance's weapons is an Israeli hand—and we will chop it off."[57]

Syria's foreign minister also asserted that 1559 was part of America's plans to rearrange the map of the Middle East. Bashar Al Assad discerned that the tide was turning. Though Assad bowed to intense international pressure and promised to pull Syrian troops back to the Beka'a, his pledge fell short of a complete withdrawal from Lebanon. When Assad finally agreed to fast-track the complete withdrawal of Syrian forces, thousands of Lebanese turned out to celebrate. Lebanon's Sunnis, Christians, Druze, and some Shi'a groups ignored warnings of civil war coming together to reject outside intervention, demand sovereignty, and reaffirm their commitment to the Taif Accord. They also embraced democracy as a vehicle for asserting their policies through the ballot box.

Nasrallah's approach to politics was transformed by Hariri's assassination. Hezbollah found itself for the first time without a foreign patron when Damascus withdrew its 20,000 army and military intelligence personnel in June 2005 and was implicated three months later in Hariri's assassination. With Syria, on the ropes, Nasrallah tried to solve the problem by creating a bigger one.

Hezbollah used the period after Israel's withdrawal from southern Lebanon to rearm its militias with Iranian missiles transported via Syria. With assistance from North Korea, it developed a vast network of tunnels and bunkers in southern Lebanon. While it waited for the right moment to attack, Hezbollah maintained operations along the Israel border in order to demonstrate its continued commitment to violence and Israel's destruction. The opportunity came in May 2006 when a car bomb exploded in Sidon killing a senior member of Islamic Jihad. Hezbollah accused Israel of assassination and launched attacks using Katyusha rockets. In response, Israeli war planes pounded suspected launch points in the worst cross-border fighting since 2000. With 300 Lebanese in Israeli jails, Hezbollah openly acknowledged its plan to take Israeli hostages for the purpose of prisoner exchange.

On July 12, 2006, Hezbollah commandos crossed the border into Israel killing eight soldiers and capturing Ehud Goldwasser and Eldad Regev. Israel's Prime Minister Ehud Olmert held the Lebanese government responsible for Hezbollah's aggression. He pointed out that, for almost two years, Lebanon had failed to implement UN Security Council Resolution 1559 calling on the Lebanese army to take control of the border and dismantle militia groups.

Concerned that Hezbollah would move the kidnapped soldiers to a third country, Olmert implemented a full naval blockade. He also ordered the Israeli air force to bomb the runways of Rafik Hariri International Airport and destroy the main highway between Beirut and Damascus. When Hezbollah escalated its firing of rockets into the Galilee, IDF mechanized units and infantry crossed the border into southern Lebanon. Olmert's goal was to drive Hezbollah across the Litani River where its rockets would be out of range of towns in northern Israel. Operations also sought to degrade Hezbollah's capabilities and, if possible, kill Nasrallah.

Nasrallah promised total war. Hezbollah had "no choice" but to launch reprisals against civilians, he maintained. "As long as the enemy acts without limitations or red lines, it is our right to continue the confrontation without limits."[58] Despite the heavy air bombardment using precision-guided munitions, Hezbollah continued its daily fire of Katyushas on towns of the Galilee. Thunder 1, Fajr 3 and Fajr 5 missiles struck Haifa, Israel's third largest city with a population of 300,000. Hezbollah even used an Iranian C-802 computer guided land-to-sea missile to attack an Israeli naval ship. Nasrallah promised to attack Tel Aviv with its arsenal of long-range Iranian Zelzal missiles.

Hezbollah's capabilities took Israel by surprise. Israel's intelligence services were caught flat-footed and its vaunted ground forces got bogged down in southern Lebanon. Just like the Six Day War, Israel hoped for a decisive victory. It was not to be. Olmert and Defense Minister Amir Peretz were responsible for a series of miscalculations. On the military side, they misjudged the impact of air power in dislocating and eradicating Hezbollah. On the diplomatic front, Israel lost the moral high ground when Olmert and Peretz decided to launch reprisals across Lebanon. Israel's intensified use of cluster bombs in the final days of the conflict was condemned worldwide.

Hezbollah gained public support in Lebanon as the conflict escalated. The war forged a sense of social cohesion and common purpose among Lebanon's factions united by their view of Israel as the common enemy. Even Israel's friends making up the anti-Syrian coalition in Lebanon were fiercely critical of Israel's decision to launch reprisals across the country.

With war raging, Prime Minister Fouad Siniora presented a seven-point peace plan at a conference in Rome on July 26, 2006. The plan formed the basis for UN Security Council resolution 1701 that called on Israel to withdraw from Lebanon and for the Government of Lebanon to assert its control in the South and disarm militias. For its part, the international community initially pledged $900 million for reconstruction and agreed to expand the United Nations Interim Force in Lebanon (UNIFIL) into a more capable peacekeeping force. The resolution was approved by the

Lebanese cabinet, which includes ministers from Hezbollah. It was also endorsed by Iran, Syria, and the Arab League.[59]

The war ended after thirty-four days. Hundreds died on both sides, thousands were displaced, and there was extensive damage to civilian infrastructure and businesses. Olmert tried to claim victory but his appeal was drowned out by domestic critics and calls for an investigation into the conduct of the war. In fact, Hezbollah was the big winner. With the Lebanese government largely invisible in war-ravaged parts of southern Lebanon, Hezbollah stepped into the breach using money from Iran to make cash payments of up to $12,000 per family. Rather than the Lebanese government, Hezbollah's yellow flags were visible in rubble-strewn villages that had suffered the brunt of Israel's attacks.

For standing up to Israel, Nasrallah was celebrated in Lebanon and across the Shi'a and Arab worlds. The thity-four-day war positioned Hezbollah and Amal on the cusp of power. Hezbollah organized massive street protests when Siniora refused to increase Hezbollah's representation in the cabinet thereby giving it veto power. The government ground to a halt when Hezbollah ministers resigned in protest. Beirut's cafes were buzzing with discussion about Hezbollah's efforts to control the government in order to block the UN tribunal investigating Syria's involvement in Hariri's assassination and prevent implementation of other provisions in Resolution 1701.

Though it failed to publicly pressure Israel to end its bombardment, the United States and other donors rallied behind Siniora as soon as the fighting ended. At the Paris donors' conference, reconstruction funds were pledged and political support extended to Siniora's government. The United States also urged Siniora to resume the disarmament dialogue with Hezbollah, which had come to a crashing halt. Progress was undermined, however, when conflict erupted between the Lebanese army and Fatah Al Islam militants on May 20, 2007.

Siniora inherited Fatah Al Islam from Hariri who, it is believed, established the Sunni militant organization as a counterweight to Hezbollah. Hariri coordinated support through the Information Bureau (*Maa'loumat*) of the National Police. At Hariri's behest, Saudi funds were channeled through the Mediterranean Bank, which Hariri owned.

After Hariri's death, Siniora decided to distance his administration from Fatah Al Islam. When the Fatah Al Islam representative went to the bank to collect the organization's monthly stipend, he learned that funding was suspended and decided to rob the bank. Commandos from the Maa'loumat responded by raiding a Fatah Al Islam safe house in Tripoli killing 20. The army's Second Bureau (*El-Maktabthani*) was targeted for reprisal by Fatah Al Islam in an operation that killed thity-three soldiers. Violence escalated from there.[60]

Many Al-Islam fighters came from Iraq and were inspired by Al Qaeda. They infiltrated some of the twelve Palestinian refugee camps in Lebanon including Nahr Al Bared. American military transport planes from Kuwait steadily delivered aid to assist Siniora's government in its fight against Fatah Al Islam. With U.S. financial and technical support, the Lebanese Army established a cordon around Nahr Al Bared. It shut off electricity, water, and other essential services. More than 25,000 defenseless civilians fled the camp. Fatah Al Islam sleeper cells instigated operations from other camps in the south such as Ain Al Hilwe. As fighting spread to Sidon, Lebanese became increasingly alarmed by the prospect of violence spreading across the country. The confrontation with Fatah Al Islam highlighted weaknesses of the Siniora government and underscored the risk of deadly violence escalating between Lebanon's ethnic, religious, and political factions.

These fears were confirmed when street clashes broke out in early 2008 between the Lebanese Army and supporters of Hezbollah and Amal. The struggle between Siniora and Hezbollah incapacitated Lebanon, which was unable to select a president for months as rival parties jockeyed for power. It also undermined the Arab League's plan for resolving Lebanon's crisis, which involved the formation of a national unity government with a compromise candidate as president and plans for a new election based on an improved electoral law. Street violence gave rise to questions about the viability of power-sharing embodied in the Taif Accord. It also cast a long shadow over Lebanon's future as the ideological confrontation intensified between Lebanese with a western orientation and those with a more eastern perspective.

The impasse was finally resolved on May 21, 2008, averting a civil war, the deal to form a new government empowered Hezbollah and its backers, Syria and Iran. While General Michel Suleiman became president, and Hezbollah and its opposition allies were awarded enough cabinet seats to veto any decision. The Electoral reform involved the creation of the country's sects. Hezbollah kept its arsenal pledging not to use its weapons against Lebanese.

International Actors

United States

Nasrallah maintained, "[The United States] has been exploiting the events of September 11 to achieve its long term strategies around the world."[61] "We are not against the American people," insisted Fadlallah. "We are against the policy of the American administration, especially as it relates to Israel."[62] He insisted, "The U.S. does not have an American policy in the Middle East, but an 'Israel policy' which stems from its ideological commitment to Israel."[63] He asked, "Is it in the interest of the people of the United States to make enemies of 400 million Arabs and 1.4 billion Muslims in the world for the sake of a small country like Israel, which is an occupying country?"[64]

Fadlallah tried to strike a more conciliatory tone. "We are not against the American people, but we are against the policy of the American administration," he said.[65] "We don't hate the American people, on the contrary, we love them. We ask the Congress and all the U.S. politicians: Why do you hate us?"[66]

U.S.-Syrian relations were also a flash point. The United States placed Syria on its original list of state sponsors of terrorism in 1979. The Bush administration was unrelenting in its criticism of Syria. U.S. Secretary of State Condoleezza Rice described it as "a shield for terrorist activities in southern Lebanon."[67] The State Department criticized Syria as a "safe haven and logistical support to a number of terrorist groups" including Hezbollah.[68] The Iraq War further exacerbated tensions between the United States and Syria. Secretary of Defense Donald H. Rumsfeld warned Damascus that allowing Syria to become the insurgency's headquarters and financing center constituted "hostile acts."[69] The U.S. Congress agreed. It passed the Syrian Accountability Act of 2004 imposing additional restrictions on private investment, banking, and air travel.

Hezbollah drew parallels between America's occupation of Iraq and Israel's invasion of Lebanon in 1982. "We don't believe that the United States has come to free Iraq, but to install a new dictator with democratic features, one that can protect its interests more than Saddam did," said Nasrallah, "The United States has made alliances with most dictatorial states the cruelest states in the Arab, Islamic, and third worlds as long as this is in line with its interests.... I believe that the Iraqi people, especially Shi'a Muslims, reject any occupier. This war has united the Islamic world from border to border against the United States."[70] Hezbollah responded cynically to U.S. policy that emphasized, "Helping create the conditions for a political environment in Lebanon that is free of violence, free of intimidation and that is responsive to the desires of the Lebanese people."[71]

President Bush called Hezbollah "pathetic."[72] His antipathy was just as strong towards Syria. Linking Syria and Hezbollah, he declared, "The time has come for Syria to fully implement Security Council Resolution 1559. All Syrian military forces and intelligence personnel must withdraw before Lebanese elections for those elections to be free and fair."[73] According to Bush, "Syria is out of step with the progress being made in the greater Middle East. Democracy is on the move, and this is a country that isn't moving with the democratic movement."[74]

In response to Bush's support for an international tribunal to try suspects in the Hariri assassination, a Hezbollah spokesman said: "[The resolution] is a violation of the sovereignty of Lebanon and an aggressive interference in its internal affairs. The resolution [is] illegal and illegitimate. The ruling coalition has presented a great gift to the American administration as they put in its hands a political card that it can use for political pressure."[75] Nasrallah was convinced that the United States would assert its leverage over Siniora to force him into signing a peace treaty with Israel. Nasrallah warned the West not try to control events in Lebanon. "Your plans are wrong," he exclaimed. "Lebanon is not Ukraine."[76]

Israel

Since Israel was established in 1948, Arab countries have only suffered defeat at the hands of the IDF. Hezbollah's guerilla war against the IDF in southern Lebanon, which culminated in the 2000 withdrawal of Israeli troops, had a huge psychological impact across the Arab world. "This is the first Arab victory," claimed Hezbollah. "It is the first time the Israelis have left an Arab land in defeat."[77] A Hezbollah spokesman indicated, "We have liberated the South. Next we will liberate Jerusalem."[78] "Israel's final departure from Lebanon is a prelude to its final obliteration from existence and the liberation of venerable Jerusalem from the talons of occupation."[79]

Nasrallah adamantly opposed negotiations. According to Nasrallah, negotiating with Israel represented a compromise validating Israel's existence. "We strongly condemn all the plans for mediation between us and Israel and we consider the mediators a hostile party because their mediation will only serve to acknowledge the legitimacy of the Zionist occupation of Palestine."[80] He insisted that, "Negotiations alone would not make Israel withdraw. They are giving so little to Arafat and humiliating him," Nasrallah complained. "In the best of cases, there will be a tiny, fragmented state, with all borders dominated by Israel, with no returning refugees, no Jerusalem [as a capital], no army."[81] Negotiations are not the right way … future resistance in Palestine will be even more violent and strong."[82]

After Israel's withdrawal, a growing number of Lebanese criticized Hezbollah for pursuing regional interests to the detriment of Lebanon's national interests. Even within Hezbollah's leadership, a debate ensued between hardliners who supported the pan-Islamic goal of resistance against Israel and those who advocated greater focus on constituent relations and Lebanese domestic politics.

European Union

France took the lead on EU policy towards Lebanon. Over dinner in Brussels in February 2005, France's President Jacques Chirac persuaded Bush to defer decisions on Hezbollah until after Syria's withdrawal. He argued that confronting Hezbollah would undermine the immediate priority of getting the Syrian security services out of Lebanon and putting the country on a path to democratic elections free from foreign interference. France and the EU also took a strong position supporting the establishment of a UN Tribunal to try Hariri's killers. After the Israel-Lebanon War, the EU pointedly criticized Israel for its "disproportionate use of force" and declared that, "the imposition of a land and sea blockade cannot be justified."[83] The EU, including member states and the European Investment Bank, has historically been Lebanon's largest donor. At the 2007 Paris donors conference, the EU generously pledged assistance for Lebanon's reconstruction and economic rehabilitation.

United Nations

UNSC 1701 reaffirmed respect for Lebanon's unity, autonomy, and territorial integrity. It also imposed an arms embargo and called for regional cooperation to prevent the flow of weapons to militias (i.e., Hezbollah). UNIFIL was originally established in March 1978 as a monitoring force on the Israeli-Lebanon border. After the cessation of hostilities between Israel and Lebanon in August 2007, the UNSC agreed to expand UNIFIL to a force of 15,000. France was originally expected to be the backbone of the expanded force. However, Italy stepped forward pledging 3,000 troops to take the leading role. The UN made clear that the force was intended as an expanded monitoring mission. Its mandate did not include disarming Hezbollah.

Russia

Russia sought to extend its influence in the Middle East at a time when, as a result of the debacle in Iraq, America's power and prestige were waning. Russia entered into commercial trade deals with Iran including the sale of nuclear technology. It pledged an extensive package of military sales to Syria. Moscow's trade ties with Iran and Syria indirectly increased its influence over Hezbollah in Lebanon. It also reestablished Russia as a player in Middle East peace by enhancing its influence over Hamas.

President Bashar Al Assad visited Moscow for the first time in January 2005. His summit meeting with President Vladimir Putin was an affirmation of improved relations between Moscow and Damascus. Practical steps were also taken. Russia wrote off 73 percent of Syria's $13 billion debt. Syria committed to buy a big package of sophisticated Russian military technology whose acquisition threatened to fundamentally change the balance of power between Syria and Israel. The procurement was underwritten by Iran.

The procurement included Scud-D surface-to-surface missiles capable of reaching any target in Israel as well as the radar jamming mobile SS-26 tactical missile. Countering Israel's mechanized armor advantage, Syria acquired several thousand anti-tank missiles, the laser-guided Kornet E with a range of 5.5 Km. Syria is also seeking the sophisticated S-300 air defense system, as well as Sukhoi SU-30 attack aircraft. The combined effect of these systems would be to significantly reduce Israel's control of Syrian air space and provide an affective ground deterrent to Israeli infantry and mechanized divisions.[84]

Iran

Elie Wiesel, the 1986 Nobel Peace Prize recipient, maintains: "Hezbollah is Iran."[85] As Hezbollah's original patron, Iran has continually provided weapons, money, and spiritual guidance. After overthrowing the Shah, Iranian Revolutionary Guards (*Pasdaran*) fervently sought to spread Ayatollah Khomeini's teachings and do battle with Islam's enemies. Up to 2,000 Pasdaran came to Lebanon right after Israel's 1982 invasion. The following year, Hezbollah's first plenary meeting was convened under the auspices of the Office of Islamic Liberation Movements, an arm of the Pasdaran. At the conclave, Hezbollah endorsed the Iranian system of divine rule (*Wilayat Al Faqih*). Iran's Supreme Leader was given ultimate authority to intervene and resolve differences. The 1985 Open Letter asserted that Hezbollah "abides by the orders of the sole wise and just command represented by the supreme jurisconsult who meets the necessary qualifications and who is presently incarnate in the Imam and guide, the great Ayatollah Ruhollah al Musawi al Khomeini."[86]

The Iranian embassy in Beirut designated liaison officers responsible for relations with Nasrallah. Pasdaran members were placed in other key embassies abroad to coordinate activities with Hezbollah, which liaised with representatives of Iranian Intelligence (VEVAK) and coordinated combat operations and hostage taking with Iran's Supreme Defense Council. After Khomeini's death in 1989, Musawi became more pragmatic and aligned himself with Iran's President Ali Akbar Rafsanjani who wanted to focus on Iran's economic development and normalizing its international relations. But ties with Hezbollah stood in the way.

With Hezbollah becoming increasingly self-sufficient from its investments and involvement in narcotics trade, Iran cut its aid by 90 percent as of 1992.[87] The number of Pasdaran was also reduced by about two-thirds in the early 1990s. Hezbollah also started to rethink the utility of holding Western hostages the last of which was released in 1992. Its decision to end the hostage impasse was influenced by Iran's more pragmatic approach. This trend continued when, in 1998, the some Iranian officials began to waver on Iran's commitment to Israel's destruction suggesting that Hezbollah could suspend its struggle with Israel if the IDF left Lebanon.[88]

Upon assuming office, President Ahmed Ahmadinejad resumed Iran's hard-line supporting Hezbollah's confrontation with Israel. He intensified contact between Hezbollah and the Pasdaran. Once again Iranian weapons flowed through Syria to the Beka'a. Iran provided funds to Hezbollah that were distributed to families whose homes and livelihoods were destroyed in the war. Through Hezbollah's construction company (*Jihad Al Bina*), Iran also paid to rebuild many schools, health clinics and mosques.

Ahmadinejad fully endorsed Hezbollah's role as Iran's proxy and took vigorous steps to strengthen the organization as a counter to interests of the West. Israel and the United States were convinced that Iran was behind the attack of July 2006. They believed that Iran sanctioned the raid as a way of diverting attention from a show-down with the UN Security Council over its nuclear enrichment activities. Ahmedinejad saw America's support for Israel's bombing campaign as part of a broader strategy to degrade Hezbollah's ability to retaliate in the event of an attack by the United States against Iran's nuclear facilities. Once again, Iran succeeded in transforming Lebanon into a proxy battlefield.[89]

Syria

According to the U.S. Office of Counter-Terrorism, Hezbollah "Receives substantial amounts of financial, training, weapons, explosives, political, diplomatic, and organizational aid from [both] Iran and Syria (1999)."[90] While Pasdaran trained Hezbollah militia in the Beka'a starting in the early 1980s, Syria was transporting weapons for anti-Israel operations from Tehran to Damascus and then via truck to Hezbollah bases adjoining the southern security zone. Syria also assisted the transfer of hostages and the logistics of their release, as well as opium production and drug trafficking to the West.

President Hafez Al Assad viewed Hezbollah as a "buffer" against Israel and was content for Hezbollah to be a thorn in Israel's side.[91] Syria embraced Hezbollah to advance its own struggle with Israel over the Golan Heights, which were occupied in the 1967 war. Syria finds value in Hezbollah because its existence reminds Israel of the consequences of occupying the Golan. Damascus also sponsored Hezbollah in order to undermine a comprehensive Arab-Israeli peace accord, as well as a separate Israeli-Palestinian agreement that would leave Syria isolated and with little chance of regaining lost territory. Hafez Al Assad was adamant about maintaining deniability; Syria's overt support for terrorism risked a backlash and direct Israeli reprisals.

While supporting Hezbollah, Hafez Al Assad was wary and watchful. He had an ambivalent relationship with Hezbollah simultaneously arming Amal as a counterbalance. Supporting Hezbollah with one hand, Damascus constrained it with the other. Syria's Ba'ath Party is staunchly secular and Assad rejected Hezbollah's Islamist vision of governance. In 1985, he threatened to kill Fadlallah if he endorsed an Islamic Republic in Lebanon.[92]

Hafez Al Assad was also concerned about the domestic response to Syria's involvement. He belonged to the A'alaui tribe, which only accounts for slightly more than 10 percent of Syria's population. He was careful not to draw attention to his support for Hezbollah, because he feared that the deprived Sunni of Syria—more than 70 percent of the country—might come to resent the costs associated with Syria's involvement.

Bashar Al Assad was considered weak and indecisive compared to his father. During his rule, Syrian forces were forced out of Lebanon. His government was accused of masterminding the Hariri assassination resulting in sanctions by the United States and postponement of a trade agreement between Syria and the European Union. Bashar was able to deflect pressure from the United States by closing several Palestinian offices in 2003. However, Palestinian figures were left at-large and allowed to use cell phones to coordinate logistics and media relations. Bashar Al

Assad cracked down on internal dissent and intensified repression against domestic political opponents. He was overwhelmingly supported in a national referendum to a second term of seven years.

Bashar Al Assad maintains that Syria is merely trying to prevent Lebanon and other Middle Eastern states from becoming puppets of the West. To this end, he took steps to secure Syria's regional role. Despite commitments to secure its border with Lebanon and prevent the shipment of arms, "a steady flow of weapons and armed elements across the border" allowed Hezbollah to re-arm.[93] Syria also became the primary conduit for weapons and money flowing to insurgents in Iraq. The Bush administration pledged to isolate Syria but Rice was finally forced to sit down with her counterpart on the margins of an Iraq contact group meeting on May 10, 2007. Bashar Al Assad had successfully made Syria indispensable to Middle East peace.

Saudi Arabia

When Hezbollah attacked Israel, several Persian Gulf states such as Saudi Arabia and the United Arab Emirates (UAE), as well as Jordan and Egypt accused it of "unexpected, inappropriate, and irresponsible acts."[94] Saudi Arabia's official news agency declared that, "A distinction must be made between legitimate resistance and uncalculated adventures undermining elements inside Lebanon and those behind them."[95] But as Lebanon's civilian death toll continued to rise, Egypt, Jordan, and the UAE took pains to tone down their criticisms of Hezbollah lest they be perceived as expressions of support for Israel. Saudi Arabia was the largest donor to Lebanon's reconstruction pledging $1.1 billion in credits and grants at the 2007 Paris donors conference.[96]

Saudi Arabia's regional approach was increasingly inspired by concerns over Iran's growing influence and meddlesome tendencies. Sunni Arab leaders in the Middle East were more and more concerned about the emergence of a Shi'a crescent stretching from Tehran to Beirut. Not only did they adamantly oppose Iran's nuclear enrichment activities. They also worried about Iran's support for regional terrorism and its ability to foment unrest among their own Shi'a minorities.

In response to Iran's growing influence in the Middle East—and its influence with Hezbollah and Hamas—Saudi Arabia's King Abdullah bin Abdul Aziz Al Saud took steps to reassert the Kingdom's influence by asserting its pivotal role in the Middle East peace process. Abdullah personally invited Palestinian factions for talks that culminated in the Fatah-Hamas Mecca Accord of February 2007. In addition, Foreign Minister Prince Saud bin Faisal bin Abdul Azziz attended Bush's Annapolis conference with other Sunni Arab countries who were concerned about the Shi'a crescent extending from Tehran to Beirut. Worried that the country's delicate power-sharing formula would collapse causing civil war, many Lebanese clamored for Saudi Arabia to mediate differences between factions in a repeat performance of its role leading to the Taif Accord of 1989. Hezbollah dismissed Saudi Arabia's role. Hezbollah's leaders have a deep disdain for Saudi Arabia's royal family, which they accuse of pouring money into Lebanon to support Sunni sects and their pro-Western protégés. That Qatar convened the May 2008 negotiations ending Lebanon's political deadlock signaled Saudi Arabia's diminished role.

The Way Forward

Hezbollah's raid into northern Israel proved that the organization misrepresented its intentions and is still far from making the strategic decision to abandon violence and pursue its goals through a political process. Nasrallah has surely grown in stature as a result of the Israel-Lebanon War. However, his celebrity status may be short-lived. Many Lebanese blame him for foolish adventurism and acting as a pawn of Iran and Syria.

Moreover, Hezbollah is under mounting pressure from constituents who demand accountability. Its middle-class supporters want Hezbollah to emphasize domestic issues rather than pursue a regional policy. Lebanese families are increasingly focused on reconstruction, investment and access to social services such as education. They want their children to become breadwinners not martyrs.

UNSC Resolution 1701 offers a program to stabilize Lebanon. It prescribes security assistance, as well as political and economic resources in order to restore the country's territorial integrity, sovereignty, and political independence. The international community can play a vital role. However, the government of Lebanon must first create conditions for effective international cooperation by implementing the Lebanese constitution and institutionalizing the Taif Accord.

Taif was surely innovative at its time. Critics maintain, however, that the system of structured confessional proportionality stopped working due to demographic shifts and the manipulation of external powers. The complete failure of Lebanon's public sector raises pressing questions about the structure and capacity of the country's governance system. Lebanon is already fragile and does not need another convulsive and potentially violent transition. It should let the process of internal change proceed gradually while making the best of its current arrangement. Persistent and even-handed engagement by the international community is the best way to realize equal rights for all Lebanese citizens.

By the time of this book's publication, Lebanon should have a president and a national unity government. Further measures to enhance effective governance in Lebanon must include with revising the country's electoral law. Reconvening the National Committee for Electoral Reform (*Al-Hay'a al-Wataniya Li-Kanoun al-Intikabh*), which includes wise men and notables from civil society, would help to energize and secularize the process. In addition, the parliament should adopt legislation enshrining independence of the judiciary and, to strengthen rule of law, the judiciary should be empowered to appoint judges without political interference. Steps are also needed to build the capacity of government agencies. Issuing administrative regulations defining the authority of government departments would be a good first step.

With more effective governance, the Government of Lebanon will have a better chance of implementing UNSC Resolutions 1559 (2004), 1680 (2006), and 1701 (2006). Deploying Lebanon's national armed forces in southern Lebanon is critical to extending the government's authority over all Lebanese territory. UNIFIL can help stabilize the area, but it needs material and manpower from the international community. It would also benefit from more reliable field intelligence on Hezbollah. The UN Security Council reviews UNIFIL's mandate every six months. It should extend UNIFIL's term for as long as Lebanese forces need assistance.

Demilitarizing and disarming militias will be the ultimate test of the government's capabilities. As individuals not militia units, Hezbollah fighters can be co-opted by bringing them into the Lebanese military. This move would preserve Hezbollah's self-declared role as guarantor of security while satisfying demands that Hezbollah disband. To reduce foreign influence on Lebanon's independence, the government should evict members of Iran's Revolutionary Guard who have worked side-by-side with Hezbollah. Since Lebanese and Syrian agencies have failed to cooperate on preventing arms flows, the Lebanese government will need more assistance from international monitors to prevent overland weapons transfers from Syria to Hezbollah.

Lebanon's problems cannot be addressed through security assistance alone. As called for in 1701, the UN Secretary General and his special representative should consult with all parties to encourage implementation of the Taif Accord. By reaching out to more moderate elements in the Shura Council, it is possible to make Hezbollah a more responsible stakeholder in Lebanese politics. Encouraging its participation in the cabinet and giving its civilian representatives senior administrative posts in the government bureaucracy would support voices of moderation within the Party.

It is also critical to eliminate issues that could radicalize relations and spark violence among Lebanese factions as well as between Lebanon and Israel. Addressing the status of Shaba'a Farms would help neutralize Shaba'a as a flash point for conflict and obviate claims by Hezbollah that its militia is needed to liberate the territory. With the authority given him under 1701, the secretary general should appoint an international commission of arbitration to study relevant cartographic, legal and political issues. The commission's finding—in all likelihood awarding Shaba'a to Lebanon—would be binding on Israel, Lebanon, and Syria.

Hezbollah finds a fertile field among Lebanese Shi'a in large part because of the widespread poverty that exists at the grass-roots. Governance reform would increase the impact of development assistance and enforce transparency on government agencies involved in overseeing reconstruction activities. The government must not abandon to Hezbollah and its Iranian financiers the task of assisting war victims in southern Lebanon. Initiative could be taken in conjunction with multinational corporations active in Lebanon to establish a special economic development and jobs creation fund using private equity matched with contributions from donor countries. Governance reform would also encourage Lebanese expatriates and oil-rich countries in the Persian Gulf to expand their investment in local industries. Led by community leaders working in tandem with central government officials, a special bureau for economic rehabilitation of the South could support grass-roots economic development. De-mining and cluster bomb collection might also be a tool for local job creation enabling economic and agricultural development. The international community can help Lebanon's economic rehabilitation by accelerating its accession to the World Trade Organization (WTO).

Both Israel and the United States have an interest in Lebanon's success. Israel can help reduce tensions by respecting the Blue Line. It should find a role for Lebanon in activities of the Quartet.[97] It is also important to engage Syria as a way of advancing Lebanon's interests and furthering the goal of comprehensive Middle East peace. The outlines of an agreement between Israel and Syria are not hard to determine. Israel would withdraw from the Golan Heights over an extended period of time—say fifteen years. The border area would be demilitarized. Israel would have access to water supplies emanating from the Jordan River and Lake Kinneret. As part of the package, Syria would end its support for Hezbollah and Hamas. It would also pledge to distance itself from Iran.

Negotiating an arrangement between Israel and Syria is more problematic than just envisioning one. Syria should be handled cautiously given its history of duplicity and meddling in Lebanon's affairs. Before launching into negotiations, the Quartet should focus on confidence-building measures such as the release of Lebanese prisoners in Israeli detention and resolving the dispute over the Hasbani River and Wazzani Springs.

Extracting Bashar Al Assad from Iran's influence should be a priority. This can only be accomplished with the active involvement of the United States. The Bush administration can maintain the appearance of isolating Syria while using back channels to communicate. If Syria wants to make progress towards normalizing relations with the United States, it must first prove its goodwill by closing the offices of Hamas and Islamic Jihad in Damascus, ending money and weapons transfers to Hezbollah, and sealing its border with Lebanon as well as with Iraq.

Likewise, Saudi Arabia's unhelpful role must be addressed. Support for Al Qaeda-linked groups like Fatah Al Islam is unacceptable. If Saudi Arabia wants to provide support, it should fulfill its pledges from the Paris Conference and make sure that the entirety of its assistance is conveyed through government agencies. Doing so would bolster the government's credibility and reduce the risk of funds being siphoned by radical Sunni groups who might instigate violence that could upset tenuous ethnic and religious power-sharing arrangements in the constitution.

Lebanon is at a tipping point. It risks resurgent civil war if Siniora does not move vigorously to implement reforms and to assert the government's authority across the country. As the government's authority collapses, Lebanon could become a failed state run by warlords. Lebanon would fall further under the control of Iran and Syria becoming a staging ground for terrorist activities and a base for attacking Israel. Heroin production and transport from the Beka'a would increase. Rather than a refuge for stateless Palestinians, the camps would become breeding grounds for extremism and violence much like the take-over of refugee camps by the Interhamwe in Eastern Congo.

The Israel-Lebanon War of 2006 was a wake-up call. Despite its terrible human toll, armed conflict can create opportunities for political and diplomatic progress. In Lebanon's case, the cost of failure is especially high. Resurgent sectarian strife and fragmentation would not only exact a terrible toll on Lebanon. It would also cause instability with regional repercussions making Israel less secure and setting back U.S. interests already ill-served by problems in Iraq.

Notes

1.   *The Qur'an*, Chapter 5, Verse 56.
2.   Figures as of 2005.
3.   The 1932 census determined that Lebanon's population consisted of 26.4% Sunnis, 26.1% Shi'a, 22.2% Christian Maronites, 19.7% other Christians, 5.6% Druze, 0.8% Alawites, and 0.2% Jews.
4.   Martin Kramer, "Hezbollah: The Calculus of Jihad," in *Fundamentalisms and the State Remaking Polities, Economies, and Militance*, eds. M. Marty and R.S. Appleby, University of Chicago Press, 1993, pp. 539-56.
5.   Augustus Richard Norton, "Hezbollah of Lebanon: Extremist Ideals vs. Mundane Politics," *The Council on Foreign Relations*. 1999.
6.   *Agence France Presse*, "Hezbollah renews threats to defend Lebanese with Rockets," June 30, 1999.
7.   Magnus Ranstorp, Hezbollah's Command Leadership: Structure, Decision-Making and Relationship with Iranian Clergy and Institutions," *Terrorism and Political Violence*, Vol. 6, No. 3 (Autumn 1994), Published by Frank Cass, London, pp. 303-339.
8.   Sam F. Ghattas, "From Guerilla Fighter to Powerful Leader," *The Associated Press*, March 13, 2005.
9.   "Hezbollah: Rebel without a Cause," *The International Crisis Group*, July 30, 2003.
10. William Dowell, "A Voice of Hezbollah," *Time Magazine*. October 9, 1989, p. 58.
11. Judith Miller, "Faces of Fundamentalism," *Foreign Affairs*, Vol. 73, No. 6, November/December 1994.
12. Rod Nordland, "Sheikh Fadlallah," *Newsweek*, March 22, 2004, p. 68.
13. Augustus Richard Norton, "Hezbollah of Lebanon: Extremist Ideals vs. Mundane Politics," *The Council on Foreign Relations*. 1999.
14. Open Letter from Hezbollah to the Disinherited in Lebanon and the World, Beirut, February 16, 1985.
15. Interview with a Lebanese Journalist. Cited by the International Crisis Group *Middle East Report* No. 7, "Old Games, New Rules: Conflict on the Israel-Lebanon Border, November 18, 2002.
16. Nizar Hamzeh, "Lebanon's Hizbullah: from Islamic revolution to parliamentary accommodation, *Third World Quarterly*, Vol. 14, No. 2, 1993.
17. Intelligence and Terrorism Information Center at the Center for Special Studies. Special Information Bulletin. December 2003. http://www.intelligence.org.il/eng/bu/iran/jerusalem.htm.
18. Interview with Husayn al-Musawi. Beirut: *Dar al-Shira*, 1984, pp. 226-27.
19. "Hezbollah: Rebel without a Cause," *The International Crisis Group*, July 30, 2003.
20. Speech by Sayyid Hasan Nasrallah, *Al-Ahd*, February 7, 1986.
21. Martin Kramer, "Hezbollah: The Calculus of Jihad," in *Fundamentalisms and the State Remaking Polities, Economies, and Militance*, eds. M. Marty and R.S. Appleby, University of Chicago Press, 1993, pp. 539-56.

22.   Augustus Richard Norton, Hezbollah and the Israeli Withdrawal from Southern Lebanon," *Journal of Palestinian Studies*, Vol. 30, No. 1 (Autumn 2000), pp. 22-35.

23.   Sami G. Hajjar, Hezbollah: Terrorism, National Liberation, or Menace?," August 2002, p. 14.

24.   Scott Peterson, "Lebanon's Top Muslim Cleric: 'No Justice Means No Peace'," *The Christian Science Monitor*, October 1, 1997, p. 18.

25.   Lara Marlowe, "A Fiery Cleric's Defense of Jihad," *Time Magazine*, January 15, 1996, p. 24.

26.   Scott MacLeod, "No Man's Land," *Time Magazine*, April 10, 2000, p. 40.

27.   Lara Marlowe, "A Fiery Cleric's Defense of Jihad," *Time Magazine*, January 15, 1996, p. 24.

28.   Jeffrey Goldberg, "In the Party of God," *The New Yorker*, October 14, 2002, p. 180.

29.   *Ibid.*

30.   Adam Shatz, "In Search of Hezbollah," *The New York Review of Books*, Vol. 51, No. 7, April 29, 2004.

31.   Hasan Nasrallah, Interview with Egyptian Television, June 2, 2000.

32.   *Al Safir*, December 15, 2001.

33.   Nicholas Blanford, "Hezbollah Sharpens its Weapons in Propaganda War," *The Christian Science Monitor*, December 28, 2001, p. 6.

34.   Judith Miller, "Faces of Fundamentalism," *Foreign Affairs, Vol. 73, No. 6*, November/December 1994.

35.   Gary C. Gambill, "Hasan Nasrallah," *Middle East Intelligence Bulletin*, Vol. 6, No. 2/3, February-March 2004.

36.   Donna Abu-Nasr, "AP Interview: Senior Hezbollah official Says Guerillas are not a Syrian Tool," *Associated Press*, March 11, 2005.

37.   Daniel Bynam, "Should Hezbollah be Next?" *Foreign Affairs*, November/December 2003.

38.   Sonni Effron, "Bush Sees Hezbollah in Politics," *The Los Angeles Times*, March 16, 2005, p. A1.

39.   *Ibid.*

40.   Ken Ellingwood, "Hezbollah will not disarm," *The Los Angeles Times*, March 17, 2005, p. A3.

41.   American Arab Anti-Discrimination Committee, *Action Alert*, July 31, 2000. http://freelebanon.org/articles/a254.htm.

42.   Anonymous interview with the author. October 17, 2005. Note that most estimates are lower.

43.   Magnus Ranstorp, *Hezbollah's Command Leadership: Structure, Decision-Making and Relationship with Iranian Clergy and Institutions, Terrorism and Political Violence*, Vol. 6, No. 3 (Autumn 1994), Published by Frank Cass, London, p. 303-339.

44.   *Ibid.*

45.   Global Witness. "For a Few Dollars More: How al-Qaeda Moved into the Diamond Trade." April 2003.

46.   *The Daily Star*, February 15, 2002.

47.   Daniel Bynam, "Should Hezbollah be Next?," *Foreign Affairs*, November/December 2003.

48.   *The Los Angeles Times*, April 17, 2003.

49.   U.S. Department of State, Background Information on Foreign Terrorist Organizations, Office of Counterterrorism, October 8, 1999.

50. *Ibid.*
51. Nicholas Blanford, "Hezbollah Sharpens its Weapons in Propaganda War," *The Christian Science Monitor*, December 28, 2001, p. 6.
52. Nicholas Blanford, "Hizbullah Reelects its leader," *The Christian Science Monitor*, August 19, 2004, p. 6.
53. Matthew A. Levitt, "Hezbollah's West Bank Terror Network," *Middle East Intelligence Bulletin, Vol. 5, No. 8-9*, August-September 2003.
54. Anthony H. Cordesman, Israel and Lebanon: The New Strategic and Military Realities, *Center for Strategic and International Studies*, Washington D.C., p. 33.
55. Hasan M. Fattah, "Hezbollah backs Syria in Lebanon," *The International Herald Tribune*, March 7, 2005, p. 6.
56. UNSC 1559.
57. *Al Safir*, (Lebanon) April 20, 2005.
58. Interview on al-Manar Television with Hassan Nasrallah. July 16, 2006.
59. Security Council Report. September 26, 2006.
60. Anonymous interview with a Lebanese Shi'a leader. July 28, 2007.
61. Nicholas Blanford, "Hezbollah Chief Offers Carrot, Stick," *The Christian Science Monitor*, July 31, 2003.
62. William Dowell, "A Voice of Hezbollah," *Time Magazine.* October 9, 1989, p. 58.
63. Sami G. Hajjar, Hezbollah: terrorism, National Liberation, or Menace?, August 2002, p. 13.
64. *ABC News: Nightline*, Interview with Ted Koppel, October 19, 2000.
65. William Dowell, "A Voice of Hezbollah," *Time Magazine.* October 9, 1989, p. 58.
66. Tom Masland, "'We Don't Trust America'," *Newsweek Web*, April 7, 2003, p. 1.
67. Tyler Marshall, "Syria is Out of Step, Bush Says," *The Los Angeles Times*, February 18, 2005, p. 27.
68. United States Department of State, Patterns of Global Terrorism 2001, May 2002.
69. Associated Press, March 28, 2003.
70. Tom Marshland, "'We Don't Trust America'," *Newsweek Web*, April 7, 2003, p. 1.
71. Transcript of the State Department Daily Briefing, March 10, 2005.
72. Press Conference with Chancellor Angela Markel, July 13, 2006.
73. "Hezbollah leads pro-Syrian show of force as troops prepare pullback," *Agence France Presse*, March 8, 2005.
74. Tyler Marshall, "Syria is 'Out of Ste' Bush says," *Los Angeles Times*, February 18, 2005, p. 27.
75. Hassan M. Fattah. "Mixed Reaction in Lebanon to U.N. Assassination Tribunal." *The New York Times.* June 1, 2007.
76. Scott McLeod, Hizballah's Herald," *Time Magazine*, March 21, 2005, p. 48.
77. Brian Whitaker, "Hezbollah heroes face the test of peace," *The Guardian* (London), June 1, 2000. p. 20.
78. ABC News Nightline, Interview by Sheila MacVicar, October 19, 2000.
79. Augustus Richard Norton, "Hezbollah of Lebanon: Extremist Ideals vs. Mundane Politics," *The Council on Foreign Relations.* 1999.
80. A.R. Norton, Amal and the Shi'a (1987), p. 179.
81. Scott Peterson, Hizbullah's Stance: Ambiguity, *The Christian Science Monitor*, January 21, 2000. p. 6
82. *Ibid.*

83.   Statement by the EU President, July 13, 2006.

84.   Ed Blance. "Better the Devil you Know." *The Middle East*. May 2007. p. 8.

85.   Interview with the author. Greenwich, CT. August 20, 2005.

86.   Open Letter from Hezbollah to the Disinherited in Lebanon and the World, Beirut, February 16, 1985.

87.   Magnus Ranstorp, *Hezbollah's Command Leadership: Structure, Decision-Making and Relationship with Iranian Clergy and Institutions," Terrorism and Political Violence*, Vol. 6, No. 3 (Autumn 1994), Published by Frank Cass, London, p. 303-339.

88.   Anthony Shadid, *The Associated Press*, March 28, 1998.

89.   According to Richard Armitage, who served as Deputy Secretary of State in Bush's first term, "If the most dominant military force in the region, the Israeli Defense Forces, can't pacify a country like Lebanon with a population of four million, [the United States] should think carefully about taking that template for Iran, with strategic depth and a population of 70 million." *Raw Story*. "Seymour Hersh: U.S. involved in Israeli plans to invade Lebanon." August 13, 2006.

90.   U.S. Department of State, Background Information on Foreign Terrorist Organizations, Office of Counterterrorism, October 8, 1999

91.   Daniel Bynam, "Should Hezbollah be Next?," *Foreign Affairs,* November/December 2003.

92.   *Ma'aretz,* March 10 and 19, 1985.

93.   Statement by Terje Roed-Larsen to the United Nations Security Council. June 11, 2007.

94.   Arab League Statement. Cairo. July 15, 2006.

95.   Statement by Saudi Arabia's official news agency. July 17, 2006.

96.   Crispian Balmer and Ashar Mohammed. "Paris Conference pledges $7.62 bln for Lebanon." *Reuters*. February 22, 2007.

97.   The Quartet includes the United States, Russia, the United Nations, and the European Union.

3

Hamas

The secret tunnel ran 600 yards from Gaza to the gates of an Israeli army outpost straddling the Kerem Shalom kibbutz and the Egyptian border. Palestinian commandos stormed out of the tunnel firing rocket-propelled grenades at an Israeli tank and an armored personnel carrier. The raid killed two soldiers and nineteen-year-old Cpl. Galid Shalit was taken hostage.[1] The incident had broad repercussions. It scuttled plans for a summit between Israeli Prime Minister Ehud Olmert and Palestinian Authority (PA) President Mahmoud Abbas. It also undermined plans for Israel's withdrawal from the West Bank. Emboldened by its sweep of parliamentary elections, the Hamas-led government reiterated its refusal to recognize Israel and vowed to liberate Palestine from the Mediterranean to the Jordan River.

History

The First Intifada was launched in December 1987 as a grass-roots uprising against Israel's occupation of the West Bank and Gaza.[2] A month later, Sheik Ahmed Yassin, a blind cleric committed to establishing a caliphate in Palestine, founded the Movement of the Islamic Resistance (*Harakat al-Muqawama al-Islamiyya*) otherwise known as Hamas, which means "zeal" in Arabic. Hamas began as a branch of the Muslim Brotherhood with the goal of destroying Israel and imposing Islamic law (*Shari'a*) in greater Palestine.

Prior to the emergence of Hamas, the Palestinian struggle for nationhood was dominated by Yasser Arafat and the Palestinian Liberation Organization (PLO) that was founded in 1964. The PLO's armed wing, Fatah, was responsible for decades of terrorist attacks in Israel and against Israeli interests around the world. Israel initially supported Hamas as a counterweight to Arafat. It saw advantage in fomenting divisions between Palestinian factions and promoting dissent among the younger generation of Palestinians who were discouraged by the lack of progress to realization of a Palestinian state and hostile to Fatah's entrenched leadership.

Though the PLO and Hamas both embraced armed struggled, Arafat was a secular nationalist who came to believe that Palestinian national aspirations could be realized through a *modus vivendi* with Israel. Hamas has always been committed to wiping Israel off the face of the map.

Hamas rejects UN Security Council Resolution 181 that called for the partition of Palestine into two states, one Jewish and the other Arab. It objected when Arafat endorsed Security Council Resolutions 242 and 338 calling for Israel to withdraw from territories that came under its control during Six Day War of 1967. It scorned Arafat for promulgating the 1988 Algiers Declaration that committed Fatah to a two-state solution and renounced attacks on targets within Israel. Hamas also rejected the Declaration of Principles commonly known as the Oslo Accord of 1993. Oslo accepted Israel's right to exist and created the Palestinian Authority (PA) to govern Palestinian autonomy in the West Bank and Gaza as an interim step towards the establishment of a Palestinian state. Hamas viewed the accord as a mechanism to keep counter-elites out of power and as an attempt by Israel to control Palestine by other means.[3] It also rejected the accord for failing to designate Jerusalem as the capitol of Palestine or address the right of return claimed by Palestinians who fled their homes when Israel was established in 1948.

More than strategy and tactics divide Hamas and Fatah. Hamas rejects Fatah's secular nationalist ideology and accuses it of selling out Islam and the Palestinian cause. When the PA was established, Hamas rebuffed Arafat's invitation to join the government, opting instead to form a coalition with the Democratic and Islamic National Front based in Damascus.[4] Insisting that the PA was illegitimate, Hamas boycotted the first elections for the Palestinian Legislative Council (PLC) and the PA presidency in January 1996.[5] Arafat deeply resented Hamas' opposition, which he viewed as a threat to Fatah's monopoly on decision-making—and a personal challenge to his authority.

Arafat blamed Hamas for Israel's decision to crack down and adopt a policy of targeted killings. In 1996, the Israeli Defense Forces (IDF) successfully killed Yahya Ayyash, Hamas' chief bomb maker who was known as the "Engineer." Hamas responded with a series of reprisals, including suicide terrorist attacks on Israeli civilians. The subsequent crackdown affected all Palestinians regardless of their political affiliation.

The cycle of violence was a recruitment bonanza for Hamas. In the 1990s, Hamas' ranks swelled with Palestinians disenchanted with Oslo and Arafat's conciliatory approach. The burgeoning Hamas-Fatah rivalry soon involved gun battles between rival militias. However, Palestinians set aside their differences when the mediation efforts of U.S. President Bill Clinton collapsed in July 2000. They came together to launch the Second Intifada.

Despite their apparent unity, Fatah grew increasingly concerned that Hamas' commitment to violence was not in the national interest of Palestinians. It tried to convince Hamas to stop suicide bombings and attacks on civilians in Israel at a November 2002 meeting in Cairo. Hamas spurned Arafat's entreaties noting that a majority of suicide terror attacks were actually carried out by the Tanzim faction of Fatah. Israel's response did not distinguish between Hamas and Fatah. Not only did it conduct targeted killings of Hamas leaders, it also razed PA infrastructure including Arafat's personal compound in Ramallah.

Arafat was growing increasingly concerned about the groundswell of popular support for Hamas, which was successfully capitalizing on rage and humiliation to broaden its grass-roots support. He tried to mollify tensions between Hamas and Fatah by releasing several prominent Hamas personalities from detention. He also worried that continued conflict between Israelis and Palestinians would play into Hamas' hands. Arafat was a shrewd politician who understood that Hamas could play the role of spoiler to negotiations with Israel.

King Abdullah of Saudi Arabia proposed a peace initiative at the Beirut Summit of the Arab League in 2002. He called on Arab countries to normalize diplomatic and economic relations with Israel in exchange for the creation of a Palestinian state based on the pre-1967 borders. Abdullah's proposal was groundbreaking. Up to that point, only Egypt and Jordan had full diplomatic relations with Israel. Interaction between other Arab states and Israel had been largely suspended since the outbreak of the Second Intifada.

Other peace proposals were put forward. The Quartet—consisting of the United Nations, United States, European Union and Russia—proposed a roadmap for peace in 2003. Following a cessation of hostilities and reciprocal steps, the roadmap envisioned the creation of a Palestinian state with borders to be set in 2005. Arafat endorsed the road map and worked with the Hamas leadership to orchestrate a period of calm (*Hudn'a*) for three months beginning in early 2003.

The PA scheduled a series of municipal elections. It reasoned that elections would bring Hamas into the political system thereby enabling the PA to exert greater control. However, Arafat died at a Paris hospital a month before the first local election and the mantle of Fatah's leadership was passed to Arafat's longtime deputy, Mahmoud Abbas, also known as Abu Mazen in November 2004.

Under pressure from the United States, Israel and Fatah acted against their better judgment and agreed to schedule PLC elections in July 2005. Postponed six months, while a debate raged on whether Hamas should be allowed to participate without renouncing violence, elections were finally held in early 2006. Hamas had by then honed its electoral skills emerging victorious with 56 percent of seats in the PLC.

Despite efforts by Abbas to bring Israel back to the negotiating table, Prime Minister Ariel Sharon rejected talks. Sharon insisted that Hamas' election meant there was no peace partner and ordered construction of a separation barrier walling off Palestinians from Israeli towns and cities. In 2005, he broke with Likud to set-up the Kadima Party. Sharon came to see Gaza and parts of the West Bank as strategic liabilities and pursued a policy of unilateral disengagement from the Palestinians. He put in process the removal of Israelis from Gaza and four settlements in the West Bank. Before Sharon could complete the withdrawal, however, he was stricken with a stroke and Kadima's leadership passed to Ehud Olmert.

Olmert was a former mayor of Jerusalem who had served in the cabinets of Prime Ministers Shamir and Sharon. Respected as a technocrat but lacking military experience, Olmert led Kadima to victory in elections on March 28, 2006. Though Kadima's margin was less than expected, the elections represented a significant milestone by both repudiating the Likud ideology of a greater Israel and rejecting the Labor Party and the Oslo process with which it was associated. Kadima represented a generational shift of leadership from the generals to civilians. It won by capitalizing on the centrist tendency in Israeli society and an overwhelming desire among Israelis to move beyond conflict with the Palestinians.

Hamas took credit for Israel's withdrawal from Gaza claiming its resistance was responsible for Israel's retreat. At the same time, Hamas criticized Olmert for exploiting Kadima's victory to continue Sharon's unilateralist approach. It also condemned Olmert's unilateral determination of Israel's borders that retained East Jerusalem as well as parts of the West Bank and the Jordan Valley.

Some in Israel and the international community hoped that the responsibility for governance would cause Hamas to moderate its militant approach. Unfazed by pressure from the international community, Hamas refused to abandon violence, abide by existing agreements between the Palestinians and Israel, and accept Israel's right to exist. Soon after forming a government, Hamas leaders praised the suicide attack by Islamic

Jihad of a Tel Aviv café in April 2006. Though Abbas condemned the attack, Israel held both the PA and Hamas responsible. The decision by international donors to suspend financial aid to the PA also exacerbated tensions between Hamas and Fatah. The Palestinian national dialogue broke down with each side casting blame on the other.

The rift in Palestinian society worsened when Marwan Barghouti, a Fatah member serving a life sentence for conspiracy to commit murder, worked with fellow-detainees (including Hamas members) to draft the so-called prisoner's document calling for a coalition government and implicitly recognizing the existence of Israel. Hamas leaders rejected the initiative but were trumped by Abbas who announced a referendum to approve the document.

After an explosion on a Gaza beach killed a family of seven in June 2006, Hamas' Qassam Brigades ended the sixteen-month ceasefire launching a barrage of rockets from Gaza and deploying suicide bombers. Northern Gaza became the launch point for a steady stream of Qassam rockets fired at Sderot and other Israeli towns bordering Gaza. The constant attacks reaffirmed for many Israelis that Hamas' vow to destroy Israel was more than rhetoric and that it would use all means at its disposal to inflict harm on the Jewish people. Overtaken by events, the referendum on the prisoner's document was never held.

On June 25, 2006, Hamas launched a raid from Gaza into Israel killing several soldiers and abducting Cpl. Galid Shalit. In response, Israeli troops attacked central Gaza and engaged in fierce fighting. Israeli gunboats reigned shells onto Gaza. Artillery was used to bomb roads and bridges. Power stations and government offices were disabled. Government ministers and members of parliament were arrested. Israel also intensified targeting of Hamas officials suspected of terror activities.

The violence became a regional conflagration when, a few weeks later, Hezbollah took a page from the Hamas playbook launching a cross-border attack and abducting two Israeli soldiers. The spiral of deadly violence between Israelis and Palestinians and the onset of war between Israel and Hezbollah marked the death knell of the road map. With both Israelis and Palestinians feeling under siege, plans for disengagement from the West Bank were put on indefinite hold.

Ideology

Hamas views violent armed struggle as a response to the humiliation caused by past and present injustices. To Hamas, Israel is a subjugating power that dehumanizes Palestinians and must be destroyed.

"The Charter of Allah: The Platform of the Islamic Resistance Movement (Hamas)" was published in August 1988. The Charter is a call to arms. It represents the convergence of Palestinian nationalism with religious ideology. Article 13 asserts that, "There is no solution to the Palestinian problem except jihad.... [When] enemies usurp some Islamic lands, jihad becomes a duty binding on all Muslims." To this end, the Charter calls on martyrs (*Shahids*) to liberate Palestine and enshrine Islamic law.[6] It describes Palestine as an endowment (*Waqf*) entrusted by God unto the Palestinians that must not be renounced until the day of resurrection.[7] "Palestine is an Islamic land accommodating the first Qibla, the third Holy Sanctuary, and the place where the messenger ascended."[8] "It is forbidden for anyone to yield or concede any part of it. The solution of the problem will only take place by holy war. Hamas owes its loyalty to Allah, derives from Islam its way of life, and strives to raise the banner of Allah over every inch of Palestine."[9]

The Hamas Charter insists that the Qur'an, as the embodiment of holy law, should be Palestine's constitution. However, most Palestinians believe that the conflict with Israel is political not religious. A 2006 post-election survey found that only 1 percent of Palestinians believed that Hamas should make the establishment of Islamic law a priority; 73 percent supported a two-state solution.[10] The Palestinian struggle for self-determination has historically been a national rather than a religious movement.

Many Palestinians—especially leftists, secularists, and Christian Palestinians—worry about Hamas' efforts to impose Shari'a on their personal lives and lifestyles. Hamas has taken steps to restrict the sale of alcohol and, though Hamas does not require women to wear headscarves (*Hijabs*) or a full veil (*Nikab*), Hamas-run social institutions put women under a lot of pressure to adopt the appearance of piety.

Islam has a played a central role in Hamas since the organization's inception. Hamas members have not become more religious as a result of their struggle. However, Hamas has increasingly invoked Islam to incite and radicalize Palestinians. It uses a vast network of mosques and social service institutions for both incitement and recruitment. Rhetoric is virulently anti-Semitic drawing on stereotypes from *The Protocols of the Elders of Zion*.[11] Israel is referred to as the new "Crusader state."[12] Jews are "unclean transgressors (*Harem*) ... [who stand for] ... filth, impurity, and evil."[13] Hamas leaders refer to Jews as "the brothers of monkeys and pigs" and pledge to annihilate Israel "from river to the sea."

Hamas is not Al Qaeda, although they share roots with the Muslim Brotherhood. There are, however, ideological similarities and operational links between the organizations. Both share a worldview that is deeply hostile to Israel and the United States. Palestinians have enjoyed prominent roles in Al Qaeda and some Palestinians have received terrorist training at Al Qaeda camps in Afghanistan. However, only a few Hamas leaders advocate a caliphate in Palestine and, unlike Al Qaeda, Hamas is focused on territory and status—not world domination.

Structure

The Hamas Charter maintains that the organization is a branch of the Muslim Brotherhood. Regional Shura councils are chosen through elections. Members of the regional Shura councils elect representatives to the central Shura council, which in turn elects a political bureau that is responsible for day-to-day decision-making.

Hamas' military wing (*Izzad-Din al-Qassam*) was founded in 1991. The Qassam Brigades was named after a notorious Islamist killed by the British in 1935. Resistance policies are determined by the central shura council, but military operations are decentralized. When Israel arrested hundreds of Hamas leaders and activists in May 1989, the central shura council took steps to further diffuse operations through the creation of a regional command system.

Hamas asserts that it has distinct political, military, and humanitarian wings. In fact, activities are integrated and closely coordinated. According to Sheikh Yassin, "We cannot separate the wing from the body. If we do so, the body will not be able to fly. Hamas is one body"[14] Despite claims to the contrary, Hamas commanders are subordinate to the organization's political leadership. According to the U.S. government, "Hamas is loosely structured with some elements working clandestinely and others working openly through mosques and social service institutions to recruit members, raise money, organize activities, and distribute propaganda."[15]

Political and social service activities are also coordinated. Several Hamas members in the PLC were recruited from non-governmental organizations controlled by Hamas. Their social service work helped them win the trust and admiration of affected populations. Hamas filled an important niche left vacant by the Fatah-dominated PA. The PA's inability to deliver services to the grass-roots reinforced the view of many Palestinians that Fatah was an elite organization riddled by incompetence and corruption.

Leadership

Hamas emphasizes collective rather than individual leadership. It is not a monolithic organization. The most hardline members are based in Gaza or live in Damascus, Beirut, or Tehran.[16] As part of its struggle to liberate Muslim lands (*Dahr-el-Islam*), they focus on radicalizing Palestinians and inciting them to violence. Hardliners revere and associate themselves with the resistance policies of Hamas' founder and spiritual leader, Sheikh Yassin.

When he was alive, Yassin effectively controlled factionalism by admonishing his colleagues to avoid infighting that, he argued, would only benefit Israel. Yassin became a target because of his vitriolic denunciations of the "Zionist entity" and fiery rhetoric calling for Israel's destruction. He was killed by an Israeli helicopter gunship in March 2004. Abdel Aziz Rantisi succeeded Yassin. Just as strident in his denunciation of Israel, Rantisi was assassinated one month later in a similar gunship operation.

Today the hard-line faction is led by Khaled Meshal. Though he was born in Ramallah, Meshal has spent most of his life outside of Palestine. He received a physics degree from Kuwait University in 1978 before settling in Damascus. Meshal is rabidly anti-Semitic and anti-Zionist. During a trip to Tehran in December 2005, he supported the pledge by Iran's President Mahmoud Ahmadinejad to wipe Israel off the face of the map and endorsed Ahmadinejad's denial of the Holocaust.[17] For Meshal, "Being in power is only a means to an end for Hamas. Our fate is to combine resistance and politics, but resistance remains the basis and politics only a branch."[18] Hamas' armed wing, the Qassam Brigades, is under the nominal command of Meshal.[19] Meshal's views enjoy broad support from Palestinian refugees who are especially averse to a two-state solution because it would abandon their right of return.

Mahmoud Zahar, who is perhaps Hamas' most influential leader in Gaza, is another prominent hard-liner who served as foreign minister in the Hamas-led government. Trained as a surgeon, Zahar was asked about his medical specialty. "Thyroids," he replied. "I'm very good at cutting throats."[20] Zahar was singled out by Israeli forces in 2003. However, only his son, Khaled, and daughter in-law were killed in an Israeli air raid that year. In February 2008, Mahmoud's second son and a member of the Qassam Brigades, died during a missile strike on his car. Zahar rose to prominence by being an outspoken critic of the 2002 Arab peace initiative that endorsed a two-state solution and still opposes talks with Israel.

As interior minister in the Hamas-led government, Said Siam controlled Hamas' 5,000-man Executive Force. Beginning with street battles in 2006, Siam repeatedly warned that any effort by Fatah to bring Hamas paramilitaries under its control would be met with violence. Siam has been personally implicated in atrocities committed during Hamas' takeover of Gaza.

Many pragmatic rank-and-file come from the West Bank where they experienced the difficulties of day-to-day life under Israeli occupation. Gaza and the West Bank are very different societies. After Israel was created in 1948, Gaza was administered by Egypt which tolerated Palestinian nationalism. Many Gazan leaders studied in Egypt and were influenced by the Muslim Brotherhood. Whereas Gaza opened to the sea, the West Bank was a landlocked, agricultural society that was annexed by Jordan. Palestinians who studied or did business in Jordan, Syria, and Lebanon were influenced by the secular nature of these societies. Separated by about forty miles, the two territories are actually world's apart.

Though they are few and far between, Hamas pragmatists take a long-term view. Their willingness to engage Israel represents tactical flexibility rather than a strategic shift in the organization's approach. Though Hamas scorns Oslo for endorsing a two-state solution, pragmatists have shown some flexibility. "The new government does not reject coordination and cooperation to resolve routine problems with anyone, including Israel."[21]

In October 2004, Hamas' political directorate circulated a memo asking whether it was time to abandon armed struggle and focus instead on the social service aspects of its agenda. It proposed a truce if Israel withdrew from the West Bank, recognized the right of return, and dismantled all settlements.[22] However, the initiative was rejected by Meshal and other hardliners who control the organization.

The pragmatists are led by Ismail Haniya who resides in the Gaza Strip not far from the congested beach camp where he was born. Haniya studied Islamic literature at the Islamic University of Gaza City in the mid-1980s. Upon graduation, he got involved in the intifada and was arrested three times by Israel. After Hamas won PLC elections, Haniya assumed the post of PA prime minister.

Haniya does acknowledge the possible evolution of Hamas' approach in the event that Israel recognizes Palestinian rights and statehood.[23] However, he rejects Israel's right to exist, refusing to negotiate and preferring instead a unilateral ceasefire. During the escalation of conflict between Hamas and Fatah in 2006, Haniya's spokesman urged an end to attacks that "do not serve the interests of the Palestinian government."[24] Abdel Aziz Rantisi summarized the approach of moderates: "The main aim of the intifada is the liberation of the West Bank, Gaza, and Jerusalem—and nothing more. We have not the force to liberate all our land. It is forbidden in our religion to give up part of our land, so we can't recognize Israel at all. But we can accept a truce with them, and can live side by side and refer all the issues to the coming generations."[25] Ahmed Yousef, Haniya's political adviser, explained:

> A Hudna is recognized in Islamic jurisprudence as a legitimate and binding contract. A Hudna extends beyond the Western concept of a cease-fire and obliges the parties to seek a permanent, non-violent resolution to their differences. The Koran finds great merit in such efforts at promoting understanding among different people. Whereas war dehumanizes the enemy and makes it easier to kill, a Hudna affords the opportunity to humanize one's opponents and understand their position with the goal of resolving intertribal and international dispute....When Hamas gives its word to an international agreement, it does so in the name of God and will therefore keep its word.[26]

Meshal condemns accommodation. The rift between Haniya and Meshal surfaced in June 2006 when Meshal denounced Haniya's call for an end to Qassam rocket attacks from Gaza. After donors suspended their support for the Hamas-led PA, other differences emerged. Despite their tactical differences, Hamas factions came together when Abbas dismissed the government and the international community moved to isolate Hamas in Gaza.

Financing

Hamas' annual budget ranged from $50 to 150 million during the 1990s. About 85 percent of its expenses were allocated to social welfare activities. However, funding dedicated to Hamas' social services is not always used for the stated purpose. The social service network is also used to raise, launder, and transfer money for terrorist operations.

Funding streams are both local and international. Local charities are supported by donations from ordinary Palestinians and religious alms collected by clerics in neighborhood mosque. In addition, Hamas controls charities in Europe and the Middle East where host country governments are reluctant to take action against efforts apparently intended to address the humanitarian needs of the Palestinian people. Iran also supports Hamas operations. It encourages Hamas to remain in a state of constant of war with Israel and pays on performance. Rewarding terror attacks with grants and financing earmarked for future attacks, Iran uses Lebanon's Hezbollah to transfer funds.

The United States has taken the lead in cracking down on terrorist financing for Hamas and other groups on the State Department's list of Foreign Terrorist Organizations (FTOs). In December 2001, it closed the Muslim Holy Land Foundation, one of the largest Muslim charities in North America, for transferring funds it maintained the Foundation knew would be used for terrorist operations. Though many donors to the Muslim Holy Land Foundation gave money to the organization thinking that they were supporting basic humanitarian activities, Holy Land Foundation financial records confirm that it transferred funds to the Islamic Relief Agency that in turn provided funds to the families of suicide bombers and detainees.[27]

In August 2003, the United States designated five other Hamas-linked charities as terrorist entities. The U.S. Treasury Department is also investigating U.S.-based corporations that it believes have ties to Hamas. As a result, it has become increasingly difficult for both charities and corporations worldwide to transfer funds to Hamas. Any bank with an affiliation in the United States is subject to serious penalties for violating restrictions imposed by the Treasury Department's Office of Foreign Assets Control (OFAC).

Hamas originally focused on bona-fide charitable activities targeting the neediest members of Palestinian society. Under Sheikh Yassin, Hamas set up parallel institutions and charitable societies for raising funds and delivering assistance. Services include kindergartens and day care centers, schools, and hospitals, sports clubs, and special activities benefiting women.

Services were also envisioned as an instrument for advancing the struggle against Israeli occupation. Charitable work overlapped with Hamas' political agenda. It was also part and parcel of the organization's military activities, as well as its recruitment and incitement efforts. In addition, charitable organizations were used for political mobilization, particularly targeting women.

Recruitment focused on Palestinian victims of targeted killings, collective punishment, and settlement expansion. To socialize youth and engender loyalty to Hamas, young people were reached via mosques, student unions, sports clubs, and charity committees that predominate in Palestinian society. Hamas also operates summer camps that it uses for recruitment. It pays the tuition of older students at universities across the Middle East and then places them at prominent institutions in Palestinian society.

Hamas historically used the media to foment violent resistance. Its communications strategy is also designed to serve the organization's recruitment and incitement goals. Hamas has five official websites, including *Al Fata*, which is geared towards children and youth. During the run-up to elections in 2006, Hamas websites were also used for political mobilization and voter education.

Hamas makes informal use of many Islamist newspapers that profile young suicide bombers and glorify suicide operations. Propaganda is also disseminated via its leading daily newspaper, *Palestine* (*Felesteen*). Media that resist Hamas' manipulation is subject to more direct forms of intimidation. For example, *Al Ayyam* decided to discontinue printing in the West Bank after repeated threats.

The Gaza-based television station, Al Aqsa, acts as a mouthpiece for the organization. Its programming focuses on religion, current affairs, and entertainment such as talent competitions and depictions of sympathetic anti-Semitic Palestinians on shows such as "Uncle Hazim."[28] A Hamas-inspired organization, Swords of Truth, threatened female anchors of official Palestinian television for not wearing veils and using makeup. The group also attacked Internet cafés, music stores, and other commercial establishments it deemed to be disseminating Western culture.

Incitement is part of the socialization process. Materials condoning suicide terrorism can be found in hospital waiting rooms and on the walls of kindergarten classes. The Jenin Hospital waiting room displays posters of suicide bombers. Hanging in Hamas-run pre-schools are posters reading: "The children of the kindergarten are the martyrs of tomorrow." Summer camps are also used for indoctrination and recruitment. During the graduation ceremony of Al Jam'iya Al Islamiya kindergarten, a five-year-old girl covered her hands with red paint in order to reenact the bloody hands of Palestinians who murdered two Israeli soldiers in Ramallah. Najah and Islamic universities display banners declaring "Israel has nuclear bombs; we have human bombs." The Hamas Islamic Student Movement distributes photographs of suicide bombers with slogans encouraging others to follow in their footsteps. As a result, an Islamic University in Gaza public opinion survey found that 73 percent of respondents age nine to sixteen hoped to become martyrs.[29]

Charitable activities also provide technical assistance to terror operations. Charities provide day jobs to personnel involved in terrorism. Social service agents stake-out targets and probe IDF checkpoints. They also act as weapons couriers and help transport operatives.[30] Hamas uses mosques as "dead drops" for munitions and other equipment, such as suicide belts. It hides weapons by burying them in the courtyards of Hamas-run kindergartens. Hamas-run hospitals provide chemicals used as explosive precursors. Photocopy machines at Hamas-financed libraries produce incitement flyers.[31]

Humanitarian programs assist the widows of suicide bombers. The families of martyred Hamas members or personnel imprisoned in Israeli jails usually receive a one-time payment of up to $5,000 and then a monthly stipend of about $100. Compensation functions like a life insurance policy. Families applying for funds are required to document their personal sacrifice. When Israel has held the families of suicide bombers accountable by bulldozing their homes and by practicing other forms of collective punishment, Hamas countered by letting its operatives know that their families would be cared for.

The Hamas Charter refers to women "as the factory of men" who take "care of the home and [raise] children of ethical character.[32] Despite its apparent chauvinism, Hamas has successfully won the loyalty of Palestinian women by offering programs that mitigate the burden of child rearing and providing services sought after by young women such as beauty parlors and women-only fitness centers.[33] In November 2006, women from the northern Gaza town of Beit Hanum showed their support for Hamas. Hundreds dressed in black abayas volunteered to act as human shields for Hamas militants holed up in a local mosque. Palestinian radio, which urged the women to participate in the first place, praised them for helping the fighters and taking casualties in their service.

Known as the "mother of martyrs," Mariam Farhat is considered by many to be the ideal Hamas matron. She had three sons killed in the intifada, including one who died storming an Israeli settlement to launch a suicide attack. Rather than grieving over her loss, she expressed her wish for 100 sons so that many more of her offspring could be sacrificed.

Elections

When Arafat and Abbas returned together from exile in Tunis, they comprised a clique of secular nationalists called "The Tunisians." Arafat believed that violence might get Israel to the negotiating table, but that military means alone were insufficient to realize the goal of a sovereign, independent, and viable Palestinian state. Despite their agenda of confrontation, the Tunisians were looked down upon as corrupt foreigners by many Palestinians who fought and suffered through the first intifada.

Fatah adopted a strategy to co-opt Hamas by encouraging the organization's participation in local elections. Hamas was inexperienced with politics, but it honed its electoral skills during four rounds of local elections over twelve months beginning in December 2004. Local elections were a proving ground for Hamas. Not only did they provide an opportunity for Hamas to broaden its base of support, they also helped Hamas develop its infrastructure for voter outreach and mobilization. Hamas increased its popular support by capitalizing on Israeli provocations such as targeted killings, collective punishment, and settlement expansion that inflicted harm and collateral damage to civilians.

The Bush administration pushed Israel and the PA to have PLC elections in July 2005. Abbas agreed against his better judgment. He warned U.S. officials that Hamas had garnered far more support than anticipated and could very well emerge as the winner of parliamentary elections.

The PA postponed elections; Abbas hoped to use the delay to better organize Fatah's campaign. Abbas also tried to take advantage of the postponement to mobilize funds from international donors thus demonstrating Fatah's capacity to engage in meaningful relations with the international community. Abbas also calculated that the delay would place elections after Israel's withdrawal from Gaza. He was convinced that Fatah would be credited for Israel's disengagement and thereby gained electoral support. Abbas did his best to project confidence that Fatah's message of pragmatic nationalism would resonate with voters. Fatah candidates ran on a platform emphasizing job creation, internal security, and a negotiated two-state solution with Israel. Fatah presented itself as the only party able to garner support from donor countries upon whom the PA depended.

Hamas drew a sharp distinction with Fatah. It rejected a two-state solution, flaunted its use of violence to end the occupation, and minimized the importance of international support to the realization of Palestine's national aspirations. Not only did it castigate Fatah for rampant corruption, Hamas criticized Fatah for delaying elections because it feared the outcome. Moreover, it accused the PA of failing to deliver on the core concerns of Palestinians. Making a compelling case, Hamas campaign workers pointed out that unemployment had increased, security had worsened, and negotiations were stalled. Hamas also capitalized on issues of morality in Palestinian society, castigating Fatah for condoning the liberal lifestyles of women.

Fatah's electoral strategy was fraught with miscalculations. Boasting about its international reach did not play well with Palestinians who, primarily concerned with local issues, were fed up with the cronyism, incompetence and lawlessness of the PA. Abbas was let down by the Bush administration, which failed to shore up his position by providing more resources and getting concessions from Israel. Official development assistance and private investment would have gone a long way to demonstrating Fatah's ability to deliver progress. The trickle of funds was not enough.

Mostly, Abbas failed to appreciate the extent to which humiliation caused Palestinians to become disenchanted with the peace process. Sharon's unilateralism also caused many Palestinians to lose confidence in negotiations as a vehicle for furthering their national aspirations. Increasingly skeptical of Fatah's conciliatory approach, Palestinians turned to Hamas as an alternative to failed efforts at achieving statehood through negotiations.

Fatah was also hurt by its inability to run a disciplined campaign by bringing intra-party factions into line. It tolerated multiple candidates for single seats, which divided the vote and enabled Hamas candidates to win some constituencies with a mere plurality. In contrast, Hamas ran an effective and disciplined campaign. Highlighting Fatah's corruption, its slogan was "Change and reform." Hamas fielded well-regarded candidates with close ties to their communities. Many Hamas candidates had worked at the grass-roots as educators or with organizations that deliver social services, which helped burnish their popular standing and credentials.

There were other reasons for Fatah's defeat. Significantly, it took the support of women for granted thinking it would have their votes simply because of its reputation as the more secular party. Instead of emphasizing social welfare and the delivery of services that are important to Palestinian women, it wrongly assumed that women would support Fatah out of concern that a Hamas-led government would restrict their dress, lifestyle, and careers.

Hamas swept to victory ending forty years of dominance by Fatah. Though it won only 44 percent of the popular vote, Hamas gained outright seventy-four of the 132 seats in the legislature with six more members pledging cooperation. Fatah emerged with forty-three seats, just enough to block changes to the Basic Law establishing the PA structure and defining its activities.[34]

Fatah supporters were stunned. Though two-thirds of Palestinians maintained support for Fatah's policy of a permanent settlement with Israel, many jumped ship to vote for Hamas as a protest against corruption and as a call for reform. Party workers demanded the resignation of

Fatah's Central Committee. However, Abbas vowed to stay the course: "I am committed to implementing the program on which you elected me a year ago,"...."It is a program based on negotiations and peaceful settlement with Israel."[35] If necessary, Abbas indicated that he would by-pass Hamas. He pointed out that, although Hamas won the election, 84 percent of Palestinians want a negotiated peace agreement with Israel and that 60 percent of Hamas supporters support an immediate resumption of negotiations.[36] Abbas insisted that Fatah had learned from its mistakes. He vowed to eliminate corruption in order to regain the trust of voters; Fatah would remain in opposition rather than take cabinet seats in the Hamas government.

Electioneering required Hamas to be more transparent about its goals and platform. Saeb Erakat, Fatah's long-time negotiator with Israel, was convinced that Hamas would change when it had to deal with the Israelis on a daily basis. "A negotiated and lasting peace may now be closer than many of us could have imagined just weeks ago," predicted Erakat.[37]

Erakat was right when it came to the pragmatists of Hamas who recognized that, once in power, they would have to engage Israel on practical matters from garbage disposal to electricity transmission. They offered to extend the current cease-fire and enter into a long-term truce if Israel pulled back to its 1967 boundaries and ceded East Jerusalem. Candidates like Mohamed Ghazel, a Hamas leader in Nablus, sought to assuage concerns that Hamas would radically reshape Palestinian society by declaring, "The [Hamas] Charter is not the Qur'an."[38]

Meshal and the hard liners had a different message. They insisted that a Hamas-led government would promote an Islamic way of life. They disavowed Israel's right to exist and pledged more violent resistance to restore the dignity of Palestinians. They promised intensified attacks against both Israeli army personnel and civilians, especially settlers. "We and the Zionists have a date with destiny," proclaimed Meshal. "If they want a war, we are the sons of war. We have more stamina than Israel and will defeat it, God willing."[39]

Escalation

After Hamas' electoral sweep, some Israelis argued that Hamas could be transformed or neutralized by fostering divisions to split the organization. They believed that Israel would have to deal with Hamas sooner or later and that any agreement would require Hamas' concurrence. Hamas built its identity opposing elections and institutions of the PA. With elections, they became a part of the system. Having assumed the mantle of power, Hamas would have to face the reality of relations with Israel. If Hamas could be coaxed into the mainstream, it could be leveraged to disavow violence, abandon terrorism, and recognize Israel's right to exist.

Others advocated measures aimed at eliminating Hamas. They argued that its ascendance was proof that the era of pretend peace was over. The victory of Hamas revealed the true face of the Palestinians. Worried that Hamas would orchestrate more suicide and rocket attacks, they called for a separation barrier and other steps to disengage and isolate the Hamas-led government. They maintained that Israel had the right to use all necessary measures until Hamas renounced its commitment to Israel's destruction.

Olmert ordered a robust response when Hamas blessed the suicide attack by Islamic Jihad of a Tel Aviv café less than a month after forming the government in April 2006. Israel beefed up security at checkpoints and closed the Gaza crossings—Erez in the north, Karni to the east, and Rafah on the border with Egypt.

Travel and transportation from Gaza into Israel were already difficult given transit restrictions imposed after the outbreak of the second intifada. Typically about 100 truckers would start queuing up at the Karni crossing as early as 3:00A.M. Their wait might take all day. When tensions were especially high, delays could last up to a week. The roadside by Karni was littered with rotting fruit and other produce that spoiled in the hot sun while truckers waited. Unable to get their produce to market, Palestinian farmers lost about $500,000 every each day that the Karni crossing was closed.

Day laborers were also affected. In 2006, an average of about 5,000 workers crossed from Gaza into Israel each day. They worked at jobs paying about $40, a far higher daily wage than they could earn in Gaza with its depressed economy and rampant unemployment. Though Israel did not formally ban Palestinian workers from entering the country, their passage became so arduous that many were delayed or not able to make it to work at all. Palestinian laborers blamed Israel for depriving them of their wages. Those that did make it to work had to spend hours waiting at checkpoints. The entire security screening process deepened the Palestinians' sense of humiliation fueling frustration and resentment.

In addition to regulating the flow of trucks and day laborers, Israel also collected taxes on behalf of the PA. When Hamas formed the government, Israel started holding taxes in escrow in order to prevent funds from being used by Hamas to legitimize their rule or fund terrorist activities. By withholding about $50 million in tax and customs revenue each month, Israel deprived the PA of an essential revenue source and contributed to worsening conditions for ordinary Palestinians.

Since Oslo, the international community had emphasized foreign aid in order to strengthen Palestinian institutions and prepare for the establishment of an eventual Palestinian state. Beginning in 1994, the PA was bankrolled to the tune of about $1 billion each year. Most of the money went to pay for welfare benefits and salaries. Donors provided about $600 million annually to the United Nations Relief and Works Agency (UNRWA) for Palestinian Refugees. Generous support was provided to local government via the Municipal Fund.

In several instances, donors linked their assistance to political objectives. In 2003, the United States threatened to withhold financial assistance for the purpose of leveraging a change in Palestinian behavior. Then the goal was to wrest control of finances from Arafat and strengthen the role of prime minister. The U.S.-led effort seemed to succeed when Arafat allowed then Prime Minister Abbas additional powers. However, progress was short-lived. Abbas resigned after only four months following a dispute with Arafat over command of the security services. In another instance, donors conditioned assistance with a crackdown on corruption. To enforce stricter standards of fiscal governance, they established a trust fund under supervision of the World Bank and asked the PA's Finance Ministry to be accountable for contributions. The reward for compliance was considerable: the Group of 8 offered a multi-year pledge of $9 billion at its 2005 meeting.

Consistent with the principle of conditionality, the EU suspended support to local governments after Hamas won several municipal elections in mid-2005. The Quartet exercised conditionality after Hamas won the PLC by demanding a modification of its radical policies and threatening to cut-off funds. Surprising consensus existed in the international community to condition direct aid to the Hamas-led government. When support was suspended, the PA was forced to discontinue paying salaries to 140,000 civil servants. Suspending payments all but shut down the PA after Hamas formed the government in March 2006. Not only did it cause economic hardship for 900,000 Palestinian family members dependent on their civil service salaries. Withholding revenues also had a devastating impact on the Palestinian economy as a whole.[40]

The World Bank warned that withholding revenues would result in dire consequences including a 30 percent reduction in personal incomes, a 27 percent contraction in the economy, and a doubling in unemployment to 40 percent. The Bank forecast an increase in the poverty level from 60 to 72 percent and a reduction in per capita real gross domestic product rates of 49.4 percent from 1999 levels.[41] The total GDP of Palestine averaged just $4.5 billion/year.[42] The largely donor-dependent Palestinian economy was already in shambles when steps were taken to limit financial flows.

Abbas warned that suspending foreign aid would have serious consequences. He cautioned that the suspension would undermine the West's ability to influence events leaving Hamas more dependent on Arab countries and Iran. He was especially alarmed that cutting off financial support to members of the Palestinian security services would drive them into the ranks of radical militias and exacerbate tensions between Palestinian factions

Javier Solana, the EU foreign policy chief, took Abbas' concerns on board. Solana worried that withholding financial support could backfire and increase popular support for Hamas. He wanted to make sure that problems associated with the PA's empty coffers were seen as Hamas' failure rather than Fatah's or shortcomings of the international community. To assuage concerns, he insisted: "The European Union will not abandon the Palestinian people. We have never done so and we never will."[43]

The EU considered several creative financing mechanisms that would allow it to show support for Abbas while pressuring Hamas and mitigating hardship for the Palestinians. Its Temporary Interim Mechanism (TIM) enabled direct assistance to the Palestinian population especially humanitarian activities such as health care and teachers' salaries. Donors also tried to carve out other loopholes by, for example, providing assistance to the Central Elections Commission so that elections could occur, which they hoped would result in Hamas' political demise.

Withholding assistance worsened an already difficult financial situation for the PA. Even before elections, the PA was broke and had a deficit of $700 million for 2005. With debts of $1.3 billion, the PA found itself out of money. It was unable to secure additional credit as a result of pressures by the United States to restrict bank financing for the Hamas-led government. Hamas blamed Abbas for holding back funds in the PA's accounts and conspiring with Western donors to cut off the PA's lifeline.

Facing a financial crisis, Hamas sought relief from countries in the Islamic world. Haniya went on a fund raising trip; Iran and Qatar each pledged $50 million. Other Arab League members also pledged support. Haniya brought millions back in his suitcase, but contributions were too meager and slow in coming. Countries belonging to the Organization of

Islamic Conference are notorious for making late payments or reneging on their pledges.

Facing economic isolation and fiscal collapse, Hamas still refused to change course or back down from its hard-line positions. According to Muhammad Dahlan, who headed Palestinian security forces for Arafat, Abbas asked Haniya: "What's your program. How will you get out of this crisis? And Hamas always says, 'God will help us.' Fine. We all believe in God, but politics requires an answer."[44]

In September 2006, civil servants went on strike to protest the fact that the PA had not paid salaries for six months. Schools failed to open and 1.5 million students were left with no classes to attend. Postal service was suspended. Activities at hospitals were curtailed to emergency services.[45]

Relations between Hamas and Fatah grew increasingly acrimonious. Branches of the security services under the control of Fatah and Hamas wound up in direct confrontation. Prior to elections, Fatah controlled the preventive security services, the presidential guard and about a dozen other security agencies with 70,000 members. When Hamas announced plans to build a Palestinian army, Abbas took steps to consolidate his control of the security apparatus by appointing his interior minister as deputy commander of all Palestinian forces. His goal was to integrate armed groups and paramilitaries under the slogan "One authority, one gun."[46]

Hamas rejected Abbas' initiative. It warned Abbas not to make any changes in the leadership structure or appoint new ministers without first seeking approval from Hamas. It appointed Jamal Abu Samhadana, leader of the Popular Resistance Committees, an umbrella group of militant organizations including Hamas, as senior supervisor in the Interior Ministry. "This is a message to Abu Mazen and other brothers in the Authority to stop issuing decrees and decisions (before consulting us) as if to throw them in our face," warned Meshal. "We will not deal with them as legitimate. No one can deceive us."[47]

Compounding the political impasse, Hamas also rejected efforts by Abbas to form a government of national unity. Abbas called for early presidential and parliamentary elections. He hoped to establish a government of technocrats that would be agreeable to all parties and, by removing Hamas ideologues from leadership positions, get international donors back on board.

As acrimony intensified so did the frequency and ferocity of armed conflict between Hamas and Fatah. Clad in camouflage pants and black

T-shirts, Hamas commandos associated with the executive force tried to break-up Fatah rallies protesting unpaid government salaries. Violence spread to Khan Yunis in Southern Gaza and across the territory. In October 2006, daily gun battles erupted across Gaza despite the observance of Ramadan. Against the backdrop of failed talks on establishing a government of national unity, the conflict looked increasingly like a Palestinian civil war.

Olmert castigated violence between Palestinian factions during his visit to Washington, D.C. in May 2006. Presenting a strategy for disengagement, he argued that Israel faced no option other than to take unilateral steps establishing its borders and withdrawing settlers. He announced the suspension of contact with the PA, which he called a "hostile entity." His address to a joint session of the U.S. Congress was interrupted by 16 standing ovations.

In their joint press conference, Bush endorsed Olmert's "bold ideas." Bush also warned against Israeli unilateralism urging Olmert to restart serious negotiations with Abbas as the democratically and legitimately elected leader of the Palestinians. Rice reiterated that, "No one should try and unilaterally predetermine the outcome of the final status agreement."[48] Israel could simply disengage and throw the key over the fence, as it did in Gaza. Or it could work with Abbas to strengthen him as a peace partner. Though he was concerned that failed negotiations would rekindle a new round of conflict, Olmert relented allowing the possibility of "personal" contact with Abbas.[49]

Hopes were high after Elie Wiesel, the 1986 Nobel Peace Prize recipient, and King Abdullah II of Jordan brought Olmert and Abbas together at a conference of Nobel Laureates in Petra, Jordan on June 22, 2006. While the symbolism of the meeting was important, substantive differences were also apparent. Abbas wanted to address final status issues; Olmert insisted that discussions focus on security concerns and that any political process be predicated by progress steps dismantling militant groups.

Palestinians were meanwhile pre-occupied with Marwan Bhargouti's prisoner's document. Rather than calling for Israel's destruction, the document implicitly recognized the existence of Israel by insisting that Israel pull back to its pre-1967 borders and cede control of East Jerusalem. Hamas rejected the document, but was trumped by Abbas who called for a referendum to approve the plan. Abbas hoped that the prisoner's document could be leveraged by Fatah to recoup some of its lost leadership. He also hoped that negotiations on the document could segway into talks on a government of national unity.

Hamas succeeded in distracting Palestinians from the prisoner's document by attacking an IDF base near Kerem Shalom just outside of Gaza on June 25, 2006. The raid killed two soldiers and led to the abduction of Shalit. The Popular Resistance Committees and the Islamic Army claimed responsibility. They announced that the raid was revenge for the assassination of Jamal Abu Samhadana. Shalit's seizure came three days after Abbas and Olmert met in Petra. The abduction succeeded in scuttling future talks between Abbas and Olmert, as well as negotiations between Fatah and Hamas on the prisoner's document.

Palestinians viewed the capture of Shalit as a legitimate act of resistance since 10,000 Palestinians were held in Israeli jails. Despite the withdrawal of all troops and settlers, Hamas argued that Israel's control of the airspace, coastal waters, and of passages in and out of Gaza meant that the occupation continued. Olmert responded, "The government of Israel will not yield to extortion by the Palestinian Authority and the Hamas government, which are led by murderous terrorist organizations."[50]

The IDF launched incursions into Gaza in response to Shalit's abduction. Operations involved mechanized vehicles and infantry as well as air strikes. Air-launched missiles disabled Gaza's electricity plant thereby cutting off power to more than 1 million people. Israel suspended supplies of benzene and diesel fuel. Roads and bridges in southern Gaza were targeted ostensibly to prevent Shalit's removal. Haniya's office was attacked by helicopter gunships and burned to the ground. So was the office of Interior Minister Said Siam. About one-third of Palestinian Parliament members as well as half the Hamas ministers from the West Bank were arrested. Israel reiterated its policy of targeted killings aimed at decapitating the Hamas leadership.

Meshal welcomed Israel's reprisals and the resulting rise in tensions. He was totally uninterested in negotiating Shalit's release. Egypt's President Hosni Mubarak claimed to have worked out a deal to free Shalit, but accused an unnamed third party of scuttling the arrangement. Moreover, an emboldened Meshal resisted calls by Abbas for dialogue on a government of national unity. The Shalit crisis made both Haniya and Abbas look increasingly irrelevant, which was fine with Meshal and other Hamas hardliners.

Within weeks, the confrontation between Israel and Hamas was overshadowed by Hezbollah's raid into northern Israel and the ensuing war. Resurgent conflict with Lebanon had a chilling effect on Olmert's plans for unilateral disengagement. The withdrawal of troops from southern Lebanon in 2000 and the pull-out from Gaza enjoyed broad popular support at the time. But the actions of Hamas and Hezbollah convinced a large majority of Israelis that ceding land was a sign of weakness. Israelis worried about civilian casualties should the West Bank become a launching point for Katyushas, which would be within range of almost every major Israeli population center. Concerned about the perils of unilateral withdrawal, disengagement from the West Bank disappeared from Olmert's agenda.

In July 2007, the Hamas executive force led a bloody take-over of Gaza. Wearing black ski masks, Hamas militias overwhelmed Fatah forces. Fatah figures were shot in the kneecaps and thrown from rooftops. Dahlan's luxurious home was looted and murals of Arafat defaced. The Palestinian civil war discredited the Palestinian cause convincing many that neither Hamas nor Fatah was ready for responsible self-rule. Intra-Palestinian violence was also a setback to Israel as well as the United States. By not doing more to support Abbas after Arafat died and before legislative elections that swept Hamas to power, the Bush administration contributed to the crisis.

When Hamas began launching 122 millimeter Katyusha rockets with a ten-mile range on Ashkelon, a city of 120,000 on the coast, Israeli officials accused Hamas of seriously escalating the conflict. UN Secretary General Ban Ki-moon responded by criticizing "Israel's disproportionate and excessive use of force [that] has killed and injured many civilians, including children."[51] Bush was also seized by the risks of intensified conflict and dedicated his administration to finalizing an Israeli-Palestinian Peace accord by the end of 2008.

Bush summoned the parties to an American-led peace conference in Annapolis. The fact that the conference happened at all was an accomplishment. The presence of forty-nine countries and international organizations affirmed the seriousness of Bush's initiative aimed at "resolving all issues, including all core issues without exception, as specified in previous agreements."[52] Olmert affirmed, "We want peace ... [and] are prepared to make painful compromise, rife with risks, in order to realize these aspirations."[53] The presence of Saudi Arabia and Syria were noteworthy. Uninvited, Iran was conspicuous in its absence.

International Actors

United States

The United States has no rival when it comes to influencing events in the Middle East. American politicians may differ on ways to realize Israel's security, but there is broad bipartisan agreement that the United States has no better friend in the Middle East than Israel.

More than any other president, Bill Clinton was personally engaged in trying to work out an arrangement to end the Israeli-Palestinian conflict. Clinton rolled up his sleeves and tried to mediate a settlement. That Clinton failed revealed the degree of Palestinian intransigence. It also underscored the limits of U.S. leadership, particularly during the final days of Clinton's administration.

Bush adopted a more needs-based approach. Initial U.S. efforts focused on the 242 formula that emphasized land for peace as well as the roadmap to peace that promised an independent, sovereign, and viable Palestinian state. Focusing on elections as the cornerstone of its democracy agenda, the Bush administration pushed Israel and Abbas to have elections for the PLC. It did not, however, fully appreciate the extent of popular support for Hamas. U.S. officials knew that Hamas would do well, but they had no idea that Hamas would do that well. The result was a nightmare scenario in which Hamas, an organization labeled as an FTO by the U.S. government, assumed power through democratic means.

The fact that U.S. officials called for sanctions against the Hamas-led government prompted fierce criticism in Palestinian circles and across the Arab world. It confirmed the suspicion that America supported elections only when the outcome advanced America's interests. The United States was lambasted for adopting a double standard. The Bush administration flatly stated that it would not deal with the Palestinian government unless Hamas met the demands of the international community. Absent compliance, he called for "swift, decisive action against [Palestinian] terror groups such as Hamas, to cut off their funding and support."[54]

OFAC enforced the decision to suspend assistance to the PA. The U.S. Agency for International Development (USAID) demanded that the PA return $50 million in unspent funds earmarked for infrastructure projects. After 9/11, USAID demanded that all grantees sign a certificate affirming that no funds would be used to support militant or terrorist activities. Aid was restricted to groups that adopted transparency and audit procedures. The United States also adopted a multilateral approach putting pressure on European and Asian financers, as well as the Arab Bank to restrict the flow of funds to Hamas.

By isolating Hamas and starving the PA of funds, the United States sought to show the Palestinians that Hamas was incapable of fulfilling its campaign pledge to better their lives. Either the Hamas-led government would collapse resulting in new elections that would bring Fatah back to power. Or Hamas would accept the realities of responsible governance, agree to a long-term truce, and fold its military wing into the Palestinian security services.

After the Gaza take-over by Hamas, the United States adopted a "West Bank first" policy. It released funds earmarked for the PA. In addition, Lt. Gen. Keith W. Drayton, the U.S. security coordinator for Palestinians, was given $80 million to train and equip Fatah's Presidential Guard. To bolster Abbas, Bush convinced Olmert to distribute tax revenues of the PA that Israel was holding in escrow. The West Bank first policy sought to accentuate differences between Palestinians in Gaza and the West Bank so that Gazans would abandon Hamas and throw their support behind Fatah.

United Nations

Enshrining the principle of land for peace, the Quartet adopted "a performance-based roadmap to a permanent two-state solution to the Israeli-Palestinian Conflict" in line with relevant UN resolutions (i.e., UNSCRs 242, 338 and 1397). The 2002 initiative envisioned progress in parallel starting with an end to violence, normalization of Palestinian life, and the building of Palestinian institutions. However, the roadmap led nowhere. The process was undermined by the PA's failure to stop incitement, curtail terrorism, or consolidate its security services.

The United Nations focused its efforts on Middle East peace through a plethora of special envoys. Tony Blair is the latest. Upon stepping down as prime minister of Great Britain, he accepted a mandate from the Quartet to build Palestinian institutions.

UNRWA was established in 1950 for the purpose of providing assistance to approximately 4.4 million Palestinians who fled their homes after Israel's creation. Originally envisioned as a temporary mechanism, UNRWA exists to this day. In addition to services and reconstruction, UNRWA also plays an advocacy role. When Israel closed access to Gaza after the civil war, UNRWA's head called for the Karni crossing to be opened. He pointed out that closing the Karni crossing was causing serious damage to Gaza's already ailing economy. He estimated that 120,000 workers in Gaza would lose their jobs; noted a shortage of basic supplies such as rice, vegetable oil and baby milk; and warned that farmers, unable to import fertilizer or export goods, faced a worsening crisis. According to UNRWA, Israel's security cordon around Gaza would make the enclave 100 percent dependent on foreign aid.[55]

The UN's most effective advocate is the Secretary General. Ban Ki-moon responded to the civil war in Gaza by calling for an international force to stabilize the situation. However, the Security Council never even discussed the proposal. The United States and other countries had no appetite for paying the bill. They were also convinced that few troops would be contributed as long as conflict was underway. Ban Ki-moon's unsuccessful intervention revealed the UN's limitations in Middle East affairs. The Secretary General is only able to exercise authority given to him by member states, especially permanent members of the Security Council.

European Union

Countries in Europe are traditionally more sympathetic to the Palestinian cause than the United States. Taking EU contributions and those of European member states together, Europe provided more than half a billion euros each year—making it the largest donor to the PA. The EU also played a leading role in the World Bank Consultative Group. In 1997, the EU made the PA a full partner in the Barcelona process designed to promote Euro-Mediterranean cooperation.

In addition to education, EU assistance traditionally focused on institution building, the rule of law, judicial reform, and capacity building of local government. Working through the Ministry of Planning, EU assistance also sought to strengthen public finances by requiring transparency and consolidating all finances in a single account monitored by the IMF. About a quarter of the EU's contributions are channeled through UNRWA.

In September 2003, the European Union bowed to U.S. pressure and placed Hamas on its list of terrorist organizations. This set the stage for suspending assistance to the PA and boycotting Hamas. To avoid the impression that it was punishing all Gazans, the EU created the Temporary Interim Mechanism (TIM) enabling direct assistance to the Palestinian population. TIM provided essential supplies and operating costs for hospitals and dispensaries. It supplied fuel and utilities. It was also the channel for making direct payments as social allowances to the most vulnerable segments of Palestinian society. About 1 million Palestinians benefited. The EU and Norway contributed 200 million Euros to TIM in 2006.

Russia

Hamas officials made a high-profile trip to Moscow soon after forming the government in March 2006. After stops in Iran and Turkey, it was their first visit to a non-Muslim country. Vladimir Putin's invitation angered U.S. officials who had been urging him to support efforts aimed at isolating Hamas. Putin retorted, "It would be a big mistake to suspend aid to the Palestinians. When we talk about the causes and roots of terrorism we refer to social injustice, misery and unemployment. If we stop helping simple Palestinian citizens, are we going to eradicate terrorism and criminality? Of course not."[56] While demonstrating Russia's new assertiveness in foreign policy, Putin was careful not to contradict consensus of the international community or undermine efforts by the Quartet.

Iran

Iran's tactical goal is to foment conflict between Israel and Palestinians and, in so doing, damage Israel, diminish the United States and demonstrate Iran's power projection capabilities. Israel takes seriously Ahmedinejad's threat to wipe it off the map. Iranian leaders still call the United States "the Great Satan." They chasten the United States for its efforts to promote democracy in the Muslim world. According to Ali Larijani, then Secretary over Iran's National Security Council, "America showed that it is not after democracy in the region after it cut aid to Palestine" even after "Hamas was elected by popular vote."[57] The United States and Iran are on a collision course over Iran's nuclear program. Tehran may have encouraged Hamas to attack Israel and keep Cpl. Galid Shalit hostage in order to distract the international community from its refusal to suspend enrichment activities.

Syria

Iran works hand in glove with Syria using Hezbollah as a conduit for its performance payments to Hamas and Islamic Jihad. Israel has vowed to use all legal means to block Iranian money from reaching Hamas. However, Meshal and the Damascus-based leadership is out of reach. Syria has ignored pressure from the United States to close down Hamas and Islamic Jihad offices in Damascus. According to Israeli Defense Minister Amir Peretz, "Hamas' terror headquarters operates from Syria. I suggest that Basher al Assad, who is trying to conduct himself blindly, open his eyes, because he bears the responsibility. We will know how to strike those who are involved."[58] Shalit's abduction came at a time when Syria had an interest in distracting the international community from pursuing a UN investigation of its role in the assassination of Lebanon's President Rafik Hariri.

Arab States

Proposed by Saudi Arabia's then Crown Prince Abdullah, the 2002 Arab Peace Initiative called for the normalization of relations between Arab countries and Israel in the context of a comprehensive settlement that addressed the refugee issue, the status of Jerusalem, Israeli-Syrian and Israeli-Lebanese relations. The proposal was unanimously endorsed by the Arab League at the Beirut Summit (March 28, 2002) and again in 2007 at the Riyadh Summit.

Some persons close to the Saudi Royal Family as well as members of the Royal Family itself are ideologically aligned and financially supportive of Hamas. King Abdullah officially uses Saudi Arabia's religious prestige and vast oil wealth to play a helpful role. When Hamas-Fatah tensions turned violent, he invited Palestinian leaders to Mecca for negotiations with the goal of establishing a government of national unity and averting a full-blown civil war. The Mecca Accord of February 8, 2007, laid the foundation for reconciliation between Palestinian factions and an end to intra-Palestinian violence.

King Abdullah rarely deviates from America's positions. The Bush administration did not, however, look kindly upon his efforts to forge a government of national unity. He was motivated, at least in part, by the need to strengthen Saudi Arabia's role as a counterweight to Iran's growing influence in the region. Saudi Arabia's intervention did not sit well with Ayman Al Zawahiri, Al Qaeda's No. 2. Al Zawahiri accused Hamas of selling out by participating in Saudi-sponsored talks. According to Al Zawahiri, "Hamas went on a picnic with the American devil and its Saudi agent."[59] He accused Hamas of surrendering Palestine to the Jews maintaining that "Hamas' leadership has finally caught Sadat's train of humiliation and surrender."[60]

Foreign Minister Prince Saud Al Faisal linked the rise of radical ideologies with stagnation in the peace process during his remarks at the Annapolis Conference. "Feelings of despair and frustration have reached a dangerously high level," he said. "The Middle East has the capacity of becoming a haven in which all the children of Abraham can live normal and prosperous lives, free of fear and insecurity."[61] Despite his high-minded rhetoric, Saud Al Faisal was deeply unhappy that the conference communiqué failed to reference the Arab League Peace initiative and refused to shake Olmert's hand.

Beginning in 2007, Egypt, Jordan, and other Gulf States such as Qatar also engaged in more pro-active diplomacy. Egypt has a long history of mediating disputes between Palestinian factions, as well as with Israel. Beginning with Camp David in 1979, Egypt was the driving force behind the peace process. Egypt called for a UN Security Council resolution endorsing a comprehensive peace between twenty-two Arab countries and Israel after the 1991 Gulf War. It endorsed the 2002 Beirut Declaration of the Arab League and worked assiduously behind the scenes to secure the release of Cpl. Galid Shalit. Hosni Mubarak encouraged Hamas and Fatah to enter into power-sharing arrangements and work together on security and ceasefire implementation. He publicly urged Islamic Jihad to stop firing Qassams and Katyushas from Gaza. He also tried to broker a truce between the Al Aksa Martyrs Brigade and Israel, but Mubarak was rebuffed by Palestinian groups that refused his mediation.

Egyptians are passionate about the Palestinian cause. However, Mubarak supported Bush's approach—"West Bank First," and found himself in an awkward position when Hamas bulldozed a gap in the Rafah crossing. Prior to the breach, Mubarak had taken steps to tighten security around Gaza and disrupt the flow of money and weapons via an elaborate system of tunnels from Egypt to Gaza. He closed Egypt's diplomatic offices in Gaza and moved them to the West Bank in a demonstration of support for Fatah. At the same time, Mubarak tried to maintain the appearance of independence from Washington lest his compliance with the Bush administration further alienate him from Egyptians critical of his passive subordination to the West.

Hamas' rise to power represents Egypt's worst fear. Mubarak now confronts the reality of a terrorist state on Egypt's border under the supervision of Iran, with ties to Hezbollah and inspired by his nemesis, the Muslim Brotherhood of Egypt. Mubarak walks a fine line. He wants Hamas to fail, but is careful not to be implicated in efforts to further its demise.

Jordan's King Abdullah II shares many of the same concerns as his counterparts in Egypt and Saudi Arabia with whom he coordinates mediation efforts. Abdullah is especially concerned that the radicalization of the Palestinians would have a destabilizing affect in Jordan where more than half the population is Palestinian. Jordan strongly supported the Arab Peace Initiative. According to Marwan Muasher, then Jordan's foreign minister: "For the first time since the conflict started, the whole Arab world is promising Israel collective security measures. The whole Arab world is promising Israel a collective peace treaty and normal relations—not with neighbor Arab states, but with every single one of them."[62]

Like Mubarak, Abdullah must balance his engagement with Israel and domestic critics who accuse him of being too accommodating. Within days of Hamas' election, Abdullah warned the United States not to cut off aid to the PA. In a sign of popular discontent with Abdullah's perceived kowtowing to the West, more than one million people protested in Amman when Abdullah criticized Hezbollah for its provocative raid in northern Israel in July 2006.

Qatar stepped up to play a constructive mediating role in 2006. Foreign Minister Sheik Hamad Ben Jassam made several trips to Palestine in September and October trying to facilitate discussions between Hamas and Fatah on a national unity government. Qatar's efforts broke down because Hamas refused to implicity recognize Israel. Qatar expanded its efforts in December when it held the UN Security Council Presidency. It organized a debate on sustainable peace in the Middle East and issued a strong presidential statement on the worsening violence in Gaza. Despite the Bush administration's veto of a Qatari-sponsored resolution condemning Israel for operations in Beit Hanum, the United States encourages Qatar to play an active role. U.S.-Qatar cooperation is extensive. With U.S Central Command based in Qatar, Qatar has emerged as a key U.S. ally and staging ground for military operations.

The Way Forward

Hamas rose to power because it promised Palestinians a better life. Ultimately the Palestinian electorate will judge whether Hamas has fulfilled its pledge. If it rejects Hamas, Hamas will be forced to face the reality that more can be accomplished for the Palestinian people by dealing with Israel rather than trying to destroy it.

The best way to promote moderation in the Palestinian polity is to eliminate the social, economic, and political conditions that gave rise to extremism in the first place. To this end, Israel and the international community must improve the quality of life for Palestinians in the West Bank. The hope is that when Palestinians see dramatic benefits—change and reform, security and order—they will put pressure on Hamas to reconcile with Fatah thereby creating conditions for improved relations with Israel.[63]

Tangible carrots and sticks are required. Unilateral steps by Israel are the easiest. Israel should release all customs duties that rightfully belong to the PA so that resources flow to the emergency government of Salam Fayyad. Implementing the 2005 Agreement on Movement and Access would address many hardships of ordinary Palestinians. Dismantling more checkpoints would stimulate commerce within the West Bank, allow access to health care facilities, and facilitate contact and cooperation between Palestinian universities. Eliminating the daily humiliation experienced by Palestinians would also help erode the culture of hate towards Israel that is endemic in Palestinian society. Humanitarian gestures are desirable. These include releasing from detention Palestinians, especially women and children who are innocent of capital crimes. Palestinians must feel that they are treated with dignity.

In addition to these steps by the government of Israel, communication, contact, and cooperation between Israeli and Palestinian civil society representatives can help reduce negative stereotypes and demonization. Palestinian contact with Israelis is restricted to checkpoints, which makes them feel that all Israelis participate in their harassment and humiliation. Likewise, Israelis have come to believe that Palestinians are terrorists bent on killing civilians and destroying their country. Track two activities between Israelis and Palestinians can help change these perceptions. Track two can also usefully explore the underlying conditions that give rise to conflict while developing joint strategies for addressing shared problems through reciprocal efforts. NGO activities are not a substitute for official diplomacy. They can, however, create a climate conducive to diplomatic efforts while generating practical benefits.

More than confidence-building, Israel can show that it is serious about Palestinian national goals by fulfilling its pledge at Annapolis to engage in continuous talks on core issues and the "political horizon." While talks are underway, Israel should avoid security operations that Palestinians believe are intended to scuttle negotiations. In addition, Israel should not take unilateral actions that are construed as steps to predetermine the outcome. Since retaining large settlement blocks in the West Bank makes sustainable peace impossible, Israel should publicly announce an end to settlement expansion. It also needs a plan and timetable for dismantling unauthorized outposts and withdrawing Israeli settlers and security forces from non-essential areas.[64] Occupation is not conducive to progress or Israel's long-term security.

Fatah must do its part to prove that is a real peace partner. Withdrawing from settlements will meet fierce resistance from Kadima's coalition partners, Shas and the Yisrael Beiteinu Party. The settlement movement is quick to point out that Gaza and southern Lebanon quickly turned into staging grounds for attacks after Israel's unilateral withdrawals. Rolling back settlements must be carefully managed to prevent Hamas from claiming a victory for its policy of confrontation.

The PA can help address Israel's security concerns by disarming Palestinian militias. It should require members of the Al Aksa Martyrs Brigade to relinquish their weapons and sign a pledge to cease all violent activity against Israel. As part of the disarmament and demobilization plan, militia members would be given jobs as civil servants or integrated into official security services under civilian control. Israel could catalyze their reintegration through amnesty arrangements.

Fatah will not regain popular support among Palestinians until it shows a genuine commitment to fundamental reform. More effective and accountable governance can be achieved by designating a cabinet designating of technocrats, empowering the prime minister, and clearly separating powers. A political bloc that is independent from both Hamas and Fatah could coalesce around the articulation of a political program for Palestine when the present PLC term ends in 2010. The rule of law, including further refining the electoral law, is critical.

When it comes to economic reform, improving the management of public finances and curtailing corruption are priorities. Reform would also enable greater foreign direct investment. Job creation is essential. Donors can assist by providing funds for special projects such as construction of an airport in the West Bank. A road-building project connecting Ramallah with enclaves in the West Bank would employ tens of thousands and infuse cash into the local economy. Palestine youths are tired of isolation or aspire to be part of a knowledge-based economy focusing on information technologies.

It goes without saying that involvement by the United States and the international community is indispensible to Middle East peace. After Annapolis revitalized the road-map, regular conferences could be convened by the Quartet to help engage Arab states and mobilize diplomatic support for bilateral negotiations. Working groups on specialized topics such as economic development could help focus know-how and resources. Tony Blair, the Quartet's new special representative, must be given every opportunity to succeed. To this end, donors should support Blair's efforts and earmark funds through the TIM, including support for the election commission. Cash flow is important to keep the PA from relying solely on revenue from Arab states.

The United States needs to restore its credibility as an honest-broker. Many Palestinians believe that America's boycott of Hamas meant it was never given a chance to succeed. U.S. officials need to publicly encourage Israel to change policies that adversely affect the Palestinian people. For example, Rice criticized Israel rightly for pre-determining the outcome of final status negotiations when the Israeli Defense Ministry announced plans to build thirty homes in Maskiot on the West Bank. Israel's leaders concede that criticism is not necessarily unwelcome; they can use it to deflect domestic criticism by blaming Washington. A more pro-active and balanced U.S. approach would also mollify America's critics in the Arab and Muslim world.

While bolstering Fatah and improving conditions for ordinary Palestinians in the West Bank, the pressure must be maintained on Hamas. While allowing humanitarian and electricity supplies, all funds and political contact with Hamas should be suspended until it satisfies benchmarks of the international community. Hamas is not going away. There is only one future Palestinian state and it will include both Gaza and the West Bank. If there is any hope of bringing Hamas in-line with international norms, a ceasefire is the necessary and pivotal first step. Israel refuses to negotiate directly with Hamas. However, a third-party could facilitate the cease-fire and encourage Hamas to enter into a verifiable long-term truce. Only then should Hamas be entitled to participate in elections.

A truce may be more realizable by driving a wedge between the pragmatists in Hamas and the organization's more radical leaders. Unfettered by constraints imposed by Meshal and the hardliners, Haniya may be more willing to compromise. Israel can test Haniya's flexibility by setting down specific markers that define reasonable conduct. Hamas has previously enforced a lull in hostilities. It may be convinced to do so again. The government of Israel should be willing to stop targeted killings, collective punishment, and attacks against Palestinian in Gaza and the West Bank if Haniya can effectively prevent terrorism by Islamic Jihad and other terror groups.

The question is how to separate Haniya from Meshal and other hardline colleagues. Experience suggests that Syria can be turned if it is required to pay a high enough price for hosting and supporting Meshal.[66] President Bashar Al Assad might close the offices of militant Palestinian groups and evict Meshal if he understood the personal costs involved in his continued support. Unless Syria gives up Meshal, the United States should push for sanctions targeting Bashar in the UN Security Council. Sanctions should include a travel ban for Bashar, his family and inner circle of political and business allies, as well the freezing of their private financial assets and the assets of corporations that they control. Turkey, which has a proven track record confronting terrorism, should threaten to limit Syria's access to water from the Euphrates unless Bashar stops harboring terror groups and their leaders.

Other Arab states can help ratchet up pressure on Hamas. Egypt should interdict weapons smuggling via tunnels and regulate its border with Gaza more effectively. Other Arab states could follow Egypt's lead by closing their diplomatic offices in Gaza and moving them to the West Bank. The international community can put international charities that front for Hamas out of business by arresting their officials, closing their offices, and seizing assets. Actions should also be taken against banks and individuals that transfer funds to Hamas. In addition to Interpol issuing warrants for persons implicated in terror, a list of Hamas hardliners should be published and their travel banned.

It would be wrong to abandon Palestinians living in Gaza. It is also not in anyone's interest to allow the enclave to become a terrorist entity inspired by Al Qaeda and under the control of Iran. The challenge is how to squeeze Hamas financially without imposing further hardship on the Palestinian people.

While restricting Gaza crossings, humanitarian supplies—especially for schools and hospitals—should be exempt. To replace the Hamas network, donors could resource international humanitarian agencies to set-up alternative grass-roots social service mechanisms. Donors should also support the Municipal Development Fund with assiatance restricted to non-Hamas localities. So that Gaza does not become entirely donor dependent, it should be possible to relax the crossings for day laborers and ease restrictions on the transport of agricultural goods from Gaza to Israel.

More than confidence-building measures, the ultimate goal of sustainable peace can only be achieved via a two-state solution that resolves the Israeli-Palestinian conflict. The contours of a compromise are well known: boundaries roughly based on the pre-1967 borders; a just, fair and realistic solution to the refugee issue that compensates Palestinians while ensuring Israel's identity as a Jewish state; and some remapping of Jerusalem that preserves the city's sanctity to all peoples. Comprehensive peace would also require some accommodation between Israel and Syria and between Israel and Lebanon. While Turkey is playing an important role on the former, details of a comprehensive Middle East peace agreement are, beyond the scope of this chapter.

Notes

1.   June 25, 2006.
2.   December 7, 1987.
3.   September 13, 1993.
4.   Includes Islamic Jihad, the Popular Front for the Liberation of Palestine, the Democratic Front for the Liberation of Palestine, and five other rejectionists groups.
5.   January 20, 1996.
6.   The Charter of Allah: The Platform of the Islamic Resistance Movement (Hamas). http://www.fas.org/irp/world/para/docs/880818.htm.
7.   *Ibid.*
8.   *Ibid.*
9.   *Ibid.*
10.   "The Palestinian Political Pulse." *Near East Consulting*. February 28, 2006.
11.   Adopted on August 18, 1988.
12.   The Charter of Allah: The Platform of the Islamic Resistance Movement (Hamas). http://www.fas.org/irp/world/para/docs/880818.htm.
13.   *Ibid.*
14.   *Reuters.* May 27, 1998.
15.   Testimony of David Aufhauser before the U.S. House of Representatives Committee on Financial Services, Subcommittee on Oversight and Investigations. September 24, 2003. http://www.treas.gov/press/release/js758.htm
16.   Jeroen Gunning. "Peace with Hamas? The Transforming Potential of Political Participation." *International Affairs*. March 2004. Vol. 80, Issue 2.
17.   *Al-Hayat*. December 16, 2005.
18.   Statement by Khaled Meshal. Damascus. March 16, 2006.
19.   *The Economist*. "Hamas in a bind." June 17, 2006.
20.   Greg Myre. *The New York Times*. "Hamas is Silent on leaders as the Power Tilts to Gaza." February 3, 2006. p. A10.
21.   Henry Siegman. "Hamas: The Last Chance for Peace." *The New York Review of Books*. Vol. 53, No. 7. April 27, 2006.
22.   *The Daily Star*. "Hamas demands say in decisions." February 9, 2006.
23.   Henry Siegman. "Hamas: The Last Chance for Peace." *The New York Review of Books*. Vol. 53, No. 7. April 27, 2006.
24.   *The Economist*. "Hamas in a bind." June 17, 2006.
25.   John Kifner. "How Hamas Rose from Wild Card to Power." *The New York Times*, Week in Review. January 29, 2006. p. 4.
26.   Ahmed Yousef. "Pause for Peace." *The International Herald Tribune*. November 2, 2006.
27.   Mathew Levitt. "Hamas from Cradle to Grave." *Middle East Quarterly*. Winter 2004. Vol. 11. Issue 1.
28.   Chris McGreal. "New-look Hamas spends on an image makeover." *The Guardian*. January 20, 2006.
29.   Mathew Levitt. "Hamas from Cradle to Grave." *Middle East Quarterly*. Winter 2004. Vol. 11. Issue 1.
30.   U.S. State Department. Patterns of Global Terrorism 2000. http://www.state.gov/s/ct/rls/pgtrp/2000/2438.htm.
31.   Mathew Levitt. "Hamas from Cradle to Grave." *Middle East Quarterly*. Winter 2004. Vol. 11. Issue 1.
32.   The Charter of Allah: The Platform of the Islamic Resistance Movement (Hamas). http://www.fas.org/irp/world/para/docs/880818.htm
33.   Dogu Ergil. *Turkish Daily News*. "Hamas and Peace?" February 6, 2006.

34.   Thomas L. Friedman. *The New York Times* (op-ed). "The Weapon of Democracy." February 15, 2006. p. A23.
35.   Steven Erlanger. Hamas Routs Ruling Faction, Casting Pall on Peace process. *The New York Times.* January 27, 2006. p. A1.
36.   Saeb Erakat. *The New York Times* (op-ed). "What the PLO Has to Offer." March 1, 2006.
37.   *Ibid.*
38.   Fotini Christia and Sreemati Mitter. Hamas the held (op-ed). *The New York Times.* January 27, 2006. p A23.
39.   Statement by Khaled Meshal. Damascus. March 16, 2006.
40.   Statement by James D. Wolfensohn. Senate Foreign Relations Committee. March 15, 2006.
41.   George Gavrilis. "The Forgotten West Bank." *Foreign Affairs.* January/February 2006. Vol. 85, Issue 1.
42.   "Enter Hamas: The Challenges of Political Integration." International Crisis Group. Middle East Report No. 49. January 18, 2006.
43.   Statement by Javier Solana. Ramallah. February 16, 2006.
44.   Steven Erlanger. "A Gaza Political Figure Says He's Becoming a Scapegoat." *The New York Times.* June 17, 2006. p. A5.
45.   *IPCRI News Service.* September 4, 2006.
46.   George Gavrilis. "The Forgotten West Bank." *Foreign Affairs.* January/February 2006. Vol. 85, Issue 1.
47.   *The Daily Star.* "Hamas demands say in decisions." February 9, 2006.
48.   Transcript of remarks by U.S. Secretary of State Condoleezza Rice. Benjamin Franklin Room, U.S. Department of State. February 8, 2006.
49.   Press conference with President George W. Bush and Prime Minister Ehud Olmert. The White House. May 24, 2006.
50.   Statement by the Office of the Prime Minister. July 3, 2006.
51.   Statement by United nations Secretary General Ban Ki-moon at the Organization of Islamic Conference in Senegal on March 13, 2008.
52.   Joint understanding issued by the Israeli and Palestinian delegations in Annapolis on November 27, 2007.
53.   Statement by Prime Minister Ehud Olmert in Annapolis on November 27, 2008.
54.   White House News Release. June 25, 2003. www://whitehouse.gov/news/re-leases/2003/06/20030625-12.html
55.   UN News Centre. "Failure to open Israel-Gaza crossing will have 'disastrous consequences'—UN official." August 9, 2007.
56.   *The Daily Star.* "Hamas demands say in decisions." February 9, 2006.
57.   Steven Erlanger. *The New York Times.* "Iran Pledges Financial Aid to Hamas-Led Palestinians." February 23, 2006.
58.   Ian Fisher. "Olmert Rejects Ultimatum on Soldier by Palestinians." *The New York Times.* July 4, 2006. p. A9.
59.   *Associated Press.* "Al Qaeda's al-Zawahri blasts Hamas government." March 11, 2007.
60.   *Ibid.*
61.   Statement by H.R.H. Prince Saud Al Faisal, Foreign Minister of Saudi Arabia in Annapolis on November 27, 2007.
62.   Statement by Marwan Muasher, Jordan's Minister of Foreign Affairs. Council on Foreign Relations. September 23, 2002.
63.   *Ibid.*
64.   Martin Indyk. "A 'Two-State Solution' Palestinian Style." *The Washington Post.* June 15, 2007. p. A21.

65. The State of Israel official position is that the Territories are "Disputed" territories, rather than "Occupied" because: (1) the Territories were part of the British Mandate, (2) the Arab states rejected the 1947 partition plan, (3) no attempt was made to establish a Palestinian state between 1949 and 1967, (4) the Geneva Conventions relating to occupied territories applies only to sovereign territories captured from a signatory to the conventions, and (5) Israel took control of the Territories as a result of a *defensive war*.

     In general, the Israeli Supreme Court of Justice has held that Israel holds the Territories in "Belligerent Occupation," thereby limiting the application of the IV Geneva Convention, to the extend adopted by the Israeli government on an humanitarian basis, rather than a legal obligation. The International Community, with the limited exception of the U.S. in some cases, but including the International Court of Justice, position is that the Territories are "Occupied" territories because: (1) they were captured by force of arms and against the will of their population, (2) the residents in those areas were stateless, and (3) Israel has put the Territories under military rather than civilian administration, creating *de facto* state of occupation.

66. This was shown in 1989 when Syria evicted Abdullah Ocalan, head of the Kurdistan Worker's Party, under threat of military action from Turkey.

4

Kurdistan Worker's Party

Turkish Special Forces dragged Abdullah Ocalan, the notorious chief of the Kurdistan Worker's Party (PKK), from his car in Nairobi on February 15, 1999. A Turkish private plane whisked Ocalan out of Africa and deposited him at a remote prison on Imrali Island in the Marmara Sea. The maximum-security facility was ringed by warships; F-16 warplanes provided secure air space overhead. On February 16, 1999, Turkish television showed images of Turkey's most wanted fugitive—hooded, drugged, and dazed. Turks celebrated blaming Ocalan for the deaths of more than 30,000 people during the PKK's fifteen year separatist war. But not everyone approved. Across Europe, Kurds stormed embassies, seized hostages, and burned themselves in protest. They were expressing solidarity with Ocalan, who they view as an icon for demanding political and cultural rights for the Kurds and standing up to Turkey.

History

Kurds are the largest stateless minority in the world. There are an estimated 30 million Kurds in various parts of "Greater Kurdistan," a geographic area encompassing territories in Turkey, Iraq, Iran, Syria, and Armenia. More than half of the world's Kurds live in Turkey where they represent 20 percent of the population.

Mustafa Kemal, known as Ataturk ("the father of all Turks"), assembled the remnants of the Ottoman Empire to create the Republic of Turkey in 1923. Though Ataturk was committed to building a truly modern state on par with its European neighbors, he was wary of European intentions. Not only did the Sevres Treaty of 1920 partition Turkey and reduce it to one-third of the Empire's size, it also promised the Kurds a country of their own. Ataturk rejected Sevres and rallied Turks in a "war of liberation." Victorious, he succeeded in scuttling Sevres and replacing it with the Lausanne Treaty in 1923.

To address the aspirations of Turkey's minorities, Lausanne pledged:

> No restrictions shall be imposed on the free use by any Turkish national of any language in private intercourse, in commerce, religion, in the press, or in publication of any kind, or at public meetings. Notwithstanding the existence of the official language, adequate facilities shall be given to Turkish nationals of non-Turkish speech for the oral use of language before their own courts.[1]

Such provisions did not placate restive Kurds. In 1925, Kurds launched an insurgency with the goal of establishing an independent homeland. The rebellion was brutally put down. Its ringleaders were hanged in the central square of Diyarbakir, a teeming Kurdish city along the Silk Route in southeastern Turkey.

Turkey tried to suppress Kurdish identity following another uprising in 1937. It went so far as to deny the very existence of Kurds in Turkey. According to Andrew Mango, a scholar of Turkish history, "In 1938 when Ataturk died, it was forbidden to speak of Kurds and the authorities could fine people who spoke Kurdish in public. The assimilation of linguistic minorities was official policy."[2] The "Kurdish reality"—the existence of Kurds in Turkey—was denied. Kurds were called "Mountain Turks." Their language, culture and geographical place names banned. Minority rights were extended only to non-Muslims identified in the Lausanne Treaty.[3]

Kurdish nationalism gained ground in the mid-1970s despite efforts by the Turkish state to forge a common national identity.[4] Restrictions on Kurdish-language periodicals and music cassette tapes were initially relaxed, but these privileges were short-lived. Ultranationalists worried that cultural rights would lead to greater demands. They feared a campaign for independence or, at the very least, efforts to establish a federal entity called "Turkish Kurdistan."

The crackdown on Kurdish cultural rights intensified after Turkey's military coup on September 12, 1980. The military junta pushed through a draconian constitution further curtailing Kurdish rights. Under martial law, the military banned all demonstrations of Kurdish cultural identity. A big banner was hung at intersections throughout Turkey and across the main boulevard in Diyarbakir, which read: "Happy is he who can call himself a Turk."[5]

Ideology

Abdullah Ocalan—also known as "Apo," Kurdish for "uncle"—founded the PKK in 1978. The PKK was influenced by the ideological struggle that defined the Cold War and the worldwide anti-colonial movement of the 1970s. Its charter espoused a Marxist proletarian revolution for Turkey. It envisioned "the fundamental force of the revolution would be a worker-peasant alliance" and that the organization would act as the "vanguard of the global socialist movement."[6]

The charter also outlined the organization's political agenda. It "condemned the repressive exploitation of the Kurds" and called for a "democratic and united Kurdistan." Ocalan envisioned the establishment of a northern Kurdish state in southeast Anatolia (Turkey).[7] To Ocalan, this would be the first step towards creation of an independent, united greater Kurdistan. Rejecting Turkish state institutions and ideology, Ocalan's goal was to meld all Kurds into a union that included Kurds with different dialects (*Zaza, Kurmanji, Surani*) and Kurds from different Muslim denominations (Sunni, Shafii, Alevi).

Ocalan's charismatic appeal and calls for social justice were compelling. He rallied Kurds by condemning traditional feudal and tribal formations that both divided and disadvantaged the Kurdish community and calling on them to rebel against wealthy Kurdish landowners (*"Agas"*) whom he viewed as instruments of oppression and agents of the state.

Ocalan successfully recruited militia members by imploring Kurds to sacrifice for an exalted cause.[8] According to Ankara University's Professor Dogu Ergil, "The state was seen as the source of everything negative. Any attack on its institutions, personnel, or symbolic supporters was both a rebellion against injustice and a call for attention."[9]

In reality, however, most Kurds were caught in the middle of conflict between the PKK and Turkish security forces. Ocalan was unmoved by their suffering. He welcomed Turkey's heavy-handed response believing it drove a generation of young Kurds into the ranks of the PKK.

Though Ocalan boasted of the organization's broad grass-roots support, the PKK experienced serious recruiting problems that gave rise to questions about the depth of its popular base. Young Kurds identify more closely with Islam than the PKK's Marxist and secular ideology. With the demise of the Soviet Union, the PKK tried to broaden its appeal by modifying its rhetoric and adopting Sunni and Shalafi Islamic beliefs. By 1989, the PKK's publications all quoted the Qur'an. The PKK also sought ties with Islamic groups. In 1990, it entered into an alliance with Turkish Hezbollah. When Refah, an Islamic party, emerged as the big winner in Turkey's parliamentary elections of December 1995, the PKK morphed from a Maoist nationalist organization into an Islamic one. It could not, however, fundamentally reinvent itself.

The United States listed the PKK as a Foreign Terrorist Organization (FTO) in 2001. Soon after, Canada and the United Kingdom classified the PKK as an FTO. Following U.S. and Turkish pressure, the European Union added the PKK to its list of terror organizations in May 2002.

Structure

Ocalan fashioned the PKK as a rigid hierarchical organization. The Party Congress is nominally the organization's governing body. It includes several hundred members and meets every four years. The nine-member Central Committee elects the Chairmanship Council, which is responsible for all ideological, political, organizational and military activities. Functioning under the Central Military Council, the Military Committee is responsible for people's defense units, intelligence operations, and "revenge teams." Party Provincial Congresses meet every two years; local committees meet more regularly.

Despite the appearance of participatory decision-making, the PKK is a well-disciplined hierarchical organization that operates as a cult of personality with Stalinist discipline. Its by-laws stipulate that the chairman is charged with leading the organization between party congresses, which are to be convened every four years. In fact, ultimate authority rested with Ocalan who dominated the Central Committee, the Chairmanship Council, and the Central Disciplinary Board that he used to suppress dissent and purge opponents.

Over the years, the PKK fine-tuned a sophisticated lobbying and public relations effort. Various European-based media outlets such as the Mesopotamian News Agency in Germany were used as platforms for issuing instructions and coordinating activities. The Kurdistan Parliament in-Exile, established in 1995, operates MED-TV, one of thirty-nine Europe-based media institutions run by the PKK. MED-TV costs $200 million/year.[10] Its successor, ROJ- TV, broadcasts pro-PKK news including interviews with PKK leaders.

The PKK also has a network of websites such as "The Freedom for Ocalan" site hosted in Cologne and a site in Düsseldorf run by the PKK political offshoot, Kongra-Gel. The Mesopotamian News Agency in Germany and Sardasht-TV/Music in Sweden were components of the PKK's extensive advocacy and communications infrastructure.

Outreach efforts successfully influenced public opinion in Western Europe garnering support for the Kurdish cause. For example, members of the Kurdistan Parliament in-Exile were treated as dignitaries and awarded laminate passes to the Council of Europe in Strasbourg. Leyla

Zana, a self-described political prisoner campaigning against a system that denied Kurds their national and political rights, received the European Parliament's Sakharov Award.[11] Denmark's Prime Minister Anders Fogh Rasmussen cited press freedom in refusing to shut down ROJ-TV. When France's First Lady, Mme. Danielle Mitterrand, wrote Ocalan in 1998, she addressed the letter to "Dear Monsieur President."

Leadership

The PKK's iconic leader, Ocalan was born to a Kurdish father and Turkman mother in a rural village named Omerli in 1948. Omerli was typical of communities in Turkey's backward and traditional southeast where Kurds were marginalized by a combination of discriminatory policies and the state's incompetence. Ocalan enrolled in the University of Ankara's Faculty of Political Science. He was soon expelled for non-attendance, but not before inculcating a radical leftist ideology that was in fashion on campus at the time.

After Turkey's 1980 military coup, the PKK organized a tactical retreat to Syria. When the military junta pushed through a constitution further curtailing Kurdish political and cultural rights, Ocalan founded a military wing called the Kurdistan Popular Liberation Army (ARGK). Beginning in 1984, Ocalan launched a series of attacks against Turkish infrastructure and facilities of the security services from PKK bases in Syria's Beka'a Valley and Iran.

Ocalan not only embraced armed struggle against Turkey. Dissenting Kurds were also targeted. Disobedience meant execution. Defectors were assassinated in Sweden (1984 and 1985), Denmark (1985), Netherlands (1987 and 1989), and in Germany (1986, 1987 and 1988).[12] Up to sixty PKK members were executed in 1986. That year, five of the original central committee members were executed, three committed suicide, and others went underground.

Violence was also used to coerce the grass-roots Kurdish community. There was no middle ground. Ocalan demanded that Kurds choose between loyalty to Turkey and support for the PKK. Brutal and swift punishment was extended to those who refused to cooperate. For example, the PKK slaughtered residents in the village of Pinarcik in June 1987 and, two months later, it killed twenty-four residents of Kilickaya including fourteen children, because the village leaders were deemed unsympathetic to its cause.

After Turkey built the Ataturk and Birecik Dams on the Euphrates River, it threatened to cut off water supplies unless Syria severed ties with the PKK. In October 1998, Syria signed the Adana Memorandum designating the PKK a terrorist organization and agreeing to evict it from Syrian territory. Ocalan's flight from Syria started an odyssey that led him to Moscow and then Rome. When Turkey demanded custody of Ocalan from Italian authorities, they refused citing Italy's prohibition against the death penalty. Turks protested by burning Italian silk ties and declaring pasta "cuisine non grata."

After Rome, Ocalan flew to Athens and then Nairobi. Kenya was teaming with FBI agents investigating the bombing of the U.S. embassy by Al Qaeda. They intercepted Ocalan's cell phone communications and alerted Turkey's Military Intelligence Service (MIT). According to former Foreign Minister Ilter Turkmen, "The United States delivered Ocalan to us like they delivered a pizza—and let us take credit for it."[13]

In December 1998, Prime Minister Bulent Ecevit proudly addressed the nation to announce Ocalan's capture. "Nothing can be achieved in Turkey through terrorism," said Ecevit. "The state has kept its vows to the mothers of our martyrs." He called on PKK fighters to surrender and warned Ocalan's followers, "You have reached the end of your road."[14] The headline in one of Turkey's largest papers announced "Victory: Turkey showed the world it was a great state by capturing the baby killer."[15]

A Turkish state security court charged Ocalan with treason, an offense punishable by death. In a surprising display of remorse, Ocalan apologized for the suffering caused by the PKK and accepted personal responsibility. He offered to end the PKK's armed struggle in exchange for his life: "The democratic option is the only alternative to solving the Kurdish question. Separation is neither possible nor necessary. We want peace, dialogue, and free political action within the framework of a democratic Turkish state."[16] He pleaded, "Give me a chance. In three months, I will bring all of them down from the mountains. I am responsible for my past. Now I want to be responsible for my future."[17] "I really love Turkey and the Turkish people. My mother was Turkish. A solution based on the unity and independence of Turkey, which would guarantee peace and real democracy, is our innermost wish."[18] A Turkish military court ultimately sentenced Ocalan to death in June 1999. However, his death sentence was commuted to life in prison.

Ocalan's plea for forgiveness and reconciliation were initially echoed by other PKK leaders. Murat Karayilan, the organization's chief commander, announced that the PKK had given up its socialist ideology and would seek to live at peace in a democratic Turkey. A leader of Kongragel, a PKK political affiliate, and member of the Kurdish Parliament in

Exile, Zubeyir Aydar, affirmed that the PKK had abandoned plans for an independent state and instead wanted equal rights for all Turkish citizens—including Kurds. Nizamettin Tas, a Central Committee member, said: "The Kurds can play a big role in favor of democracy, not only in Iraq but also in Syria, Turkey and Iran."[19] Led by the PKK's spokesman in Europe, a delegation of PKK members flew back to Turkey and surrendered to Turkish authorities at the airport in Istanbul. PKK militias also surrendered at the Turkey-Iraq border.

A gap arose in the PKK's leadership after Ocalan's arrest. Since no one stepped up to take his place in the hierarchy, Osman Ocalan, his brother, assumed temporary leadership but soon faded from the scene. Even from prison, Abdullah Ocalan remained the dominant leader of the PKK. He continued to run the organization's affairs giving instructions through his lawyers and via European-based media outlets.

Not everyone in the PKK welcomed Ocalan's change of heart or his efforts to start negotiations. Some Central Committee members accused him of treason. Other PKK factions gradually emerged. The Kurdish Diaspora in Europe opposes amnesty. Executive Council members advocate perpetual armed struggle. They insist that the Turkish state only responds to violence.

The Qandil faction in Northern Iraq has the weapons. It is made up of militant field commanders—like Fehman Hussein and Murat Karayilan—with years of experience in the insurgency. A few commanders, like Hamili Yildirim in Tunceli province, rejected Ocalan's order to disband and vowed to fight on. However, many of the Qandil faction's new members are Kurdish youth who could be convinced to leave the organization if they had a job and were assured political and cultural rights.

Members of Parliament belonging to the Democratic Society Party (DTP) are subordinate to Ocalan but privately chafe under his control. The PKK mobilized their networks demanding that Turkey negotiate with Ocalan from his prison cell. Musa Kaval, a member of the Kurdistan Parliament-in-Exile appealed, "For years, Israel refused to talk to Arafat and South Africa interned Mandela. Here too the time has come for diplomacy."[20] The government is resisting. It maintains that Turkey will never talk to terrorists or negotiate under duress. DTP members aspire to becoming the interlocutor between Ocalan and the state. Instead the judiciary has brought charges against DTP leaders and taken steps to ban the party outright.

Angered that the government would not respond to their overtures or negotiate directly with them, the PKK ended its truce in June 2004.

A month later, the PKK reversed itself, offering a permanent ceasefire if Turkey met certain conditions and unilaterally suspended attacks for thirty days. Under the guidance of Osman Ocalan, Kongra-Gel named itself the "New PKK." It allied itself with the Islamic Great Riders Front, an Al Qaeda franchise.[21] The Kurdish Freedom Falcons, a front group for Kongra-Gel, was responsible for a series of bombings including an attack on a tourist bus in Kusadasi in July 2005.

That year, PKK operations led to the deaths of 200 soldiers and civilians. More than 600 people died as a result of PKK activity the following year. During the first half of 2007, 225 people—of whom 167 were soldiers—died as a result of attacks by the PKK. Half of the victims were killed by roadside bombs and improvised explosive devices, techniques picked up in Iraq.[22] Turkish officials believe that PKK leaders have no interest in amnesty. "For the PKK it is about survival, power, and money—not just about terrorism."[23]

Financing

Support from the Kurdish Diaspora was critical. Of about 4 million Turkish citizens living in Europe, about a million are Kurds. Cultural associations and information centers such as the Germany-based Kurdish Employers Association, the Kurdish Islamic Movement, and the Kurdish Red Crescent helped raise funds for the PKK. Money was laundered through subsidiary foundations in Switzerland, Britain, Sweden, Belgium, Denmark, and Cyprus.

The PKK also financed its operations through criminal activities such as drug and arms smuggling, human trafficking, and extortion. The State Department's Bureau of International Narcotics and Law Enforcement reported that the PKK was extensively involved in heroin production and trafficking. According to Turkish authorities, the PKK refined morphine in mobile laboratories near Istanbul and in southeast Anatolia. It also smuggled heroin from Iran, Pakistan, and Afghanistan through Turkey to the Balkans and then into Western Europe. The British government asserted that the PKK was responsible for 40 percent of the heroin sold in Europe.[24]

In addition, the PKK organized protection rackets targeting Kurdish-owned businesses across Europe. It also collected a "revolutionary tax" from Kurdish businessmen in Turkey who were forced to pay or face the consequences, which included murder, kidnapping, ransoming and destruction of personal property. In 1993, the PKK earned $86 million from criminal activities.[25] At its peak, estimated annual income from combined revenue sources was as high as $500 million.[26] The Turkish Foreign Ministry cites annual income in 2005 of $150 million.[27]

Elections

The overwhelming majority of Turkey's Kurds hope to advance their goals through the political process. To this end, a series of Kurdish political parties fielded candidates to run for parliament. Though Kurdish parties were able to win control of municipal governments in areas densely populated by Kurds, they had had little success at the national level.

Turkey's electoral law prohibits parties from being seated in parliament unless they receive more than 10 percent of the national vote. No exclusively Kurdish party was ever able to pass the threshold. Despite their large numbers, Kurds are diffused across the country. Many live in remote rural areas and do not have access to polling stations. Women have few rights; most do not vote. Many Kurds—men and women alike—have limited education and, unfamiliar with the political process, do not participate.

When hybrid parties did win enough support to join the Turkish Grand National Assembly (TGNA), Turkish authorities banned them or applied other forms of pressure undermining their ability to promote Kurdish interests working within the political system. The People's Labor Party (HEP) won 18 seats in parliamentary lections of October 1991. However, Turkish legislators were incensed when Leyla Zana insisted on taking her oath of office in Kurdish, wearing a tricolor band of the PKK's traditional Kurdish colors. The HEP was banned and its leaders thrown in jail for being accessories to a terrorist organization. In 2008, charges were brought against DTP members under Article 301 of the Criminal Code that makes it an offense to insult Turkishness. Turkey's nationalist judiciary also initiated proceedings to ban the DTP.

President Turgut Ozal was a visionary. He recognized that the PKK could be undermined by giving Kurdish political parties a greater role in national politics. He also believed that reforms would placate Kurds and make them better citizens. Ozal urged the parliament to lift its ban on the use of the Kurdish language and even floated the idea of a general amnesty for PKK fighters. In August 1992, Suleyman Demirel—who served as president and seven times as prime minister—met with mayors belonging to HEP's successor, Kurdish Democratic Party (HADEP), which controlled thirty-seven municipal governments. Demirel was denounced by ultranationalists and Ozal was fiercely attacked for acknowledging the legitimacy of Kurdish political activity. Ozal died before he could implement envisioned reforms.

In April 2002, the PKK formally disbanded and became the Kurdistan Freedom and Democracy Congress (KADEK). However, PKK leaders struggled in their new role and grew increasingly frustrated by the slow pace of reforms. KADEK demanded that Turkey adopt a new constitution guaranteeing Kurdish political and cultural rights and declaring Turks and Kurds two constituent nations in Turkey. KADEK dissolved in 2003 after the State Department added it to the list of FTOs. A year later, KADEK reformed under a new name, the Kurdistan Society Congress (Kongra-Gel), which the United States and the EU also designated an FTO. That year, Dogu Ergil wrote: "The PKK suspended its attacks and they are waiting. If the bureaucratic state in Turkey turns into a democratic state, then the PKK will not resume terrorist attacks. The Kurdish people do not want to be involved in armed struggle."[28]

Recep Tayyip Erdogan's Justice and Development Party (AKP) swept to victory in November 2003. Though Erdogan is a devout Muslim, he won favor by distancing himself from radical Islam, condemning corruption, and embracing moderate, democratic positions. Erdogan nominated Abdullah Gul to become president, but the military feared his devotion to Islam and threatened a coup blocking the nomination. Erdogan scheduled early elections on July 22, 2007. In an overwhelming endorsement, the AKP won 48 percent of the vote gaining 340 of the 550 seats in the TGNA.

AKP's margin was fueled by support in the south and southeast where it received more votes than the DTP, which emerged after Kongra-Gel as the political voice of the Kurds. Of Diyarbakir's twelve parliamentary seats, the AKP won eight. The AKP was rewarded for spending lavishly on roads, schools and different social services. Kurds credited AKP for legislative reforms enabling greater cultural rights including Kurdish language broadcasts and education. In addition, the AKP's conservative values appealed to Kurdish voters who increasingly reject ethnic politics and embrace a Turkish solution to their grievances.

Though they did not fare as well as expected, the results were a significant victory for the DTP. Bypassing the barrier requirements, twenty-one Kurds were elected as independent deputies. According to a DTP Member of Parliament, "By voting for the AKP and DTP, both Turks and Kurds demonstrated that they are against their respective militaries."[29] However, the DTP protested when Erdogan demanded that they renounce PKK terror. An MP explained, "Every Kurd has a family member involved with the PKK. How can I condemn my own children?"[30]

Relations between AKP and DTP were strained when the DTP's first action was to call for improving Ocalan's prison conditions. When AKP ignored its appeal, DTP MPs abstained from the third round of voting to confirm Gul. Despite their falling out, Gul spoke directly to the Kurdish problem during his inaugural address, heralding strength in diversity, calling for greater cultural rights including more official use of minority languages, and underscoring the need for greater individual rights in the new constitution. Gul chose to visit Kurdish cities in the southeast as his first domestic trip where he was warmly received. In their meetings, DTP members emphasized the central importance of amnesty to address the PKK problem.

The military was deeply humiliated by the elections. Its bullying backfired, antagonizing Turks and further increasing support among Kurds for the AKP. Revealing the degree of its hostility to AKP, Chairman of the General Staff Yasar Büyükanit and other top generals boycotted Gul's swearing-in ceremony in the parliament and violated a long-standing tradition by skipping Gul's first official reception. Büyükanit begrudgingly waited more than two weeks to congratulate Gul on his election as president.

The ultranationalist National Action Party (MHP) capitalized on social tensions to cross the barrier for representation in the parliament winning 13 percent of the vote. In coalition with the Republican People's Party (CHP), it vowed to disrupt AKP reforms. MHP and CHP were especially fearful of plans for a new constitution to replace the 1982 constitution adopted by the military government after its coup. Drafting of the new charter is underway. It will be Turkey's first constitution written by civilians and vetted by civil society. The draft harmonizes Turkey's approach to ethnic and religious issues with standards in the European Convention on Human Rights. It also eliminates provisions for suspending human rights during martial law or a state of emergency that had been used to crack down on those who threatened "the indivisible integrity of the state."[31]

Erdogan adamantly embraced the goal of EU membership, which had broad popular appeal among all Turkish citizens. When asked if Turkey's future lay in Europe, 77.4 percent favored EU membership. Kurds overwhelmingly prefer to be a part of Europe than a landlocked "greater Kurdistan." Among Turkish citizens of Kurdish origin, 83.3 percent of respondents answered affirmatively when asked about EU membership.[32] A vast majority of Turks believed in the transformative effect the EU will have on living standards and political freedoms.[33]

Erdogan recognized that EU standards would be beneficial to all citizens, Turks and Kurds alike. He vigorously pursued legislative and constitutional reforms liberalizing the political system and relaxing restrictions on freedom of the press, association, and expression. Turkey abolished the death penalty, revised the penal code, reinforced the rights of women, liberalized minority language broadcasts, ended random searches without a court order, and implemented a policy of zero tolerance towards torture. It adopted measures to dismantle state security courts, enhance independence of the judiciary and reform the prison system. It amended the anti-terror statutes, as well as the Penal Code and the Codes of Criminal and Administrative Procedure. Turkey also signed and ratified protocols 6 and 13 of the European Convention on Human Rights.

Recognizing that, "the road to the EU passes through Diyarbakir," steps were taken to protect and promote the rights of Kurds.[34] The state of emergency was lifted in several southeastern provinces. Law No. 4709 amended Article 28 of the constitution removing the ban on the Kurdish language. In June 2004, an appeals court ordered the release of Leyla Zana and three other Kurdish parliamentarians who had languished in jail for over a decade. New regulations were adopted initially allowing forty-five minutes of Kurdish-language broadcasts to be aired on television each week. In March 2008, a television station devoted to Kurdish-language and other minority programming was announced (24 hours a day and seven days a week).

The "Homecoming Law" was adopted in August 2003. It offered provisional reintegration for Kurds who agreed to lay down their arms. A "Back to Village Program" promised grants to returnees so they could rebuild their homes, farms, and livestock. However, only 1,873 persons were reintegrated during the first six months of the program. Returning displaced persons to their homes failed due to lack of basic infrastructure such as electricity and telephone service. The continued presence of village guards also discouraged returns. Only 5,239 of 104,734 persons eligible for compensation applied and, of those, only 1,190 received any payment.[35]

In August 2005, Erdogan visited Diyarbakir. He promised to "resolve the issue with more democracy. A great and powerful nation must have the confidence to face itself, recognize the mistakes and sins of its past, and march confidently into the future.... We are ready to consult anyone ... Turkey will not retreat from the point we have reached. We will not step back from our process of democratization."[36] Erdogan also recognized the unique characteristics of the Kurdish community. "All Turks have sub-identities. No one should be offended by this. A Kurd can say I am a Kurd."[37] Erdogan's conciliatory approach drew high praise from U.S. officials. The U.S. Assistant Secretary of State for Democracy, Human Rights, and Labor maintained, "Far from hurting Turkey's territorial integrity, an inclusive policy that acknowledged (Kurdish) rights strengthens the Turkish state by giving the Kurdish community a genuine stake in the country's future."[38]

Kurds were further encouraged when, in a private meeting with Kurdish intellectuals, Erdogan reaffirmed that the PKK problem could not be solved through military means alone. After his trip to Diyarbakir, judges ordered the release of some PKK members and reduced the sentences of others. Such steps convinced Kurds that Erdogan was prepared to talk with the PKK. Yusuf Kanli, then editor in chief of the *Turkish Daily News*, described Erdogan's statement as "discreet and limited amnesty" aimed at "healing the wounds by our twenty years of trauma."[39]

Military hardliners maintained that Turkey would never talk to terrorists. Condemning overtures to the PKK, National Security Council officers insisted, "Redefinition of identity is a violation of the constitution. Discussions like those harm the structure of the state based on one nation."[40] President Ahmet Necdet Sezer added, "All citizens are Turks regardless of their ethnic origin and religion."[41]

They also resented Erdogan's efforts to tackle the thorny task of subordinating Turkey's military to civilian authority. In May 2004, a constitutional amendment terminated special off-budget accounts that were used to finance the pet projects of commanders. Military courts were barred from prosecuting civilians in peacetime. The NSC was enlarged giving civilians the majority of seats and the government assumed responsibility for appointing its secretary general. The NSC's powers were curtailed. For example, it was denied *carte blanche* to investigate civilians. Erdogan used the NSC rotation system to force hard-line generals into retirement. When measures were adopted preventing the military from convening meetings and curtailing their frequency, the NSC became a consultative body under control of the elected government.

Historically, Turkey's military has been the unflinching guardians of Ataturk's legacy—secularism, nationalism, and modernization. Officers see their task extending beyond the protection of Turkish territory to include warding off threats to public order, such as separatism, terrorism, and religious fundamentalism.

Instead of promoting the interests of individual citizens, the so-called deep state—interwoven ultranationalist interest groups including members of the armed forces and police, corrupt politicians, government bureaucrats, and mafia members—is preoccupied with preserving its privileges and power. According to Suleyman Demirel, "It is a fundamental principle that there is one state. But in our country there are two."

The state is a product of Turkey's inefficient central government. Its powers are enshrined in the Turkish constitution. The NSC is empowered to take whatever steps it deems "necessary for the preservation of the State." Its priority is ensuring security of the "sacred" state and the continuity of official institutions comprising the bureaucracy. As the primary obstacle resisting attempts to democratize the southeast, the state has failed to provide for social security thus exacerbating disaffection and contributing to the erosion of social cohesion.[42] Estrangement has been exacerbated by the state's preference for uniformity, which ignores cultural differences over unity, as well as its failure to reconcile ethnic, religious, and cultural identities.

In response to demands for greater democratic participation, a Turkish general responded: "If there is need for more democracy, we will bring it."[43] Kurds reject the state's paternalistic approach to building democracy. Many blame it for indiscriminately targeting the Kurdish community in its fight with the PKK.

Escalation

PKK hit-and-run operations initially targeted infrastructure such as utility systems, railroads, and bridges. Turkey responded with an iron fist. In 1978, the state put several southeastern provinces under martial law. It declared a state of emergency about a decade later. Army camps, police checkpoints, and military airports were established from the Semdinli Mountains in the southeast to Siirt near the border with Syria.

Turkey launched major military operations in 1989 and again in 1992. PKK activities peaked the following year when 4,198 clashes were reported between the PKK and security forces.[44] By 1995, up to 150,000 Turkish troops and police were involved in seek and destroy missions as well as hot pursuit across international frontiers. Security operations cost $8 billion/year. Turkish officials estimated the total cost of the conflict at $200 billion.[45]

Cloaking itself in the rule of law, the security services invoked Article 14 of the constitution to crackdown on activities threatening the "indivisibility of the state." It also cited Article 125 of the Penal Code stipulating, "Any person who carries out any action intended to destroy the unity of the Turkish state or separate any part of the territory shall be punished with by death," as well as Article 8 of the "Law for Fighting against Terrorism" whose broad definition of terrorism was used to criminalize free discussion about Kurdish issues.[46] Turkey's heavy-handed approach silenced moderate voices thereby enhancing the impact of Ocalan's strident appeals and call to arms.

Political assassination was also widely used to silence opposition. Government-backed death squads killed hundreds of suspected PKK sympathizers.[47] Between 1989 and 1996, more than 1,500 persons affiliated with the Kurdish opposition were victims of unidentified murders. Close to 500 disappeared between 1991 and 1997, and between 1983 and 1994, 230 people—many of them Kurds—died from torture while in police custody.[48]

A displacement policy sought to deprive the PKK of shelter and support from the local population. Up to two million Kurds were forcibly evacuated from their villages.[49] As a result, cities such as Diyarbakir and Cizre, and Nusaybin more than doubled in size. Diyarbakir's unemployment rate skyrocketed to 70 percent. Its poverty rate rose to 39.7 percent. More than 10,000 shanty-town homes sprang up in the city.[50]

Pitting Kurd against Kurd, the state hired and equipped 60,000 paramilitaries comprising the "village guard system." The authorities explained that the system was intended to help villagers defend themselves. It had the opposite affect by polarizing communities and acting as a magnet for PKK operations. In addition to the village guards, the PKK also targeted Kurdish elites who sided with the Turkish establishment as well as Kurds who worked for state institutions.

Ocalan forced Kurds to choose between loyalty to Turkey and support for the PKK. He promised brutal and swift punishment to those who rejected his entreaties. Between 1984 and 1987, the PKK kidnapped or killed 217 teachers. It burned hundreds of rural schools shutting down the education system. Hospitals were attacked; doctors and nurses killed.

After years of insurgency in exile, the PKK Central Committee realized it could not defeat Turkey militarily and moderated its demand for independence seeking an autonomous federal state instead. When its appeal was snubbed, the PKK adopted the tactic of suicide terrorism in 1997. "Suicide guerilla teams" drew from vulnerable segments of society.

About a third of the PKK's ranks were comprised of poor rural women who were given equal status with men in the organization. According to Ocalan, "It is not difficult to get on a bus, to get on an airplane. We have thousands of people who shall go with a bomb around them."[51] Between 1995 and 1999, the PKK was responsible for twenty-one suicide terrorist attacks.

Violence and martial law took a serious toll on the economy in Turkey's southeast. Seasonal herding and small-scale agriculture activities became almost impossible with the declaration of a state of emergency. Between 1983 and 1992, Turkey invested $20 billion in the GAP Project. GAP was a massive irrigation and hydroelectric scheme that sought to harness the Tigris and Euphrates by building twenty dams, including the $2.3 billion Ataturk Dam—the worlds ninth largest. Its irrigation network was meant to service 1.7 million hectares, increase agricultural production seven fold, triple per-capital income, and create 3.3 million new jobs. The "GAP Social Action Plan" emphasized human development and social services. However, GAP fell far short of expectations with financing shortfalls and the ongoing security crisis, including PKK attacks, undermining its success. Many displaced by GAP dams and related irrigation schemes were provided compensation if they held formal land-titles. Traditional land users were rarely compensated. As a result, several hundred thousand people were displaced by GAP. They were supported by Islamist charities or developed sympathies for the PKK.[52]

Ocalan's arrest in 1999 was widely celebrated across Turkey. Turkey hoped that it would break the back of the PKK. After his arrest, an overwhelming majority of Kurds favored living in peace and prosperity with their Turkish brethren and within the boundaries of Turkey. Public opinion polls indicated that Kurds did not want a separate state. Rather, they wanted to feel and to be assured that Turkey was their country as well. Non-PKK Kurds who demanded acknowledgement insisted that they had been mischaracterized as separatists. Though a Turkish military court sentenced Ocalan to death in June 1999, his death sentence was commuted to life in prison. Turkish officials hoped that showing leniency would further moderate the Kurds. They also understood that killing Ocalan would spoil Turkey's chances of becoming a candidate for membership in the European Union.

The PKK demanded that Turkey negotiate with Ocalan. When Erdogan refused, it resumed operations in 2004. With Turkey's EU prospects waning, the state tried to provoke a renewal of hostilities in the Southeast that would justify the re-imposition of martial law and provide the pretext for rolling back EU-inspired reforms restricting the military's powers.

In November 2005, a white Dogan car stopped at the curb in front of the Hope Bookstore in the town of Semdinli, Hakkari Province. A bomb was thrown from the car window killing the bookstore owner. A crowd pursued the vehicle and apprehended the bombers who turned out to be security officers. In the car, which belonged to the gendarmerie, they found an Intelligence identification badge, several AK-47 rifles, and a list of other targets. The bombing was one of twenty incidents that occurred in Hakkari. All were staged to look like PKK terrorism.

When the Turkish intelligent agents were identified, General Yasar Büyükanit, then the Deputy Chief of Staff and Land Forces Commander, announced: "I know Sergeant Ali Kaya; we worked together. He is a good boy."[53] The TGNA established a parliamentary committee to investigate the incidents, but at least one member received death threats. The Semdinli prosecutor was removed from his post and his license to practice law was revoked.

The Semdinli affair stirred great concern about the military's role and its ability to undermine the rule of law with impunity. Kurds responded with protests in towns and cities across the southeast. Peaceful protesters were violently disbursed by Turkish security services. Four civilians were killed by police. Human Rights Watch and other groups condemned Turkey's heavy-handed response charging excessive use of force.

Semdinli was compared to the 1996 Susurluk incident, which revealed a cabal between the state, security services, and organized crime to assassinate perceived civilian opponents in return for sharing the spoils from narcotics trafficking by criminal groups. Semdinli reinforced the view that Turkey's failure to democratize meant citizens did not control their welfare. Gunter Verheugen, the EU enlargement commissioner, called for an international investigation: "If security officials are involved in the bombing, severe sanctions must be taken against those responsible for such provocation. The southeast needs peace, investment, jobs, and respect for cultural rights—certainly not violence."[54]

Turkish Kurds look across the border at their brethren in northern Iraq who enjoy greater freedom and prosperity. They want what Iraqi Kurds have. Support for the PKK, which had waned dramatically after Ocalan's arrest is rebounding.

An estimated 2,000 militants in Turkey and up to 4,000 in Iraqi Kurdistan operated from sixty-five bases in eight areas with PKK headquarters high-atop the Qandil Mountains on the border between Turkey, Iraq, and Iran. About fifty miles from the Turkish border, the complex includes guest houses, a restaurant and classrooms used to school young recruits in Kurdish nationalism and Marxist-Leninist ideology.[55] The bases are in forbidding territory. Even Saddam Hussein's Republican Guard failed to bring the remote mountain peaks under control. Qandil serves as a staging ground for attacks against Turkish troops in the lowlands and across the border. As noted above, during the first half of 2007, 225 people—of whom 167 were soldiers—died as a result of attacks by the PKK. Half of the victims were killed by roadside bombs and improvised explosive devices, techniques picked up in Iraq.[56]

Both the government and the military were under intense pressure to respond. When Erdogan visited the White House in June 2005, he criticized the "failure" of the United States to evict PKK fighters and urged the United States to take action "eradicating the major thorn."[57]

Secretary of State Condoleezza Rice repeatedly assured Turkish officials that the PKK's presence would not be tolerated. So did a cavalcade of other senior U.S. officials such as National Security Adviser Stephen Hadley who affirmed, "The PKK is a terrorist organization. We condemn its activities. We understand that its activities in northern Iraq affect Turkey and cost Turkish lives. And the coalition and the Iraqi transitional government need to work together to do more to against this threat."[58]

Erdogan was skeptical, telling Bush that the PKK was trying to lure the United States and Turkey into confrontation. Addressing pressure from Turkish nationalists, Erdogan warned before elections, "We will have to do whatever it takes. And that 'whatever' is obvious."[59]

During the summer of 2007, more than 100,000 troops were massed on the Iraqi border threatening a cross-border operation to break the back of the PKK. With Turkey threatening a large-scale invasion, reports surfaced that the U.S. and Turkish officials initiated discreet discussions on a joint military operation. Involving U.S. Special Forces working with the Turkish Army. This "covert activity" would seek to neutralize the PKK by killing its leaders and field commanders. The operation was cancelled after its cover was blown by media reports in July 2007."[60]

Later that month, Turkish media revealed that the United States was using the PKK to channel money and weapons to its affiliate, the Party for Free Life of Kurdistan (PJAK) and other Iranian Kurdish groups as part of its regime strategy for Iran.[61] The U.S. Embassy/Ankara issued a vehement denial. "The United States regards the PKK as a terrorist organization. We do not supply the PKK with weapons, transport, or anything else. We are not in discussions with the PKK about Iran or any other subject and we do not meet with its personnel. On the country, we are working to oppose PKK terrorism and to isolate the organization and its leaders in Northern Iraq and Europe."[62]

International Actors

United States

Turkey is a crucial ally of the United States in its war on terror. Since it became a NATO member in 1952, Turkey has represented the Alliance's eastern flank, sharing a long border with Russia, several Caucasian states, and controlling the straits leading from the Black Sea to the Mediterranean. The country played a crucial role in containing the Soviet Union during the Cold War. In the 1990s, it monitored Saddam Hussein and protected Iraqi Kurds by permitting U.S. and British warplanes to use its bases. After 9/11, Turkey became an important staging area for coalition forces in Afghanistan and eventually assumed overall command of the International Stabilization Force. As a secular Muslim country, Turkey is committed to fight Al Qaeda and other terrorist groups. Security co-operation with NATO and EU membership are the cornerstones of its foreign policy.

After their uprising was suppressed in February 1991, 1.5 million Iraqi Kurds fled over the mountains to Turkey and Iran. Through "Operation Provide Comfort," the U.S. military set up and supplied refugee camps on the border between Turkey and Iraq. By mid-April, the establishment of a no-fly zone above the 36th parallel allowed Iraqi Kurds to return to their homes in a crescent shaped enclave along the Turkish, Syrian, and Iranian borders. The PKK took advantage of the U.S. security umbrella to set up bases in the remote mountains of northern Iraq.

Turkey strongly opposed the Bush administration's decision to attack Iraq. U.S.-Turkish relations reached a low point on March 1, 2003 when the TGNA failed to authorize the transit of the 4th Infantry Division through Turkey into Iraq. The Bush administration's failure to act against the PKK further fueled anti-Americanism. Today, antipathy among Turks towards the United States is at an all-time high. According to a 2007 German Marshall Fund survey, only 9 percent of Turks have a favorable view of the United States.[63]

Many Turks believe that the United States has a hidden agenda to establish a greater Kurdistan. They point to the fact that, after the United States occupied Iraq in 2003, the PKK was able to reconstitute itself. These concerns were mollified by Rice during a trip to Ankara in October 2008 during which she referred to the PKK as "a common enemy." When Bush and Erdogan met in the oval office on November 5, 2008, Bush not only promised to give Turkey actionable intelligence on PKK facilities in Northern Iraq, he also gave Erdogan a green light for air strikes. Though nearly thirty PKK members were killed in the first attack in December, subsequent sorties only struck some empty caves and abandoned settlements, inflicting little damage to the PPK's infrastructure or capabilities.

European Union

Joining the EU became a national obsession for many Turks in the 1990s. Turkey's prospects looked bleak when, in 1997, several former Communist countries jumped the queue and Turkey was not even considered as a candidate. Adding insult to injury, Luxembourg's Prime Minister Jean-Claude Juncker stated, "A country in which torture is still a common practice cannot have a seat at the table of the European Union." Juncker's derogatory slur convinced many Turks that, no matter the extent of reforms, the EU simply did not want Turkey to be a part of its Christian club.

Turkey demanded benchmarks to measure its progress. At the 2002 Copenhagen Summit, the EU outlined the political and economic conditions that Ankara would have to satisfy before formal accession talks could begin. These became known as the "Copenhagen criteria." They included economic reforms and stable institutions guaranteeing democracy, human rights, and the rule of law. Though hardliners balked at reforms, most military officers understood the need for civilian control over the military. They appreciate that EU membership would represent the culmination of a modernization process launched by Ataturk. Former Chief of Staff Huseyn Kivriköglu insisted that Turkey's progress towards EU membership was a "geostrategic necessity."[64]

Despite forward-moving steps, European Council reports highlighted problems with the implementation of reforms.[65] It found that the amount of time allocated to Kurdish-language television broadcasts was capped and, though Kurdish is allowed in private schools, few students can afford the tuition. In June 2005, the governor of Ankara refused to issue a business license to the Kurdish Democracy Culture and Solidarity Association claiming its agenda of cultural rights was unconstitutional. In July 2005, the governor of Bingol imposed an $800 administrative fee on a local human rights organization for printing its letterhead in Kurdish. Diyarbakir, Batman, Sirnak, Madin, Siirt, Itakarri, Bingol, and Tunceli were called "critical provinces" and governed under a special administrative law.

Turkey also failed to reform laws stifling free speech. Adopted in October 2005, Article 131 of the criminal code imposed penalties for insulting state institutions. When Orhan Pamuk stated that "30,000 Kurds and a million Armenians were killed in these lands but nobody dares to talk about it,"[66] he was charged with "insulting Turkishness."[67]

Limited progress was made reintegrating former militias and returning displaced persons to their homes. Fewer than 8,000 were granted imnesty during the program's first six months. The Back to Village Program failed to create conditions for return. Only about 5 percent of those eligible for compensation appled. Most applicants received no payment.[68]

Critics of Turkey in Europe seized on lagging implementation of reforms to try and block Turkey's EU membership. The French and Dutch votes against ratification of the European constitution were at least in part a reaction to Turkey's candidacy. Austria called for "special partnership status" short of full membership. Angela Merkel, Germany's chancellor, opposes Turkey's membership. So does Nicolas Sarkozy, who won France's presidential election in 2007. Upon taking office, Sarkozy reiterated his strong opposition to Turkey's EU membership. "Turkey has no place in Europe," he insisted.[69] Sarkozy was more concerned about winning support for an EU treaty than issues like Turkey's membership. However, Sarkozy is first and foremost a pragmatist who subsequently moderated his views. Erdogan came out of his meeting with Sarkozy on the margins of the UN General Assembly in September 2007 announcing that France would now support Turkey's membership in the EU. When an ethnic Turk was identified as a ringleader of the July 2007 German terror plot, Merkel toned down her anti-Turkish rhetoric fearful of inflaming Muslim minorities within Germany. She was especially wary of radicalizing Germany's 2.7 million Turks.

Though the EU formally initiated negotiations with Turkey in 2005, it may take up to 20 years before Turkey meets the requirements. The refusal to approve a customs union agreement with Cyprus, an EU member, makes progress more difficult. There are 60,000 pages of regulations. Even if Turkey makes decisive progress, membership is not guaranteed. The PKK's resumption of military activities in 2005 and Turkey's transgressions against Iraq's territorial integrity, in 2008 have further complicated Turkey's EU prospects.

Iraq

Turkish nationalists have an existential fear that the emergence of an independent Iraqi Kurdistan will encourage Turkish Kurds to take steps against the indivisibility of the state. They believe that the oil-rich northern Iraqi city of Kirkuk is the key.

Massing troops on the Iraqi borders was more than a threat to the PKK. It was also intended to signal the Iraqi Kurds. Turkey will not abide by Article 140 of the Iraqi constitution that requires a popular referendum on Kirkuk's status by December 31, 2007.[70] Nor would it allow the Iraqi Turkmen to become a repressed minority by Iraqi Kurds whom Turkey fears will radicalize its own Kurdish minority.

The troop build up is intended to pressure Iraq into delaying the referendum. Iraqi Kurds were upset in 2005 when the interim constitution set 2007 as the deadline. Now they are upset that it might not happen by year's end—or at all. Massoud Barzani, president, of the Iraqi Kurdistan Regional Government (KRG) has a hard time explaining the delay to his constituents. Claiming that the KRG will get Kirkuk by default is not good enough.[71]

Turkish generals are on record stating that they would deploy forces to prevent a largescale ground operation referendum on Kirkuk's status. It is unlikely that Turkey would undertake this operation without permission of the United States. Such permission will not be forthcoming. The United States badly needs Barzani's peshmarga to augment Iraqi security forces. Nor is the United States likely to pressure Barzani into a direct confrontation with the PKK. Over the past fifteen years, Iraqi Kurds unsuccessfully engaged the PKK militarily on three occasions, twice in consort with Turkish troops.

To placate Turkey, the Bush administration proposed a Tripartite Mechanism on intelligence sharing that included the United States, Turkey and Iraq. General Joe Ralston (U.S. Army, ret.) was appointed Special Envoy for Countering PKK Terrorism on August 25, 2006. Iraq's President Jalal Talabani, who also leads the Patriotic Union of Kurdistan, welcomed the initiative. "The PKK terrorist group threatens firstly the national interests of the Kurdish people," said Talabani. "Policing measures will be taken against the PKK. We will do all we can."[72] After seven meetings, however, it was clear that the initiative was going nowhere. It was undermined by the Iraqi government's lack of responsiveness, Turkey's intransigence, and the unwillingness of the United States to pressure either. Moreover, the agreement did not include the KRG that controls territory where the PKK is based.

Greece

Since its inception, the PKK received assistance from Iran, Iraq, Syria, Greece, and Armenia—Turkey's neighbors who used the PKK to settle scores and leverage their own interests. Cooperation was based on convenience rather than commitment; assistance proved to be shallow and unreliable. The PKK, and by inference, Turkish Kurds became pawns in a greater game. Greek-Turkish relations were strained by Turkey's occupation of northern Cyprus in July 1974. Tensions were exacerbated by disputes over territorial waters. When Ocalan was arrested, he was in possession of a Cypriot passport. He had flown from Athens to Nairobi in the private plane of a Greek military official. In Kenya, he was the guest of Greece's ambassador. During interrogation, Ocalan admitted that Greek churches collected money for the PKK. Greece's Prime Minister Simitis questioned whether the PKK was a terrorist organization: "The PKK is an organization fighting for the rights of the Kurdish minority and using various means to reach this end."[73] Turkey responded by accusing Greece of being a state sponsor of terrorism.

Iran

Iran's Revolutionary Guards (Pasdaran) trained the PKK in Lebanon's Beka'a Valley. Iran supported the PKK despite Turkey's strict neutrality during the Iran-Iraq War (1980-88). Its assistance was a way to strike back at Turkey for the country's secular ways, membership in NATO, and its close cooperation with the United States. Iranian mullahs hoped that their support would contribute to the PKK's transformation from a nationalist insurgency into a religious movement. Assistance to the PKK was also consistent with their broader goal of exporting Iran's Islamic revolution throughout the Muslim world.

Syria

Hafez Al Assad was enraged when Turkey built the Ataturk and Birecik Dams on the Euphrates River thereby limiting critical water flows to Syria. Assad not only sheltered, trained, and equipped Lebanon's PKK. He also enabled the organization to receive training in the Beka'a' Valley of Lebanon. Ocalan openly used his Damascus villa as a base of operations. From his front porch, he met with members of the international press and convened field commanders to coordinate activities. In 1998, Turkey threatened to cut off all water supplies unless Syria severed ties with the PKK. Facing a real threat of military confrontation with Turkey, Syria signed the Adana Memorandum in October 1998. This agreement designated the PKK a terrorist organization and required Syria to evict the organization from its territory.

Increasingly alienated from the United States and the EU, Turkey is also seeking new allies. Its outreach focuses on Russia, Arab countries in the Middle East, and on Central Asia where it has extensive trade and energy interests.

The Way Forward

A Turkish solution to the PKK problem is based on Turkey's continued democratization and improved living standards for all citizens including those of Kurdish origin. Military action against the PKK in northern Iraq would have serious negative consequences. It would undermine Turkey's democratic development, radicalize Turkish Kurds, and risk a regional conflagration with adverse affect on relations between the United States and Turkey, as well as Turkey's prospects of joining the EU.

Rather than a risky escalation of the conflict, Turkey should emphasize non-military measures that would encourage PKK members to disarm and reintegrate into civilian life. A peaceful solution to the PKK problem represents a potential win-win that would preserve Turkey's territorial integrity, strengthen its democracy, and promote peace and progress for all. PKK fighters will come down from the mountains if they believe that the AKP can effectively promote their interests.

Turkey's new "civil constitution" is a big step in institutionalizing the protection and promotion of minority rights in accordance with the European Convention on Human Rights. But instead of pressing ahead with the constitution, the AKP frittered away its popular mandate by focusing on removing regulations that restrict the wearing of head scarves by girls at public schools. Erdogan should focus instead on adopting the new constitution, fully implementing political and cultural reforms, and abolishing regressive legislation, especially Article 301 of the Criminal Code. Changes are also needed to Articles 215, 216, 217, and 220 of the Penal Code that have been used to limit expression of Kurds. Cultural rights, including use of the Kurdish language in public education, and public services should be expanded. Restrictions on religious freedom and minority rights require review. The anti-terror law still allows too broad a definition of terrorism and needs to be amended. Measures are also needed to reform the judiciary, which is rigid, unaccountable, and deeply conservative.[74]

Erdogan cannot falter in his efforts to take on the "Deep State" or satisfy the Copenhagen criteria. The prospect of EU membership is critical to reforms. "Special partnership" is a totally inadequate substitute for negotiations on full membership. Only a strong and united message of support for Turkey's candidacy from EU member states, especially Germany and France, can sustain the momentum for difficult reforms. The most pressing challenge is fully subordinating Turkey's armed forces to civilian control and disempowering state structures that impede progress to preserve the status quo. Despite the AKP's recent electoral success, the resumption of armed conflict is being used by the deep state to sustain a primary role for the military, justify expanded security expenditures, and slow down the overall pace of reform. The deep state is eager to use the resurgent PKK as an excuse to marginalize the AKP, thereby shrinking the space for democratic participation. The PKK welcomes Turkey's military action because it fuels Kurdish nationalism and undermines moderates seeking a peaceful solution.

Turkey has an unquestioned right to root out terrorist groups operating on its territory. However, in so doing, its security forces must comply with universal legal principles and international human rights standards. Turkey's armed forces should function like a "democratic army." The NSC cannot condone massive population transfers or a scorched earth policy. It cannot be complicit with shadowy forces running rogue operations or assassinating civilians in order to foment strife and civil unrest. Such operations bring discredit on the entire institution of the armed forces, as well as shame to its leaders.

Improving economic conditions in the southeast is also part of the solution. Today Turkey is reaping the benefits of macro-economic financial reforms implemented by the AKP after the 2001 financial crisis. No more telling indicator is the rise in Foreign Direct Investment (FDI). Between 1980 and 2003, total FDI was just $19 billion whereas in 2006, FDI totaled $20 billion.[75] The country's overall economic well-being allows the AKP to earmark public resources for infrastructure such as road and water works. In March 2008, Erdogan announced a $12 billion development plan for the southeast that would involve new dam projects to provide inexpensive electricity for economic growth. Upgrading Diyarbakir's airport to accommodate international flights would be worthwhile. Funds could also be dedicated to Turkey's state energy company for research and development of energy resources in the southeast.

It is important to apply lessons from GAP. Project development should involve affected Kurdish communities. Instead of a top-down approach, projects should be undertaken at the grass-roots. Creating jobs is paramount. To this end, the 30 percent unemployment rate in the southeast can be reduced by upgrading traditional agricultural and animal husbandry industries. Southeastern Turkey has abundant water resources from the Tigris and Euphrates rivers, as well as underground water supplies. Instead of flooding the Ataturk Dam, which will wipe out the topsoil, drip irrigation would be a more effective and user-friendly technology. Land reform would involve bundling multi-ownership lots to allow economies of scale when introducing new irrigation and fertilizer techniques. Improvements in animal husbandry can be achieved by introducing more efficient leather tanning and processing procedures and linking production to distribution strategies.

The Middle East represents a ripe market for agro-industry and leather products. In addition to Harbur, other border crossings to Iraq should be opened. Instead of intentionally delaying trucks carrying perishable goods and other consumer items from Turkey to Iraq, the gendarmerie should facilitate transport and the Interior Ministry expedite visas for businessmen from northern Iraq investigating investment or joint ventures in the southeast. Establishing a planning office within the Office of the Prime Minister would promote inter-agency coordination, facilitate joint actions between national and local governments, and help channel investments.

Investments can yield amcillary benefits by incorporating the goal of dismantling the tribal and feudal character of Kurdish society. Women can play a crucial role. More projects should emphasize women's employment. Rural credit would generate small-scale industries for women. Population planning programs are also needed given the large size of families and the existence of multiple marriages among Kurds. Expanded educational opportunities are needed for young girls. Investments in the Southeast could also be used to enhance social services such as health, education, and to subsidize return and resettlement efforts targeting civilians displaced by conflict with the PKK.

Through the European Regional Development Fund, the European Social Fund, or the European Agricultural Guidance and Guarantee Fund, the EU and the Government of Turkey could co-sponsor a "Peace and Development Fund." Assistance would support the Back to Village Program and provide compensation to homeowners in the event that their property has been destroyed or rendered uninhabitable. The special administrative status of provinces in the Southeast should be revoked and the village guard system would be abolished, with international donor support, helping to reintegrate village guards so they can reintegrate into society.

While Erdogan pushes for political reforms nationwide and economic progress in the southeast, he should be careful not to invite a confrontation with the military or provide a pretext for a military take-over. Improving overall conditions can go just so far. Pressure must also be brought to bear on the PKK by the international community as well as the KRG.

The international community can increase pressure on the PKK by targeting its financing and propaganda infrastructure. The European Counter Terrorism Group could take the lead, investigating money laundering. The UN Counter-Terrorism Committee, which was established to deny funding to terrorist activities, could also request that the EU and other member states suspected of hosting PKK front organizations report on efforts to cut off financing.[76] The licenses for European-based PKK media outlets that incite hatred or endorse violence should be revoked.

The conflict between Turkey and the PKK is linked to the tragedy unfolding in Iraq. Turks see the emergence of a *de facto* independent state of Iraqi Kurdistan inspiring the separatist demands of Turkish Kurds. Turkey's ground operation in February 2008 sent a clear warning to Iraqi Kurds on Kirkuk. Turkey adamantly opposes the Kirkuk governorate joining the KRG. The more it objects, however, the more likely Iraqis will be to push for a referendum on Kirkuk's status and the less likely they will be to adopt power-sharing arrangements protecting the rights of all Kirkukis.[77]

The simple fact is that events in Iraq are outside of Turkey's control. Launching a major cross-border operation runs the risk of causing a spiral of deadly violence that would engulf the region and ill-serve Turkey's security interests. As Iraq fragments, Turkey may come to realize that a stable, secular, and pro-Western Iraqi Kurdistan is a useful buffer between it and an increasingly unstable and Islamicized Iraq.

Though relations are tense now, Turkey will ultimately forge an indispensable partnership with Iraqi Kurdistan. For the time being, Turkey and the KRG need to interact, identify common ground, and take steps to build confidence. Turkey should stop vilifying Massoud Barzani and open a direct channel by sending a special envoy to meet him. As follow-up to Jalal Talabani's Ankara trip in March 2008, the groundwork could be laid by Nechivan Barzani, the KRG Prime Minister, who is a proponent of cooperation with Turkey.

The KRG must recognize that its future prospects are contingent upon ties with Turkey. Landlocked and surrounded by hostile neighbors, the

KRG needs Turkey as its lifeline to the world. The KRG must do its part to build better relations by limiting the PKK's logistics and replacing PKK checkpoints around Qandil with its own. It can also reduce financial flows by implementing screening procedures that interdict funds being transferred to the PKK by travelers arriving at the airport in Erbil. In addition, the KRG should restrict the activities of pro-PKK groups that condone violence (e.g., Democratic Solution Party).

Economic ties are essential to fostering better relations. To this end, Turkish companies should be offered preferential production sharing agreements to develop oil fields that the KRG is opening to international joint ventures. In turn, Turkey can stimulate trade/investment by expediting transit procedures at the Harbur gate and opening more border crossings to Iraqi Kurdistan. Instead of highlighting the benefits of co-mingled Turkish-KRG financial interests, Turkey threatens sanctions against the KRG for harboring the PKK. While slowing trade at the Harbur Gate on the Turkey-Iraq border, Ankara is also dragging its feet on an agreement to open a second border crossing to facilitate travel and trade with Iraq. Ankara believes its economic leverage will pressure Iraqi Kurds to confront the PKK. But economic sanctions will also hurt Turkish businesses, which have received the lion's share of reconstruction contracts in northern Iraq.

These proposed measures can ameliorate the situation. However, Turkey will never solve the PKK problem unless it is prepared to endorse an amnesty arrangement. Turkey has a long tradition of amnesties. The AKP should capitalize on its July 2007 electoral victory to make the case that amnesty is integral to Turkey's national security interest.

Amnesty would proceed in phases. First, PKK members who joined after 2002 would be eligible. Cadres without command responsibility would be next. Senior commanders would not receive amnesty. Once these initial phases are successfully completed, they would apply for asylum in their country of current residence. Turks want the commanders to stand trial in Turkey, but the commanders would never allow the process to go forward unless there was something in it for them. Leaders will not let go of the rank-and-file unless the arrangement addresses their fate as well.

Terminology is important. The term "general amnesty" (*general af*) is too contentious. The PKK interprets amnesty to mean that the Turkish government will deal with them as the representative of the Kurdish people, but it is politically untenable for any government to accept the PKK as its direct negotiating partner. Therefore, "winning to the society" (*Topuma Kazamim*) would be a more suitable reference to the DDR process of disarmoment, demobilization, and reintegation.

An interlocutor will be needed. The DTP has twenty-one deputies elected to serve Kurdish constituencies in the national parliament. Erdogan has called on the DTP to condemn PKK terror. Doing so would, however, undermine their potential as interlocutors. It is precisely because its members have ties to Ocalan, the Qandil faction, and the Kurdish Diaspora in Europe that the DTP can be an effective liaison. It is important to bolster the credibility of DTP MPs. Members of the diplomatic community should receive them at senior levels and provide counsel. Nationalists view the DTP as rogue outsiders. The AKP must compensate by treating them as genuine partners in Turkey's democratization. The judiciary's prosecution of DTP members and efforts to ban the party are ill-advised.

Turkey faces a difficult legacy from its conflict with the PKK. Establishing a Truth and Reconciliation Commission (TRC) would help build confidence and end the cycle of violence. It would also combat the culture of impunity and help entrench the rule of law. Getting to the truth will not be easy. "Multiple truths" exist. Both sides have their own version and are adamantly convinced they know what really happened. International experience could help inform the terms of reference for Turkey's TRC. Studying how other countries have developed systems for transitional justice after emerging from a long period of violence is the first step in defining the TRC's mandate, financing, and procedures for civil participation.

Continued democratization and economic development is the best way for Turkey to drain the swamp of domestic support for the PKK. Instead of giving a green light to further Turkish military actions, the United States should intensify its diplomacy to achieve a nonmilitary solution to the PKK problem. This needs to be done quickly before a new round of PKK terror attacks sabotage prospects for conciliation and cooperation among the United States, Turkey and Kurdish leaders in Iraq. Progress would also undermine the Deep state's efforts to delitimze the AKP.

Notes

1.   Article 39.
2.   Stephen Kinzer. *The New York Review of Books*. "The Big Change." January 12, 2006.
3.   Greeks, Armenians, and Jews.

4.   The author refers to ultranationalist interest groups including corrupt politicians, the army, police, and government bureaucrats as the "state" that is also otherwise known as the "deep state."
5.   The author first visited Diyarbakir in February 1992.
6.   Party program of the PKK adopted at the Fifth Victory Congress. January 1995.
7.   Dogu Ergil. "Suicide Terrorism in Turkey." *Civil Wars*, Vol. 3, No. 1 (Spring 2000). pp. 37-54.
8.   Interview with Professor Dogu Ergil. University of Ankara, Department of Political Science. February 16, 2006.
9.   Dogu Ergil. "Suicide Terrorism in Turkey." *Civil Wars,* Vol. 3, No. 1 (Spring 2000). Pgs. 37-54.
10.   Michael Radu. "The Rise and Fall of the PKK." *Orbis,* Winter 2001, Vol. 45, Issue 1. Pg. 47.
11.   Interview with the author. Ankara Maximum Security prison. February 18, 1998.
12.   MYNET/Fact Sheet. September 6, 2005.
13.   Interview with the author. August 6, 2003.
14.   Susanne Gusten. *Agence France Presse.* "Turkey announces capture of Kurdish leader Ocalan." February 16, 1999.
15.   *The Economist.* "An Ancient Tragedy." February 18, 1999.
16.   Abdullah Ocalan. "Declaration on the Democratic Solution of the Kurdish Question." *Kurdistan Information Centre*, London. Mesopotamian Publishers, 1999. p. 85.
17.   Metin Munir. *Financial Times.* "Kurdish leader gains support for deal that will end military struggle." June 3, 1999. p. 2.
18.   Statement by Abdullah Ocalan released by his lawyers on March 18, 1999.
19.   Harvey Morris. *Financial Times.* "Turkish Kurd leader drops separatism and seeks Washington talks." April 15, 2003. p. 4.
20.   Christopher de Bellaigue. *Financial Times.* Turks fearful of Kurds gaining a diplomatic base." November 17, 1998. p. 2.
21.   Interview with Professor Dogu Ergil. Faculty of Political Science, University of Ankara. February 16, 2006.
22.   Dogu Ergil. "Strange but True." *Zaman.* August 7, 2007.
23.   Interview with MOFA officials. September 14, 2007.
24.   *The Spectator.* 28 November-5 December, 1998.
25.   Michael Radu. "The Rise and Fall of the PKK." *Orbis,* Winter 2001, Vol. 45, Issue 1. p. 47.
26.   *Ibid.*
27.   Interview with MOFA officials. September 14, 2007.
28.   *Turkish Daily News.* Al-Qaeda Militants in Turkey. June 1, 2004.
29.   Interview with DTP Member of Parliament. September 13, 2007.
30.   nterview with a DTP MP on September 13, 2007.
31.   Article 14 of the 1982 constitution.
32.   Anatolian News Agency. February 18, 2005.
33.   Dogu Ergil. "Don't Worry Turkey." January 2006.
34.   *Turkish Daily News.* "Yilmaz: the road to the EU passes through Diyarbakir." December 17, 1999.
35.   *The Economist.* "Peace be unto you." August 20, 2005.
36.   Stephen Kinzer. *The New York Review of Books.* "The Big Change. January 12, 2006.
37.   AKI. January 10, 2006.

38. Michael M. Gunther. "The continuing Kurdish problem in Turkey after Ocalan's capture." *Third World Quarterly.* October 2000, Vol. 21, Issue 5.

39. Stephen Kinzer. *The New York Review of Books.* "The Big Change. January 12, 2006.

40. *AKI.* January 10, 2006.

41. *Ibid.*

42. Interview with Ilter Turkmen. Ankara. February 20, 1998.

43. Diyarbakir Metropolitan Municipality. "Democratization in Turkey and the Kurdish Question." Osman Baydemir, Mayor of Diyarbakir. September 1, 2005.

44. Dogu Ergil. "Suicide Terrorism in Turkey." *Civil Wars*, Vol. 3, No. 1 (Spring 2000). pp. 37-54.

45. National Intelligence Organization. http://www.yesil.org.terror/pkkrakamlar.htm. April 9, 2005.

46. Adopted in 1991.

47. Stephen Kinzer. *The New York Review of Books.* "The Big Change. January 12, 2006.

48. Annual Report of the Turkish Human Rights Association (2004).

49. Human Rights Watch. *World Report 2005.*

50. Diyarbakir Metropolitan Municipality. "Democratization in Turkey and the Kurdish Question." Osman Baydemir, Mayor of Diyarbakir. September 1, 2005.

51. Indictment of Abdullah Ocalan. p. 58.

52. Comment by Andreas J. Burghofer, Mesopotamia Biblioteck Linz, Austria. October 21, 2007.

53. Diyarbakir Metropolitan Municipality. "Democratization in Turkey and the Kurdish Question." Osman Baydemir, Mayor of Diyarbakir. September 1, 2005.

54. Vincent Boland. *Financial Times.* December 5, 2005. Japan edition, p. 13.

55. Liz Sly. "A Fragile stability on the border; Kurdish rebels threaten to draw regional players into Iraq." *Chicago Tribune.* July 30, 2007.

56. Dogu Ergil. "Strange but True." *Zaman.* August 7, 2007.

57. *Turkish Daily News.* June 6, 2005.

58. Peter Baker. *The Washington Post.* Hadley Makes Turkey a Priority Stop. September 24, 2005. p. A16.

59. Liz Sly. "A Fragile stability on the border; Kurdish rebels threaten to draw regional players into Iraq." *Chicago Tribune.* July 30, 2007.

60. Robert D. Novak. *The Washington Post.* "Bush's Turkish Gamble." July 30, 2007.

61. http://www.presstv.ir/pop/print.aspx. March 28, 2007.

62. *Turkish Daily News.* U.S. Embassy Denies PKK meeting." September 12, 2007.

63. GMF Survey 2007.

64. *Turkish Daily News.* January 5, 2006 cited European Council reports from 2003 and 2004.

65. Diyarbakir Metropolitan Municipality. "Democratization in Turkey and the Kurdish Question." Osman Baydemir, Mayor of Diyarbakir. September 1, 2005.

66. Scott Peterson. *Reuters.* "The case of Orhan Pamuk is being watched as a test of political freedoms. December 16, 2005.

67. Charges were brought under Article 301 of the Criminal Code.

68. *The Economist.* "Peace be unto you." August 20, 2005.

69. *Turkish Daily News.* "Sarkozy continues his unyielding opposition." June 10, 2007.

70. Article 140.

71. Interview with Joost Hilterman of the International Crisis Group. September 11, 2007.

72.   *BBC*. Turkish Premier hopeful of action against rebel Kurds after New York visit."
       September 19, 2005.
73.   MYNET/Fact Sheet. September 6, 2005.
74.   *Reuters*. "Turkey's judiciary an obstacle on the EU path." February 28, 2006.
75.   Interview with Hasan Cemal. September 12, 2007.
76.   United Nations Security Council resolution 1373 (28 September 2001).
77.   Interview with Joost Hilterman of the International Crisis Group. September 11,
       2007.

5

Free Aceh Movement

Megawati Sukarnoputri was the first Muslim head of state to visit President George W. Bush after September 11. Bush saw symbolic value in the meeting. He wanted the world to behold Indonesia's President Megawati, leader of the most populous Muslim country, expressing solidarity with the United States during its hour of grief. Megawati had her own agenda. While condemning global terrorism, she asked Bush to include the Free Aceh Movement (GAM) on the U.S. list of Foreign Terrorist Organizations (FTOs). Bush promised military and financial aid as well as trade preferences, but Megawati did not get what she wanted. Bush refused to label GAM a terrorist organization. Instead he pressed Megawati to join in his global war on terror by cracking down on Muslim hard-line groups operating from Indonesia's territory.

History

Jose Ramos-Horta, the Nobel Peace Laureate from East Timor, predicted a financial crisis in Asia that would destabilize the Indonesian rupiah and send pro-democracy demonstrators to the streets demanding the overthrow of President Suharto. Ramos-Horta also predicted that East Timor, a former Portuguese colony where 600,000 people died after Indonesia invaded in 1975, would emerge from Indonesia's collapse as an independent country.

Sure enough, Indonesia experienced a financial crisis that culminated in Suharto's downfall. He was replaced by B.J. Habibie who, in January 1999, offered the East Timorese the opportunity to select between separation from Indonesia and enhanced autonomy. Much to Jakarta's surprise, the East Timorese voted overwhelmingly for independence. Popular protests ensued when the Government of Indonesia (GOI) tried to abrogate the results. Gangs of military-backed thugs ravaged the island. Several hundred thousand refugees sought sanctuary in West Timor. Under international pressure, Jakarta invited Australia to lead a stabilization force authorized under Chapter VII of the UN Charter. From its ashes, East Timor emerged as a free and independent nation.

The events in East Timor were an omen to those who warned of a domino effect resulting in Indonesia's disintegration. In the far east of the vast archipelago, Papuans demand freedom. Oil-rich Riau in Sumatra seek self-rule. Sectarian strife in the Malukus, the original Spice Islands, and East Kalimantan also fuel separatism. Among Indonesia's hotspots, Aceh was the most volatile. Within days of the popular consultation on East Timor's status, Acehnese student groups took to the streets demanding a referendum of their own.

By virtue of its size, location, and population of 220 million, Indonesia is a critically important country in Southeast Asia. Likened to the former Yugoslavia, Indonesia is a mosaic of different ethnic and religious groups scattered across 13,000 islands covering 6,400 kilometers and five time zones. Since Indonesia declared independence in 1945, far-flung communities have chafed under Jakarta's authoritarian rule and economic exploitation.

Aceh is a remote, resource-rich yet impoverished part of Indonesia on the tip of northern Sumatra. Straddling the Malacca Straits to the north, it is strategically located as a vital link between the Pacific, the South Atlantic and the Indian Ocean. Aceh lies about 1,000 miles from Jakarta. It is, however, worlds apart from Jakarta's financial and commercial hustle and bustle. Aceh has its own culture with a language distinct from Malay. Like pockets in other parts of Indonesia such as South Sulawesi, Aceh's population of four million is known for its religious devotion.

Acehnese have a long history of resisting colonial rule and foreign occupation. Aceh was a powerful commercial empire during the sixteenth and seventeenth centuries, trading in gold and pepper, as well as ivory, tin, aloe wood and exotic spices. It remained an independent sultanate for 500 years until the late nineteenth century when the Netherlands sought to extend its colonial rule to all of Sumatra.[1] The Dutch demanded an end to piracy and slave trading, as well as Aceh's immediate surrender. They insisted that Aceh cut diplomatic and commercial ties with foreign countries, renounce loyalty to the Islamic Caliphate, and swear allegiance to the King of the Netherlands.

According to the *New York Times*, "A sanguinary battle has taken place in Aceh, a native kingdom occupying the northern portion of Sumatra. The Dutch delivered a general assault and the attack was repulsed with great slaughter. The Dutch general was killed and his army decimated and put to disastrous flight."[2] Despite their disastrous defeat, the Dutch regrouped and attacked again on Christmas Day. Major powers issued declarations of neutrality implicitly recognizing Aceh's independent and sovereign status. Though conflict continued until the beginning of World War II, the Dutch never established either legal or de facto control over Aceh.

Four years after Sukarno declared Indonesia's independence in 1945, the Netherlands ceded the Dutch East Indies to the Republic of Indonesia (RI). In violation of UN decolonization rules stipulating that no colonial power may transfer sovereignty of its former territory to another colonial power without conducting a plebiscite of the affected population, the central government in Jakarta incorporated Aceh into the province of North Sumatra and transferred sovereignty to Indonesia in 1949. Henry Kissinger observed, "Indonesia was nothing but a geographic expression until the Dutch found it more efficient to unite the islands of the Indies under a single administration."[3]

Indonesia's nation-building was interrupted by political violence that killed more than 500,000 people in 1965-66. After seizing power, General Suharto adopted a policy of "unity and nationalism." His centralized approach to governance (*Pancasila*) was anathema to the Acehnese, Papuans, and other distinct ethnic and religious minorities whose territory had been incorporated into the RI.

Suharto did not hesitate to use repressive tactics to consolidate his control. He brutally cracked down on dissent and suppressed self-determination movements. He brought the national police (POLRI) under his command. In addition, he used the Indonesian Army (TNI) and other security services such as Special Forces (KOPASSUS) and Strategic Reserve Battalions (KOSTRAD) as the primary guardians of state sovereignty. According to formal army doctrine, TNI was charged with both defending external threats and acting as a "social and political force" to "ensure the security and success of each government program in the field of development" and the "stabilization of social conditions to generate the basis for national development and security." Suharto enabled the TNI to solidify its dual function (*Dwi Fungsi*) and used a Regional Military Command Structure (*Kommando Daerah Militer/KODAM*) to establish a system of control that paralleled civilian government extending to every village.

Since the national budget provides only 25-30 percent of its overall costs, the TNI addressed the budget gap by operating commercial indus-

tries such as airlines, hotels, and banks. Its foundations subsidize welfare activities for service families such as their housing, education, and
medical care. The KODAM is the vehicle that allows TNI to engage in
lucrative economic activities exploiting resource-rich regions like Aceh.
In addition, state-owned corporations such as Pertamina, the national
energy company, paid TNI to provide security at Aceh's natural gas
fields. Without effective oversight, TNI became riddled with corruption.
It engaged in illicit activities and protection rackets. Suharto's security
services were notorious for intimidating civilians and committing human
rights abuses with impunity.

After Habibie assumed the presidency on May 21, 1998, he struck a
conciliatory tone declaring an end to martial rule, apologizing for past
abuses, and calling for an investigation of atrocities committed against
civilians. He established an Aceh branch of the National Human Rights
Commission, created an Independent Investigation Commission on
Violence in Aceh, and proposed a truth and reconciliation commission
to expose past abuses. Habibie also promised greater self-rule and more
local control of natural resources.

Though General Wiranto appeared to support Habibie's efforts, state
bureaucrats and the military establishment blocked implementation of
promised reforms. Confidence-building measures proposed by Habibie
never came to pass and those that were undertaken fell far short of expectations. For example, legislation to create a truth and reconciliation
commission was introduced in parliament but no action was taken. The
Investigation Commission was launched but lacked credibility because
its director was known to have business ties with Wiranto. While Wiranto
agreed to pull BRIMOB out of Aceh, he simultaneously threatened to
re-impose the state of emergency unless GAM abandoned its militancy
that included kidnappings, killings, burning public buildings, vandalism,
and raising of the Free Aceh rebel flag.

Abdurrahman Wahid, Habibie's successor, fared no better in con-
straining excesses by the military. Upon taking office in October 1999,
he tried to diffuse rising tensions by ordering non-organic KOPASSUS
and KOSTRAD forces to leave Aceh. He also offered a general amnesty
to rebels from GAM in exchange for an end to their separatist struggle.
Most striking, Wahid asserted that it would be unfair not to allow the
Acehnese a referendum like the one in East Timor.

A firestorm of controversy ensued. Wahid quickly backtracked, insisting that he had been misunderstood and abandoning his pledge to
conduct a referendum. When the Independent Investigative Commis-

sion on Atrocities in Aceh concluded that top army generals ordered the assassination of civilians, Wahid insisted on prosecuting the persons responsible. However, TNI and the judiciary simply refused to carry out the presidential decree.[4] Weak and indecisive, Wahid acquiesced. GAM's leaders responded by reiterating their demand for independence and vowing to use all necessary means to realize their goal of self-determination.

Ideology

Wiranto was incensed by GAM's intransigent commitment to armed struggle. Citing a visit to Aceh in June 2002 by Ayman Al Zawahiri during which he tried to forge links between GAM and Jemaah Islamiyah, an Al Qaeda franchise in Southeast Asia, Wiranto accused GAM's leaders of running a terrorist organization and working with Al Qaeda.[5] In fact, GAM had resisted Zawahiri's overtures. Instead GAM chose to focus on political objectives. At its core, GAM is a national liberation movement with a military wing that rejects Javanese domination and foreign control.

GAM undertook military operations with the goal of creating chaos. Its leadership believed that by rendering Aceh ungovernable, Jakarta would be forced to negotiate the terms for Aceh's independence. Attacks targeted Indonesian political structures and symbols of economic exploitation by the regime. Acehnese employed by the GOI or provincial authorities were also targeted. Those who objected or supported integration were subjected to harassment and other forms of violent intimidation.

Though most Acehnese reject Islamic fundamentalism, Aceh's orthodox brand of Islam is distinct from Islamic practice in other parts of Indonesia. It was one of the earliest Islamic sultanates in Southeast Asia. In 1905, *Harper's Magazine* referred to Acehnese as "Mohammedan Malays." Aceh's location on the tip of Sumatra led some to call it "the front porch of Mecca."[6]

Religious figures (*Ulama*) played a major role in the rebellion against Dutch occupation. After the RI was founded, the Ulama participated in the Darul Islam Rebellion (1953-62) opposing Javanese domination. Pro-independence clerics formed the Ulama League of Religious Schools in 1998. Its youth wing, the Rabitha Thaliban Aceh, boasted 75,000 members.[7]

Fueled by martial law and lack of respect for local customs and religion, Aceh's Muslim character became more pronounced. GAM fighters who went to Libya received not only military but ideological instruction. In August of 1999, the Muslim United Party arrived in Aceh offering aid to displaced persons and investments in development projects. Reflecting a growing public sentiment, Cut Nur Asyikin, an activist from Pidie district, asked a pro-independence rally in November 1999, "Are you ready to go on jihad if the referendum does not take place?"[8] He spoke for a growing number of Acehnese who were questioning GAM's platform of secular nationalism and commitment to negotiations. Radical splinter groups, such as the Aceh Liberation Front, started to emerge. Giving voice to an increasingly radical polity, the Liberation Front declared: "We want to free the Islamic state of Aceh–Sumatra and separate it from the toy state of Javanese Indonesia."[9]

Despite pressures from Islamic groups, GAM consistently maintained that it was secular, nationalist, and pro-Western. When Jakarta permitted Shari'a for Aceh in 2001, GAM leaders claimed that Wahid was trying to deflect the pro-independence movement by shifting the focus to religion. They called it a ploy insisting that religious law was no substitute for independence or for the justice they were seeking against those who perpetrated atrocities.[10] GAM uses the term infidel (*Kafir*) not to describe those who reject Islamic fundamentalism, but for persons who commit abuses. A prominent Indonesian columnist asserted, "Wahid decided to impose Shari'a law in order to show the political will of the government to solve the problem of Aceh. Rather than responding to Acehnese demands for a political solution to the conflict and social justice, this was a crude attempt to co-opt and empower conservative religious elite to assist with the subjugation of the Acehnese."[11]

The Front Mujahideen Islam Aceh was established in 2000 as an alternative to the GAM's secular nationalist ideology. It accused GAM of straying from the "framework of devotion to Allah."[12] GAM responded by affirming its commitment to religious tolerance. It pointed out that Christian and Chinese communities were untouched in Aceh during the riots of 1998. GAM also highlighted the fact that it refused to cooperate with Laskar Jihad, a radical Muslim group, when it tried to set up Aceh operations in 2002. GAM also rejected appeals by Laskar Jihad and other militant Muslim groups from Java to rise up against foreigners and expel Christian-aid groups after the tsunami in 2005.

Susilo Bambang Yudhoyono cynically tried to marshal international support for the GOI's struggle against GAM by characterizing it as an Islamic fundamentalist movement. At an emergency meeting of the Organization of Islamic Conference in 2006, he warned: "This war [in Lebanon] must stop or it will radicalize the Muslim world, even those of us who are moderate today. From there, it will be just one step away to that ultimate nightmare: a clash of civilizations.[13]

Structure

The Aceh-Sumatra Liberation Front (ASNLF) was founded in 1976 after the United National General Assembly recognized the legitimacy of liberation struggle, including armed struggle, waged by colonized peoples to gain their rights of self-determination and to get rid of colonial or foreign domination.[14] Declaring independence, its charter stated: "The supreme aim of the ASNLF is the survival of the people of Aceh-Sumatra as a nation; the continued existence of their national homeland, which is being confiscated and divided by Javanese settlers; the preservation of their economic and natural resources which are being plundered by the Javanese colonialists and their imperialist backers."[15]

The ASNLF later became known as the Free Aceh Movement (*Gerakan Aceh Merdeka*) or GAM. Its ranks were augmented by the central government's heavy-handed counterinsurgency tactics, which motivated uneducated, poor, young men living in rural areas to join the struggle against repression and occupation. As casualties increased, recruits driven by revenge and a desire for justice flocked to GAM. The organization's ranks include many women who were widows and the daughters of "martyrs" or victims of sexual violence.

Like the KODAM, GAM established parallel governance structures extending its reach to even the most remote communities. In 2001, GAM claimed to be in control of 75 percent of the province.[16] GAM functioned like a de facto government collecting taxes and even issuing birth and marriage certificates. It designated village heads and, reinstituting the council of elders that existed prior to the RI's establishment, assumed government functions at the district and sub-district levels.

GAM established its own justice system. Local GAM councils (*Maejlis*) harangued persons alleged "infiltrators and spies" of "interaction with the enemy."[17] GAM also controlled some media organs. A local paper, *Serambi Indonesia,* was temporarily shut down for reporting that GAM displaced civilians in a deliberate move to win sympathy and support from the international community.

MP-GAM (*Majelis Pemerintahan*) was established by Acehnese exiles in Malaysia when Hasan Di Tiro, GAM's leader, fell ill in 1999. MP-GAM viewed the GAM in Stockholm as too secular and overly influenced by their time in the West. In response to DOM in 2003, GAM's ranks swelled to 27,000 fighters. However, new recruits were motivated more by economic gain than by religious or nationalistic aims. The Army of the State of Aceh (*Tentara Negara Aceh*) was created at a 2002 leadership conference in Norway. The TNA was made up of seventeen regional commanders; each commander controlled four district level units; fighters were organized in small cells.[18] GAM's decentralized structure allowed local commanders to become warlords who behaved like gangsters exploiting conditions to enrich themselves.

Leadership

Almost all of GAM's initial members had ties to the Di Tiro clan. Hasan Di Tiro, a direct descendant of Aceh's historic sultans, was GAM's undisputed head. When Di Tiro's undisciplined and poorly armed militias were easily defeated, he fled to Sweden and announced a government in exile. To this day, Acehnese still refer to him as "Sultan" and see him as their revered head of state (*Wali Negri*).

Hasan Di Tiro lives in a dreary apartment block in the suburbs of Stockholm. He is obsessed by history. On his kitchen table, he keeps an yellowing album of yellowing newspaper clippings that he shows to visitors. In addition to news reports, the album contains a collection of sympathy and support letters he has received from world leaders over the decades. He presents the album to visitors as proof of the international community's support for Aceh's independence.

As Di Tiro's health worsened during the Geneva talks, his deputies assumed an increasingly important role. Malik Mahmud, the so-called minister of state and principal negotiator, was promoted to the post of prime minister. Other members of the negotiating team included Zaini Abdullah and Bhaktiar Abdullah who was in charge of media and international relations.

GAM's exiled leadership in Sweden insisted that it had absolute control over forces in the field. In reality, GAM's field commanders asserted more and more autonomy especially as the GOI intensified its enforcement of martial law. They increasingly viewed the government-in-exile as out of touch with the needs of ordinary Acehnese who bore the brunt of Jakarta's oppression. They also grew resentful of the Stockholm clique, which allowed them scant influence over political decisions.

The GOI pursued a three-point strategy. It tried to undermine support for GAM by questioning the government in exile's legitimacy. To this end, it pointed out that Di Tiro was a Swedish citizen and Malik was a citizen of Singapore. As foreign nationals, neither could even vote in Indonesian elections. It also tried to discredit the organization as an Al Qaeda affiliate. Jakarta repeatedly appealed to the United States to place GAM on the State Department's FTO list. It also issued repeated demarches to the government of Sweden asking it to expel Di Tiro, Malik and Zaini or to put them on trial for terrorism.

The GOI also pursued a deliberate strategy to exacerbate factionalism within GAM's command structure and among Acehnese political groups. Field commanders complained about the lack of transparency. Facing equipment and resource shortfalls, they wanted to know how their tax payments were being spent by GAM in Sweden. Hard-line field commanders rejected Di Tiro's willingness to engage in negotiations with Jakarta. They dismissed the idea of a referendum claiming that illegal colonization meant that the GOI had no authority to even conduct a consultation on Aceh's status. Some demanded negotiations with the Dutch, Aceh's original colonizers.

Lastly, the GOI sought a military solution to the conflict by ratcheting up the pressure on GAM fighters in the field and targeting both militia members as well as their civilian support base. In June 2002, TNI launched a field operation that killed Zulfahri, GAM's military commander. He was replaced by Abdullah Syafi'e who was shot together with his pregnant wife during a KOSTRAD raid six months later. Scores of local leaders were arrested and charged with terrorism following a sweep of East Aceh in May 2003. Tgk. M. Johan, GAM's District Chief, was arrested and tortured to death in July 2004. Ishak Daud, a Central Command member, was killed during a firefight in September 2004.

Financing

Wiryono Sastrohandoyo, Jakarta's former chief negotiator for Aceh, maintained that GAM derived revenues from a range of criminal activities. According to Wiryono, GAM extorted money from Exxon Mobil demanding an "allowance" of up to 10 percent of the value of its contracts with local companies.[19] GAM was routinely paid 5 percent of the profits from other foreign contractors.

Wiryono accused GAM of demanding "protection" funds from civil servants and government employees. Those who refused to pay, especially businessmen, oil executives, and local legislators with ties to the central government, were subject to kidnapping and ransoming.

GAM was also involved in narcotics trafficking. Wiryono charged that 30 percent of the marijuana in Southeast Asia was cultivated in Aceh. In addition, he accused GAM of collaborating with Medan's mafia and of colluding with local government officials in drug trafficking to countries throughout the region.[20] Acehnese expatriates in Malaysia contributed funds to GAM that came from small-arms trafficking and illegal logging.

To support its parallel governance structures, GAM received "voluntary contributions" from farmers and merchants, the equivalent of one day's income per month. It was also paid a "Nanggroe tax" from local Acehnese and especially from Chinese merchants. By 2003, GAM's monthly tax revenue was Rp. 875 million.

Escalation

About 1,000 GAM fighters returned to Aceh in 1989 to launch insurgent activities after receiving guerilla training in Libya. Operations focused on oil and natural gas industries based in Northeast Aceh. GAM was able to rally its troops by playing on their resentment of outsiders, mostly Javanese, who were benefiting from Aceh's abundant fossil fuel, natural gas, and forestry reserves.

> In 1991, Jakarta awarded ExxonMobil an exclusive concession to develop Aceh's abundant oil and gas fields. As Mobil's operation peaked in 1992, Indonesia became the world's largest exporter of Liquified Natural Gas (LNG). Almost half of its supply came from energy facilities in Lhokseumawe, Aceh.

GAM was deeply resentful of Exxon Mobil for ignoring the local economy and focusing on exports to northeast Asia. Whereas oil and gas industries generated 40 percent of Aceh's economic activity, they employed less than 10 percent of the population.[21] In 1991, GAM tried to blow up Mobil's Arun natural gas complex near Lhokseumawe causing the facility to suspend operations.

Jakarta responded to attacks in Lhokseumawe by rushing more troops to north Aceh. The deployment met fierce criticism by the Acehnese who claimed that the army was using the closing as a pretext for increasing troop levels. The Acehnese chafed under martial law, which diminished their mobility and made it hard to tend their garden plots in the hills (*Kebun*) or go to the mountains in search of food, to cut timber, grow vegetables or cassava.

Sporadic attacks on Exxon Mobil facilities went on for nearly a decade. In 2000, GAM's offensive against Exxon Mobil's intensified causing the energy giant to temporarily suspended operations. Exxon Mobil closed three of its natural gas fields the following year. It could not justify TNI's security costs for gas fields that were depleted and no longer yielding significant revenues.

Suharto understood the economic grievances of the Acehnese and tried to undermine GAM through economic development. At the beginning of the 1990s, Suharto doubled development funds and called on state firms to finance small-scale industries that train and employ local Acehnese.[22]

Two years later, he officiated at the opening ceremony of development projects totaling $219 million. Projects included flood control systems, bridge construction, and rural electrification for 708 villages. The central government also announced a new round of major infrastructure renovation projects such as the construction of an electricity grid in Pidie province and a railroad connecting Banda Aceh to Medan.

Suharto announced his investment schemes with great fanfare. However, most of the pledged funds never arrived. Suharto cronies and local government officials absconded with the lion's share of project monies. Inefficiency and corruption further antagonized Acehnese and bolstered GAM. In response, GAM intensified operations targeting rural development projects, as well as state-owned economic infrastructure, government-owned companies, and other facilities owned by companies backing the government.

Poverty in Aceh was exacerbated by the 1997-98 economic crisis. The worsening conflict caused the economy to contract even further.[23] By 2003, 40 percent of Acehnese were living under the poverty line.[24] Instead of an economic solution to the conflict, Jakarta's exploitative policies embittered most Acehnese and fueled popular support for the rebellion.

GAM's insurgency campaign focused on military convoys and army barracks. It murdered family members of security services personnel, as well as suspected military informants (*Cuak*). It targeted symbols of the GOI's plunder, as well as Javanese businessmen and transmigrants who were relocated to Aceh as part of Suharto's "New Order" national security plan. GAM would conduct sweeps, stop buses, and remove anyone with a Javanese sounding name. Some disappeared and others were executed.[25] Transmigrants who acted as informants (*Perlawanan Rakyat*) were put on a hit list. Amnesty International accused GAM of murdering civilians suspected of assisting the TNI.[26]

All told, about 50,000 Javanese transmigrants were intimidated into leaving their homes.[27]

The GOI reacted by broadening the presence of the TNI to protect the transmigrant population as well investment in Aceh's oil and gas industries. It also established a KODAM for Aceh. In response, GAM sought the withdrawal of non-organic forces in KOPASSUS and KOSTRAD, especially from GAM strongholds in Pidie and Bireuen.

It also demanded the demobilization of militia groups that had been recruited in Central Aceh such as the Youth Defense of State Ideology (*Ksatria Unit Penegak Pancasila*) that participated in intelligence gathering and joint operations with TNI. Military officials insisted that militia groups had formed spontaneously as defense units against GAM attacks.[28] In fact, TNI condoned thuggery. It looked the other way when its militias abducted young boys as child soldiers who provided a variety of services to TNI such as night guard duty (*Jaga Malam*).

In 1989, human rights conditions deteriorated dramatically when Suharto ordered massive and brutal counter-insurgency activities against GAM that were referred to as DOM (*Daerah Operasi Militer*). The national parliament (DPR) adopted a resolution authorizing the TNI to shoot demonstrators on-sight. TNI intensified its crackdown by sealing roads leading to GAM strongholds and conducting large sweeps of civilian areas to ferret out GAM leaders.

Many innocent civilians were victimized during the crackdown. In August 1989, villagers led a representative of the Indonesia Legal Aid Foundation to eleven sites containing 500 bodies.[29] In November 1990, an open pit was discovered with 200 decomposed bodies. During the period of martial law from 1990-98, 2,687 Acehnese civilians went missing, 4,563 were tortured, 1,322 were widowed, and 3,392 children left fatherless.[30] Between 1976 and 2005, about 12,000 Acehnese died as a result of the conflict. Human rights groups implicated Exxon-Mobil alleging that it knowingly provided TNI with earth moving equipment used to dig mass gràves.[31]

The repression only hardened the desire of Acehnese for independence. In April 1999, more than one million people attended a rally in Banda Aceh demanding a referendum. Rioters smashed windows and fought police to protest adoption of a bill allowing the TNI to suspend civil liberties in emergency situations."[32] About 200,000 people were driven from their homes during the subsequent crackdown.

Contradicting the GOI's long-standing policy against internationalizing the Aceh conflict, Wahid invited the Henri Dunant Centre for Humanitarian Dialogue (HDC), a Geneva-based NGO, to facilitate talks between GAM and Indoensian officials. Beginning in May 2000, discussions were held at HDC's elegant villa on Lake Geneva. The parties soon agreed to a "humanitarian pause." Over the next six months, they also agreed on procedures for GAM to transform into a legitimate political movement and a timetable for elections installing a popularly elected government.

Though Wahid was widely praised for pursuing negotiations, his bold initiative did not sit well with the military that relished its historic role as the principal defender of Indonesia's national sovereignty. Wahid was replaced by Megawati Sukarnoputri in July 200. Megawati quickly abandoned conciliation in favor of confrontation. The daughter of Sukarno, a strong nationalist, Megawati had cozy relations with the military. Upon becoming president, she authorized all necessary measures to "hold the country together."[33] She renewed the KODAM for six months, launched a military offensive, and called for the arrest of non-violent political activists thought to be supporters of GAM. Megawati also imposed a veil of secrecy by banning human rights monitors and journalists from traveling to Aceh.

Under intense pressure, GAM signed the Cessation of Hostilities Agreement (COHA) in May 2002. The COHA prohibited "attacking, shooting, engaging in torture, killing, abducting, bombing, burning, robbing, extorting, threatening, terrorizing, harassing, illegally arresting people, raping, and conducting illegal searches." It called for an end to violence, confidence-building measures, and conditions enabling the delivery of humanitarian, rehabilitation, and reconstruction assistance. In addition, the COHA created peace zones such as schools, mosques, and hospitals. It established a Joint Security Committee (JSC) to monitor and resolve disputes. It also reformulated BRIMOB's mission conforming it to regular police activities and called on the signatories to control "groups that do not share their objectives but claim to be a part of their forces." The COHA also established a five-month process of demilitarization, demobilization, and reintegration of GAM fighters into society.

Optimism was short-lived. Almost immediately after the accord, conditions on-the-ground took a turn for the worse. Jakarta accused GAM of using the COHA to buy time, consolidate its forces, and reestablish administrative control at the local level where the government had a minimal presence. In the first three weeks after the COHA, fifty incidents were reported between GAM and Indonesian security forces. The Aceh Commission for Disappearances and Victims of Violence reported that, between January and November 2002, 1,307 were killed, 1,860 tortured, 1,186 placed under administrative detention, 377 disappeared, and forty-six women were sexually harassed.[34] Members of the JSC were harassed and the JSC was ultimately disbanded.

Since the vast majority of Acehnese received information about the COHA from GAM not the government, they celebrated the COHA as a step towards independence. They believed that the UN would use the COHA to establish its presence in Aceh and that Aceh would follow in East Timor's footsteps.

Though the COHA called on the UN to assess conditions and develop a peace-building plan for donors, the world body bent over backwards to avoid parallels with East Timor. Donors were slow to raise and distribute funds. Jakarta also dragged its feet in dedicating resources. According to Wiryono, who led the Indonesian delegation in Geneva, "The government would have won the hearts and minds of the people if it had spent (more) money on food, medicine, and shelter. Peace would then be almost tangible."[35]

When HDC summoned the parties to Tokyo for another round of talks, five of the GAM negotiators were arrested on their way to the airport in Banda Aceh and placed under house arrest at the Kuala Tripa Hotel.[36] The "GAM-5" were charged under the Law on Combating Criminal Acts of Terrorism, as well as for "assisting and facilitating terrorism" under Articles 106 and 108 of the Criminal Code. In trials that fell far short of international standards, all were found guilty of "terrorism" and "rebellion" and sentenced to twelve to fifteen years in prison.

Di Tiro and the GAM leadership in Sweden were furious with the arrest of their colleagues. The Tokyo talks predictably collapsed. In response, Megawati issued Presidential Decree No. 28 declaring a state of emergency and martial law.[37]

The European Parliament responded with a resolution urging TNI to withdraw to its barracks and calling for a resumption of negotiations.[38] However, HDC's credibility as a mediator had eroded and GAM refused to participate. Agreements require a credible third party guarantor; GAM had come to see HDC as merely another NGO lacking the political clout to mediate or enforce agreements. GAM also criticized HDC for choosing to maintain a discreet profile rather than speak out and risk expulsion by Jakarta.[39]

In addition, GAM came to see HDC as an instrument of the U.S. government, which was backing Indonesia. As conflict increased, HDC invited a group of "wise men" to join the Geneva talks. The initiative was conceived by Karen Brooks, the director of Asian Affairs in the White House's National Security Council. Participation by the wise men was paid for with U.S. funds that Congress originally earmarked for humanitarian purposes. GAM expected the wise men to act as objective arbiters. However, Jakarta used them to increase pressure on the over-matched GAM negotiators.

As the HDC process unraveled, Jakarta declared it would "crush" GAM.[40] "Unidentified, suspicious looking people will be shot on sight."[41] The military issued "red and white" identity cards. Any person without one was deemed a member of GAM. Thousands of suspected GAM sympathizers were rounded up and, in accordance with Indonesion law, held in administrative detention for up to 70 days. Acting with impunity, the military threatened human rights monitors attached to the National Human Rights Commission (KOMNAS HAM) and organized attacks on local human rights groups such as the Legal Aid and Human Rights Institute.

Amnesty International reported that, "Human rights abuses are so pervasive there is virtually no part of life in the province which remains untouched."[42] However, Wiranto insisted, "No officer will be brought to trial because they were merely carrying out their duties."[43] Between the declaration of martial law in May 2003 and the tsunami on December 26, 2005, 2,300 people were killed and 150,000 rendered homeless as a result of the conflict.[44]

The COHA was doomed from the start by a fundamental misunderstanding. Jakarta insisted that the 2000 National Autonomy Law (NAD) serve as the basis for discussions on Aceh's future status. GAM insisted that it never accepted autonomy during the talks. It maintained that independence was and always would be the ultimate objective.

Acehnese are deeply skeptical of autonomy. After the RI was established, Acehnese rejected Indonesia's annexation and the All-Aceh Ulama Association rebelled against Javanese occupation. The 1953 revolt, which was sparked by the central government's refusal to grant autonomy and cultural rights, ended only when Jakarta granted Aceh status as its own province with autonomy in religious and educational affairs and provisions to respect customary law.

Jakarta lacked the administrative capacity to harmonize competing claims between central government officials and local leaders who resisted their authority. As a result, many aspects of the accord were never implemented. Limited autonomy provisions lasted only until political violence engulfed Indonesia in 1965-66.

Upon seizing power, Suharto implemented more centralized governance limiting local self-rule under the agreement. His system of Pancasila governance prevailed until Suharto's final days in power. Post-Suharto, autonomy was implemented nationwide to free Indonesia's regions from the stifling control of the central government. More far-reaching, Megawati signed Presidential Decree No. 18 in August 2001 laying the groundwork for the Special Autonomy Law for Aceh. The Special Autonomy Law required distribution of 80 percent of local forestry, fishery, and mining resources and 80 percent of oil and gas revenues to provincial authorities. It also reaffirmed traditional customary law and created institutions advancing Acehnese aspirations for greater democratic self-rule.

When it came to profit-sharing, the process of returning revenues was so opaque and riddled with corruption that Acehnese doubted whether revenues would ever flow back to them. Even if money was returned, they were convinced it would be monopolized by local elites. Rather than decentralizing power to the regency level (*Kabupaten*), the Special Autonomy Law decentralized power to provincial officials and entrenched bureaucrats with close ties to Jakarta. Moreover, Special Autonomy was a huge undertaking requiring seventy-two pieces of implementing legislation. Government institutions, particularly at the level of regencies and counties, were ill-equipped to handle their new responsibilities.

Compounding problems, GAM rejected the Special Autonomy Law. Rather than a genuine attempt at power-sharing, GAM believed that the law was imposed by the central government as an effort to reduce support for independence. GAM pledged to disrupt the implementation of autonomy in areas under its control.

Progress

The 1997-98 crisis catalyzed political and economic reforms with far reaching implications for Indonesia as a whole and for Aceh in particular. The armed forces agreed to reduce its role in politics by relinquishing reserved seats in the National Parliament. Electoral reforms required a popular vote for the position of president for the fist time in 2004. In addition to nationwide decentralization and Special Autonomy for Aceh and Papua, a Regional Representative Council was established giving provinces a stronger voice at the national level. Jakarta also took steps to stabilize its economy and improve its macro-economic indicators. Reforms reduced inflation, steadied the rupiah, and moderated interest rates.

Susilo Bambang Yudhoyono was elected president on October 20, 2004. Yudhoyono was called the "thinking general." To reduce tensions in Aceh, he maintained: "We should not just prioritize the military operation."[45] Yudhoyono contemplated an offer of amnesty to GAM and promised "safer and more prosperous Aceh" through "economic reconstruction, social rehabilitation and cultural empowerment."[46] Yudhoyono also used Vice President Jusuf Kalla to send feelers out to MP-GAM in Malaysia about restarting talks on Aceh. Setting the stage for negotiations, he contacted Maarti Ahtisaari, Finland's former president and head of the Conflict Management Institute, about acting as mediator.

On December 26, 2004 an underwater earthquake off the coast of Sumatra created a giant tsunami that inundated Aceh. Banda Aceh was literally swept away. The natural disaster killed about 130,000. Almost one million people were left homeless. The swirling brown waters did not distinguish between civilians and combatants or between Acehnese and Javanese. Entire TNI bases on the West Coast simply disappeared.

Coordinating both international and domestic aid, TNI worked with the United States and other militaries to conduct life-saving operations. It provided transitional shelter for almost a half million people. It also supervised water and sanitation projects, as well as relief activities focused on health, food, nutrition, and education. TNI also undertook cash for work programs.

TNI initially resisted international cooperation. It was concerned about the presence of foreign troops on Indonesian soil, as well as the en masse arrival of private disaster relief organizations. In a fruitless effort to monitor activities, TNI insisted that humanitarian agencies inform the government of their movements and accept military escorts. While allowing humanitarian access along the coast, it tried to bar aid workers from GAM controlled areas in the interior.

Confronted by the awesome power of nature, the tsunami had a humbling affect on many Acehnese. "[The tsunami] demonstrated there has been enough suffering in Aceh."[47] It convinced GAM that it should be flexible in order to achieve a sustainable peace. GAM declared an immediate ceasefire to facilitate the delivery of humanitarian supplies. But TNI refused to reciprocate. Accusing GAM of grabbing weapons from army bases and police stations destroyed by the tsunami, Yudhoyono vowed to continue the offensive until there was a peace agreement. Fighting continued during the six months after the earthquake during which 230 people were killed in operations.[48]

Meanwhile Yudhoyono was working behind the scenes to restart negotiations. He knew that, "A real political opportunity came knocking after the tsunami." He sent a message to Ahtisaari: the GOI was ready to send a negotiating team to Helsinki for talks.[49]

Ahtisaari gathered GAM and Indonesian officials at a secluded manor outside Helsinki. He convened five meetings over seven months. As a result, GAM and the GOI signed a peace agreement on August 15, 2005. The accord encompassed governance, including the rule of law, economic issues, political participation, human rights, amnesty and reintegration, security arrangements, and dispute settlement. Unlike the agreement brokered by HDC, it established an official International Monitoring Mission for Aceh comprised of representatives from the European Union (EU) and countries in the Association of Southeast Asian Nations (ASEAN). The central government committed $53.1 million to assist foreign peace monitors.[50]

The accord also committed Indonesia to withdraw all non-organic troops from the province except those required for external defense. Only 14,000 military and 7,000 police would remain behind. According to Bhaktiar Abdullah, "The TNI must now restrict itself to external defense only, and must immediately cease launching offensive operations. We require the Indonesian government to exercise full authority over the TNI in order to allow this process to succeed."[51]

Jakarta initially resisted allowing GAM to form a political party. Negotiators cited Indonesian law, which bans the formation of regionally based parties, requires that parties be based in Jakarta, and stipulates that parties have representation in at least half of Indonesia's thirty-three provinces. The GOI was concerned that other ethnic and religious groups across Indonesia would demand something similar thus contributing to fragmentation of the country. Though a stalemate ensued when GAM insisted on a role governing the province, Indonesia's negotiators ultimately relented allowing GAM members to stand for local elections.

More than one year after the accord, thorny issues still threatened to derail progress. Differences persisted over the concept of self-government, who is eligible to run in local elections, and the timetable for elections. Reintegration of former combatants was hampered by lack of resources as well as Aceh's economic woes and post-tsunami rehabilitation requirements.

Restoration of water, sanitation, and electricity services was unevenly restored. Many new homes were never occupied. Due to bureaucracy, corruption, and mismanagement, the construction of health clinics and schools did not proceed apace with home construction. Resources were wasted on half-baked schemes to restore corral reefs and mangrove forests as a bulwark against the next tsunami.

In addition, Acehnese were disillusioned by the Home Affairs Ministry's efforts to impede upgrading of the 2001 Special Autonomy Law. Acehnese from across the political spectrum vehemently objected when the national parliament floated a proposal to divide Aceh into two provinces. The tsunami catalyzed events leading to an end of armed conflict. After decades of fighting, however, is proving difficult to overcome enmity, restore confidence, and sustain it peace.

International Actors

United States

The Bush administration relies on Indonesia as a moderate Muslim country to support its global war on terror. Bush and Yudhoyono met in November 2006. The leaders highlighted their shared struggle against terrorism pointing out that the two nations have both suffered terrorist attacks on their soil. They welcomed the lifting of restrictions imposed by the U.S. Congress on the International Military Assistance Program and, consistent with the program's goals, agreed to expand training on the role of the military in democratic societies. Other bilateral military ties were discussed. In addition to enhancing maritime security, Bush proposed a Status of Forces of Agreement that would enable the basing of U.S. troops on Indonesian soil. To combat terrorism, they agreed to start negotiations on a Mutual Legal Assistance Treaty. Both presidents also pledged to expand cooperation in the field of disaster preparedness and assistance.[52] Though the State Department never added GAM to its FTO list, U.S. Embassy/Jakarta worked with the GOI to ratchet up the pressure on GAM by freezing the bank accounts and banning travel of some GAM leaders. At the urging of the United States, Jakarta approached the government of Sweden and asked it to evict Di Tiro and other GAM leaders.

Australia

Australia fears that a spiral of deadly violence in Aceh, West Papua, or other hotspots in Indonesia could result in a humanitarian emergency, massive population flows, and instability across Southeast Asia. After the Bali bombing on October 12, 2002, Prime Minister John Howard became a vehement defender of Indonesia's territorial integrity and an active partner in regional counter-terrorism. Emboldened by Howard's support, Yudhoyono said,: "Separatist movements must be crushed and we have international support to maintain our territorial integrity."[53] In 2004, Australia doubled its counter-terrorism assistance to Indonesia. Assistance included the establishment of a Transnational Crime Centre in Jakarta that opened in July 2004. Australia's assistance was intended to recoup goodwill with Jakarta, which accused Canberra of plotting East Timor's independence. Its support for the GOI is also motivated by the need to protect burgeoning economic ties with Indonesia including LNG supplies.

Japan

Japan's approach to Indonesia has always emphasized stability. It is concerned that security problems could affect regional trade by disrupting maritime traffic through the Malacca Straits and Singapore, major transit areas for eastbound shipping to Japan.[54] Japan is the largest donor to Indonesia. Between 1966 and 2000, Japan extended $1.2 billion in grants, $13.7 billion in loans, and $23 billion in technical assistance. Contributions from the Japan Export-Import Bank (JEXIM) and the Japanese Overseas Economic Cooperation Fund (OECF) averaged $1.9 billion a year in the mid 1990s. In addition, Japan's External Trade Organization (JETRO) actively promotes private sector engagement in Indonesia. Japanese banks own more than $30 billion of Indonesia's external debt. Japanese concerns have extensive commercial interests in Indonesia. Japan relies on Indonesia for about one-third of its LNG imports.[55]

Departing from Japan's singular focus on economic cooperation, Prime Minister Junichiro Koizumi announced a major shift from Japan's post-World War II commitment to non-interference in the affairs of Asian states. Koizumi asserted that, "Japan will consider how to increase our international role by providing an added pillar for the consolidation of peace and nation-building" to address "regional conflicts arising from religious and ethnic causes."[56] In this vein, Japan hosted the December 2002 donor conference for Aceh and was the largest contributor of funds to support the COHA.

Japan earmarked substantial sums to consolidate the Ahtisaari Accord. Through the International Organization on Migration (IOM), Japan funds conflict prevention and peace-building activities that include reintegration assistance to amnestied GAM prisoners, demobilized combatants and conflict-affected communities. Post-tsunami, Japan also played a leading role by providing humanitarian assistance, rehabilitating schools, health services and public infrastructure. It financial support was critical to rebuilding the West Coast road between Banda Aceh and Meulaboh.

ASEAN

Southeast Asia's insurgent groups cooperate across national boundaries creating an economy of scale for logistics, training, and safe havens. Jemaah Islamiyah and GAM have trained with the Moro Islamic Liberation Front (MILF) in Camp Abu Bukar in the Southern Philippines. GAM smuggled weapons from the Pattani United Liberation Organization of Thailand. The Thai Army also provided smalls arms, grenade launchers and other weaponry. Weapons from the Khmer Rouge also found their way into GAM's hands. GOI sponsored militias from East and West Timor helped arm GAM. Weapons were transported via the Malaysian provinces of Kelantan, Sarawak, and Sabah.[57]

Malaysia proved a key haven for GAM. Acehnese fleeing the conflict often landed in Kedah State in northwest Malaysia. Claiming they faced death upon return to Aceh, boat people sought protection, assistance, and political asylum. Before the DOM, up to 23,000 refugees resided in Malaysia. Many more arrived after the imposition of martial law in 2003. Violating international humanitarian law that prohibits the forcible return of asylum seekers, Malaysia implemented a policy of "refoulement." Those who were not forcibly returned were forced to live in squalid conditions. Many volunteered to go home where they faced torture, extra-judicial execution, or disappearance."[58] The GAM secretary general and interior minister resided in Malaysia.

ASEAN bodies that focus on regional security cooperation include the ASEAN Regional Forum and the ASEAN Security Community that is responsible for counter-terrorism and transnational crime. Contained in the Treaty of Amity and Cooperation, ASEAN countries are committed to mutual respect for the independence, sovereignty, equality and territorial integrity of member states.[59] ASEAN's aversion to interference in the internal affairs of member states renders it relatively useless when it comes to conflict prevention or peacebuilding. ASEAN can, however, play a helpful monitoring role. For example, five ASEAN countries helped consolidate the Ahtisaari Accord by joining with the EU, Norway, and Switzerland in the International Monitoring Mission for Aceh.[60]

Libya

Libya historically supported Muslim rebellions in Southeast Asia, including GAM. When GAM was forced into exile in the early 1980s, Libya became its most steadfast military backer.[61] Instruction focused on guerilla techniques as well as artillery, explosives, and aviation. It also included ideological indoctrination. Military assistance was personally authorized by President Muammar Gadhafi who attended graduation ceremonies for GAM militias. Di Tiro claimed that 5,000 fighters were trained in Libya, but the actual number was probably no more than 1,000.[62] Though Gadhafi generously provided training and technical assistance, no arms were provided to support GAM's front-line operations.[63]

Diplomatic relationship between Indonesia and Libya were established in October 1991. However, economic interaction was relatively stagnant until September 29, 2003 when Indonesia and Libya signed a barter trade deal involving the exchange of Libyan oil for various Indonesian goods worth an estimated 480 million dollars a year.[64] The swap involved 5,000 barrels a day in exchange for building materials, textiles, furniture, and military accessories. The following year, Jakarta announced its plan to open an embassy in Tripoli[65] and Libya distanced itself from GAM issuing a series of statements affirming support for Indonesia's territorial integrity.[66]

The Way Forward

Yudhoyono must fulfill Jakarta's commitments. Failure to implement the Aceh Accord brokered by Maarti Ahtisaari could cause renewed violence. It could also have a destabilizing effect elsewhere in Indonesia by encouraging ethnic, religious, and separatist violence across the vast archipelago.

Peacebuilding priorities include GAM participation in local elections and support for the reintegration of GAM fighters into civil society. Acehnese insist, however, that political participation and demobilization must not obviate their demands for justice. To this end, Yudhoyono should publicly condemn atrocities committed against the Acehnese and initiate legal processes in an independent court prosecuting security personnel accused of human rights abuses. The GOI, Aceh's governor, provincial parliament, as well as Acehnese civil society and religious leaders should work together to establish a "reconciliation group" charged with re-energizing the national dialogue and developing an appropriate truth, justice and reconciliation process for Aceh.

It is important to provide a peace dividend in order to demonstrate tangible benefits to Acehnese from the Ahtisaari Accord. Quick impact projects in East Aceh and other GAM strongholds would have the dual benefit of improving living conditions and marginalizing those who prefer violence to achieve political objectives. Japan could expand its support through the International Organization for Migration to reintegrate demobilized combatants, create jobs to support the amnesty program, and stimulate economic development targeting conflict-affected communities. U.S. assistance through the Millennium Challenge Corporation, which started in 2006, could also be earmarked to these ends.

Funds are also needed to strengthen governance especially at the local level. It is incumbent upon the national parliament to harmonize provisions in the 2001 Special Autonomy Law with pledges for self-government and local ownership of resources in the Ahtisaari Accord. Incendiary proposals, such as dividing Aceh into two provinces, are provocative and should be abandoned. Peace implementation must remain a concern of the international community. The Aceh Monitoring Mission should continue for as long as there is risk of violence recurring and the ASEAN Regional Forum must affirm its ongoing support for international monitoring and encourage ASEAN member states to participate.

Indonesia's rising tide lifts all boats. Yudhoyono can accelerate the country's ongoing democratization by pushing forward with plans for nationwide decentralization. Security services should be more fully resourced and brought under the control of civilian authority. In addition to human rights training, the mandate and mission of special security branches should be reformulated conforming to regular police activities. Withdrawing non-organic security units and reorganizing local police to reflect the ethnic composition of communities they serve is also important. Since the Bush administration decided to restore military assistance, exchanges and training should include instructions on the role of militaries in democratic societies.

Indonesia's corruption is endemic and threatens to derail democratization and overall progress. So that TNI does not have to offset its operating deficit with for-profit activities, its costs should be more fully covered in the national budget. Greater accountability can also be achieved by strengthening the TNI Office of the Inspector General, expanding the POLRI Office of Professional Responsibility, and creating branch offices.

To improve the investment climate, measures are needed to upgrade infrastructure and reduce red tape. Enhancing the rule of law would enable greater respect and enforcement of contracts. The United States can assist by supporting links between U.S. and Indonesian business. The June 2006 extension of U.S. Export-Import Bank coverage to private Indonesian corporations was a good step. Export-Import Bank assistance should continue and other U.S. Commerce Department programs, such as the Trade Development Program, should expand their activities in Indonesia. The bilateral Trade and Investment Framework Agreement between the United States and Indonesia could be strengthened as a vehicle to strengthen dialogue and economic cooperation.

The bond between the security services and international corporations is a source of corruption that holds back economic development. The GOI can break this bond by revising its law on the protection of national assets. Rrather than contract with TNI for project security, businesses should be allowed to hire private local security companies. Emphasizing "community-based security" and and implementing the "Voluntary Principles on Security and Human Rights," a discretionary code of conduct guiding companies in conflict zones, would increase profitability and protect corporate assets while enabling greater independence from predatory security services.

Corruption can also be mitigated via the "Publish What You Pay Initiative" adopted by international NGOs in 2003. The initiative encourages oil, gas, and mining companies to publish taxes, fees, and royalties as a condition for being listed in international stock exchanges. A system establishing greater transparency of revenue transfers to business and central, provincial, and district governments would make sure that profit- sharing agreements actually return royalties to resource-rich provinces.

Implementing autonomy requires capacity building to manage new responsibilities at the local level. The World Bank's Consultative Group for Indonesia, could take the lead assessing and improving local governance and administration. Local capacity could also be expanded via the establishment of "Aceh Professional Corps" made up of national experts and international specialists to assist social and economic development projects. International and national businesses can also play a role by emphasizing the training and hiring of ethnic Acehnese.

Aceh is not the only part of Indonesia with a pro-independence movement. The central government must learn from its experience in Aceh to peacefully resolve separatist violence in other parts of the country. The Ahtisaari Accord, which transformed GAM into a political party, earmarked funds for peacebuilding and internationalized monitoring to ensure peace implementation, can serve as a model for stabilizing other restive regions such as Papua.

Notes

1. March 26, 1873.
2. *The New York Times.* May 6, 1873.
3. Henry Kissinger. *Nuclear Weapons and Foreign Policy.* p. 256.
4. *Jakarta Post.* November 12, 1999.
5. *The Jakarta Post.* July 28, 1999.
6. *Harper's Magazine.* August 1905.
7. "Aceh: Can Autonomy Stem the Conflict?" *The International Crisis Group.* Report No. 18. June 27, 2001. p. 15.
8. *Agence France Presse.* November 8, 1999.
9. *Reuters,* July 22, 1990

10.   *Jakarta Post*. November 23, 1999.

11.   Agus Smur. *The Jakarta Post*. "Aceh in Wonderland." June 28, 2005.

12.   Kirsten E. Schulze. "The Free Aceh Movement: Anatomy of a Separatist Organi-zation." *East-West Center*. Policy Studies 2. Washington, D.C. p. 22.

13.   Statement by the President of Indonesia at an emergency meeting of the Organiza-tion of Islamic Conference. Bangkok, Thailand. August 2, 2006.

14.   UNSC Resolution adopted on October 14, 1970.

15.   Charter of the National Liberation front of Aceh-Sumatra. October 30, 1976.

16.   Aceh: Can Autonomy Stem the Conflict? *International Crisis Group*. June 27, 2001.

17.   *Human Rights Watch*. August 2001, Vol. 13, No. 4 (c).

18.   Kirsten E. Schulze. "The Free Aceh Movement: Anatomy of a Separatist Organi-zation." *East-West Center*. Policy Studies 2. Washington, D.C. p. 12.

19.   The special allowance was 250 million Rupiah.

20.   Wiryono Sastrohandoyo. "'Black Economy' threatened Aceh Peace." *The Jakarta Post*. March 25, 2003.

21.   *GOI Central Statistics Bureau*. 1998.

22.   *Financial Times*. August 2, 1990.

23.   "Aceh: Can Autonomy Stem the Conflict?" *The International Crisis Group*. Report No. 18. June 27, 2001. p. 5.

24.   *Laksamana*. "Alarming Poverty and Unemployment in Aceh." October 29, 2003.

25.   Kirsten E. Schulze. "The Free Aceh Movement: Anatomy of a Separatist Organi-zation." *East-West Center*. Policy Studies 2. Washington, D.C. p. 35.

26.   *Amnesty International* Index: ASA 21/81/99. August 4, 1999.

27.   Kirsten E. Schulze. "The Free Aceh Movement: Anatomy of a Separatist Orga-nization." *East-West Center*. Policy Studies 2. Washington, D.C. p. 39. (Note: Expulsion figures are for the years between 2000-02)

28.   *Tempo*. "Militias, by any other name." July 7, 2003.

29.   *Toronto Star*. August 6, 1998.

30.   *The Jakarta Post*. November 30, 1998.

31.   *Boston Globe*. December 26, 1998.

32.   *Washington Post*. September 24, 1999.

33.   The Indonesian Human Rights Campaign (TAPOL). January 2002.

34.   Asian Human Rights Commission. UP-68. December 5, 2002.

35.   Wiryono Sastrohandoyo. "'Black Economy' threatened Aceh Peace." *The Jakarta Post*. March 25, 2003.

36.   They are Sofyan Ibrahim Tiba, Teungku Kamaruzzaman, Amin Bin Ahmad Mar-zuki, Teungku Muhammad Usman Lampoh Awe, and Nashiruddin Bin Ahmed.

37.   May 18, 2003.

38.   June 5, 2003.

39.   Konrad Huber. "The HDC in Aceh: "Promises and Pitfalls of NGO Mediation and Implementation." *East West Center*. *Policy Studies* 9. Washington, D.C.

40.   Mathew Moore. "Indonesia fails to crush Aceh rebels." *The Age*. November 5, 2003.

41.   *Acehkita*. "TNI Claim Telah Tewaskan 2,800 Anggota GAM." September 17, 2004.

42.   *Amnesty International*. October 7, 2004.

43.   *Indonesian Human Rights Campaign (TAPOL)*. January 2002.

44.   Brad Adams. *Human Rights Watch*. "Aceh's Forgotten Victims." May 27, 2005.

45.   S.P. Harish. *IDSS Commentaries*. "Indonesia's next President: Implications for conflicts in Aceh and Papua." September 23, 2004.

46.   *Ibid.*
47.   John Aglionby. *The Guardian.* "Legacy of Tsunami brings peace to Aceh." August 15, 2005. p. 15.
48.   Brad Adams. *Human Rights Watch.* "Aceh's Forgotten Victims." May 27, 2005.
49.   *Agence France Presse.* "Peace pact only first step towards end of Aceh violence." August 16, 2005.
50.   *Agence France Presse.* "Indonesia to invest in peace process." August 16, 2005.
51.   Statement by Bhaktiar Abdullah. Released by the State of Aceh, Ministry of Information. July 17, 2005.
52.   http://www.whitehouse.gov/news/releases/2006/11/20061120-3.html
53.   Lesley McCullough. "Power before peace in Aceh." Asia Times (on-line). March 2, 2002.
54.   http://www.mofa.go.jp/region/asia-paci/indonesia/index.html
55.   Japanese Ministry of Foreign Affairs. Country Report. 2003.
       Konrad Huber. "The HDC in Aceh: "Promises and Pitfalls of NGO Mediation and Implementation." East West Center. Policy Studies 9. Washington, DC.
56.   http://www.hrw.org/reports/2001/aceh/indacheh0801.pdf
57.   Reuters. October 10, 1991.
58.   http://www.aseansec.org/92.htm
59.   http://jpn.cec.eu.int/home/news_en_newsobj1283.php
60.   BBC. November 20, 1995.
61.   http://www.heritage.org/Research/AsiaandthePacific/hl860.cfm
62.   Human Rights Watch. 1999.
63.   Rizal Sukma. *Islam in Indonesian Foreign Policy.* pg.74).
64.   coombs.anu.edu.au/SpecialProj/ASAA/biennial-conference/2004/Wardhani-B-ASAA2004.pdf
65.   http://www.fpif.org/fpiftxt/269

6

Jammu and Kashmir Liberation Front

A series of powerful bombs ripped through seven commuter trains in Mumbai during the afternoon rush hour in July 2006. Body parts were scattered everywhere; the carnage killed scores and wounded hundreds. Indian officials responded by accusing Pakistan and demanding that it dismantle its "terrorist infrastructure." Relations between India and Pakistan are defined by deep distrust and historical enmity. Pakistan trained Kashmiri militants at facilities originally established to support the Afghan Mujahadeen in their war against Soviet occupation. Backers of the militants are today looking beyond Kashmir to foment Hindu-Muslim violence and destabilize India. Kashmir—"unfinished business" of the 1947 partition—is the potential trigger for a regional war with devastating nuclear consequences.

History

Kashmir spans the Himalayas, Karakoram, and the Hindukush mountains. It is divided by the Line of Control (LoC), which was established by the ceasefire that ended the 1947-48 war between India and Pakistan. The LoC, which extends 720 km, serves as a de facto border between the two countries. Neither India nor Pakistan formally recognizes it as a permanent international boundary.

Indian Kashmir has a population of about nine million. It is twice the size of Pakistan's Azad Kashmir, which means "free," and has a population of three million.[1] Lying on the Indian side of the LoC, the spectacularly beautiful Vale of Kashmir is almost entirely Muslim (95 percent). The high dry plains of Ladakh are about evenly divided between Shi'a Muslims and Tibetan Buddhists. While about two-thirds of Jammu residents are Hindu, there are three predominantly Muslim districts in Jammu.[2] Azad Kashmir includes lush land around the Jhelum River, the arid high terrain of Baltistan, and the expansive barren Northern Areas (NA) that border China.

Kashmir was independent for nearly a thousand years under a succession of Hindu kings until it was invaded and occupied by the Moguls in 1586.[3] In 1757 it was annexed to what is currently Afghanistan before becoming part of the Sikh empire in 1846. The Dogras were rewarded by Great Britain for helping to defeat the Sikhs; Kashmir was annexed to Britain's Indian colony and accorded the status of a self-ruling "princely kingdom."[4] By the end of the nineteenth century, the Northern Areas had been fully incorporated into Jammu and Kashmir.

The Indian Independence Act of 1947 allowed Kashmiris to decide whether they would join India or Pakistan. When Muhammad Ali Jinnah orchestrated an attack on Kashmir by tribal fighters from the Northwest frontier, Kashmir's Maharaja Hari Singh sought protection from India giving it powers in exchange for security and the promise of a referendum allowing Kashmiris to determine their political status. Kashmir's right to a referendum was affirmed by the United Nations in 1948 when India brought the Kashmir dispute to the world body. Temporary autonomy measures were enshrined in Article 370 of the Indian constitution.

Since 1947, India and Pakistan have fought four wars in Kashmir. The first began within two months of their independence in 1947 and lasted more than a year. After India's prime minister Jawaharlal Nehru died in 1964, Pakistan sought to take advantage of the vacuum left by his death to press for Kashmir's separation from India. It began to infiltrate Kashmir with members of its military disguised as tribesmen and launched Operation Gibraltar designed to inspire a guerilla war.[5] When Kashmiris did not rise up, Pakistan deployed conventional forces in September 1965. The second war, which ended in a stalemate, was concluded the following year by the Treaty of Tashkent. Following the 1971 surrender of Pakistan's army in East Pakistan, India and Pakistan negotiated the 1972 Simla Agreement committing both sides to address all outstanding items, providing for a resolution of the "Kashmir question" through bilateral negotiations, and re-establishing the LoC as the de facto boundary between India and Pakistan.[6] Pakistan viewed Simla as a supplement to existing resolutions on Kashmir, which would not rule out mediation by a third party or a multilateral body such as the United Nations. For its part, India believed that Simla superceded all previous agreements and, to this day, adamantly resists third-party facilitation or mediation.

The fourth war was fought in 1999. Each winter, Indian troops withdraw from the Kargil Mountains and then return in the spring to retake their positions overlooking Highway 1A, a critical supply route for

Indian armed forces based in the Siachen Glacier region near China.[7] When Indian forces returned to their high-altitude outpost in Kargil, they encountered stiff enemy fire. Pakistan denied involvement in the Kargil operation maintaining that Kashmiri liberation groups were responsible for occupying the strategic peaks. India disputed the claim. Other countries also discounted Pakistan's assertion that the Kargil operation was solely the work of Kashmiri freedom fighters.

The Kargil offensive succeeded in putting Kashmir back in the international spotlight. Nuclear tests by India and Pakistan in 1998 underscored the dangers of a dispute over Kashmir escalating into a regional conflagration. Kashmir is still the flashpoint for violent conflict between the two countries. Up to 90,000 people having died as a result of the Kashmir conflict since 1989.[8] The cost of conflict escalation is much greater now that India and Pakistan both have nuclear weapons.

Ideology

The Jammu and Kashmir Liberation Front (JKLF) charter stipulates that Jammu and Kashmir is an indivisible entity comprised of the Kashmir Valley, Jammu and Ladakh in India, and Azad Kashmir and Gilgit-Baltistan in Pakistan. The JKLF rejects the notion that the Kashmir conflict is a territorial dispute between India and Pakistan. Refusing constitutional ties to India, Pakistan, or any other country, it demands that Kashmiris be allowed to exercise their inherent, internationally recognized, and pledged right to self-determination.

The JKLF was committed to struggle by all means as allowed to subjugated peoples by the United Nations under General Assembly Resolution 2621. It maintained that Jammu and Kashmir should be reunified as a democratic and sovereign state, pending popular approval in a referendum. It envisioned that all citizens of Kashmir would enjoy equal political, economic, and social rights and freedom to express their religious faith, irrespective of their race, religion, region, culture, and gender.[9]

The goal of economic justice was central to the JKLF. According to Yasin Malik, head of the JKLF, "The tension between [India and Pakistan] compels them to spend huge sums on defence with the result that a sizeable population of both countries is below the poverty line."[10] Kashmir's economy is largely dependent upon small-scale agriculture, handicrafts, and tourism. During the winter months, Kashmir becomes even more isolated as snow accumulation closes mountain passes. Kashmiris suffer widespread unemployment and conditions of under-development. Their economic woes are compounded by the fact that, unlike other official minorities, Kashmiris are victims of discrimination when it comes to hiring for jobs in the central government.

The JKLF proposed a ceasefire in 1994. However, the government rebuffed its offer and intensified efforts to defeat the organization militarily. Malik survived but, by 1996, the Amanullah Khan faction of the JKLF faction was all but wiped out by Indian security forces.

The JKLF subsequently became a part of the All-Parties Hurriyet Conference (APHC). Established in March 1993 by 23 Kashmiri groups, APHC adopted many of the JKLF's positions, acknowledging differences among Kashmiris but trying to unite them behind the common goal of separation from India. APHC believes that Kashmir is an unfinished item from partition that must be resolved in accordance with the aspirations of Kashmiris. According to its charter, APHC was established to:

• Wage a peaceful struggle for the people of Jammu and Kashmir in accordance with the UN charter and the resolutions adopted by the UN Security Council (including) the right to self-determination (that) shall include the right to independence.

• Make endeavors to an alternative negotiated settlement of the Kashmir dispute amongst all three parties to the dispute—India, Pakistan, and the people of Jammu and Kashmir—under the auspices of the UN or any other friendly country, provided that such settlement reflects the will of the people.

• Project the ongoing struggle in the state before nations and governments of the world in its broader perspective, as being a "struggle directed against the forcible and fraudulent occupation of the state by India."[11]

Kashmiris are tired of violence. They see India's economic boom and want to be a part of it. To this end, many believe that democracy and constitutionally defined power sharing can remedy Kashmir's ills. Hindus in Jammu as well as Buddhists and some Shi'a Muslims in Ladakh are counted in the accommodation camp.

The Kashmir conflict is often characterized as the Muslim Valley versus the Hindu state. To be sure, religion plays an important role in Kashmir's communalism. However, the movement is inspired far more by nationalism than religion.

The concept of "Kashmiriyat," which draws together Muslims, Hindus, and Buddhists based on their love of the land and their common history, is integral to the identity formation of Kashmiris. Sheikh Abdullah maintained, "[Kashmiris] are not Muslims alone, nor Hindus and Sikhs alone, nor the untouchables or Buddhists alone, but all those living in the state."

In 1939, Abdullah took steps to transform the Muslim Conference into a more grass-roots organization with a secular, socialist, and nationalist orientation.[12] Despite his efforts to secularize Kashmiri politics, there was no denying the strong religious identity of Kashmir's Muslims. Though it is accurate to characterize Kashmir as a Muslim-majority state, there are diverse sects of Muslims including Shi'a Muslims from Kargil, Punjabi Muslims in Rajouri and Poonch, as well as Sunni Muslims from Gujjar and Bakkarwal.[13] Moreover, Islam in Kashmir is inspired by Sufism, a softer and more mystical practice than the Wahhabi or Salafist traditions popular among Sunnis in the Persian Gulf.

Attempts to restrict religious activity of Kashmiris have always met stiff resistance. For example, popular protests erupted in the 1930s when the authorities imposed martial law and banned the call to prayer. When a hair from the Prophet Mohammed's beard enshrined as a holy relic at the Hazratbal Mosque disappeared in 1964, Kashmir was brought to a standstill by pilgrims and religious mourners. Pakistan's largest religious party, Jamaat-e-Islami, set up a branch in Srinigar, which was banned during the state of emergency in 1975.[14] In October 1983, the youth wing of Jamaat-e-Islami organized protests during a cricket match with a team from the West Indies that mobilized the population and caused a sectarian riot.

Madrassas also exist in Kashmir. The informal education sector was stimulated by the arrival of Bangladeshi religious teachers (*Maulvis*) in the mid-1980s. The Maulvis fled to Kashmir after a massacre in Assam and, upon arrival, established a network of madrassas to provide informal religious education to Kashmiri youth. Kashmiris who went to Pakistan for military training also received religious indoctrination at Islamic schools.

Some militant groups have a distinctly Islamist orientation or use Muslim titles for its leaders. Hizb's members use a religious honorific, "Peer Sahib," when referring to the group's founder, Syed Salahuddin. Likewise, Omar Farooq is called "Mirwaiz," a hereditary religious title bestowed upon the head priest of the Jamia Masjid in Srinigar. Many APHC members belonged to the All Kashmir Freedom Front (*Kul-Jammat-e-Hurriyat-e-Kashmir*), an umbrella organization of Pakistan-based organizations that support the establishment of an Islamic state in Kashmir.

Consistent with the concept of Kashmiriyat, the JKLF was essentially a secular organization that aspired to the establishment of an independent Kashmir where both Muslims and Hindus would be welcome. This ideal is anathema to Pakistan-based fundamentalists as well as to Afghan and Arab fighters who care far less about Kashmiri self-determination than they do about establishing Pakistani rule and creating an Islamic caliphate in Srinigar.

Structure

The JKLF is an international organization with hubs in Kashmir, Pakistan, and the United Kingdom. Two dozen branches represent nearly a quarter million Kashmiris living in Great Britain. JKLF UK-Europe also has members in the Netherlands, Belgium, France, Germany, Denmark, Norway, and Sweden. The JKLF also has a branch in New York.[15]

In India, the JKLF engaged in political and diplomatic activities organizing protests, demonstrations, and strikes. Both students and women play an important role. The Jammu Kashmir Students Liberation Front (JKSLF) and the JKLF's women's wing, called the Ladies Center (*Khawateen Markaz*), worked closely with the JKLF leadership to organize public demonstrations and acts of civil disobedience.

Other political activities focused on international relations. The JKLF's international relations bureau received many fact-finding missions and dignitaries. It also briefed diplomats, and corresponded with international non-governmental organizations (NGOs). Representatives attended conferences and other forums in capitals around the world in order to raise the profile of the Kashmir question.

The JKLF also maintained close ties with local media, which were used to promote the organization's agenda. For example, Kashmir's most widely read daily newspaper, *Aftab*, includes a column entitled "Disassociation Declaration" (*Izhar-e-Lataluqee*). Media and other advocacy tools, including the Internet, mobilized domestic support for the release of Kashmiri insurgents held in Indian jails and rallied international sympathy for the cause of Kashmir's freedom from India. Most Kashmiris ignore Indian television programming instead tuning into Pakistan radio and television for their information. This has raised the Muslim consciousness of Kashmiris and helped forge a shared identity between Kashmiris and Pakistanis.

Kashmiris are divided by three issues: union with Pakistan, armed struggle, and the role of foreign fighters. Divisions exist between homegrown dissident groups that demand independence and Kashmiris trained and financed in Pakistan who seek union with Pakistan. The greatest divide, however, is between homegrown Kashmiri groups and fighters from Afghanistan and Arab countries that came to Kashmir in order to wage holy war against democratic India. Sixty-six percent of Kashmiris believe that Pakistan's involvement over the past decade has been counter-productive; only 15 percent say it has been good for the region.[16] Sixty-five percent of Kashmiris believe that the presence of foreign fighters has damaged their cause.[17]

Hizbul-Mujahideen is a pro-Pakistan group of Kashmiris that controls the All Kashmir Freedom Front (*Kul-Jammat-e-Hurriyat-e-Kashmir*), an umbrella organization of Pakistan-based organizations that supports union with Pakistan and Shari'a for Kashmir. Hizb uses intimidation tactics to silence dissenters in their own community. Hizb has also earned the rancor of Kashmir's merchants and middle class by extorting funds to support operations. Jamaat-e-Islami is Hizb's political wing.

Pakistan disavows responsibility. According to a senior Inter Services Intelligence (ISI) official, "We did not want to involve the Afghans. At the beginning we really tried to keep them out so they would not mix with the people from Kashmir because then you could not know what would happen, but eventually the Kashmiris made their own contacts with the Afghans. We turned a blind eye to whole process and all that was happening along the border."[18] Despite his claim, the ISI operated an "Islamic Wing" designed to recruit, train, and equip Islamic holy warriors. Army of Mohammed (*Jaish-e-Mohammed*), Army of the Prophet (*Harkat-ul-Ansar*) and Army of the Pure (*Lashkar-e-Toiba*) are sponsored by the ISI Directorate and members of the Pakistan-based United Jihadi Council.

Based in Muzzafarabad, Harkat includes fighters from Pakistan, and countries such as Afghanistan, Algeria, Egypt, Lebanon, Saudi Arabia, Syria, and Sudan. Harkat was involved in the kidnapping of two British tourists in 1993 and a series of attacks in 1994-95 aimed at disrupting the pilgrimage of Hindus to the Amarnath Cave, which is believed to be the birthplace of Krishna.[19] Harkat was also responsible for occupying the Noor-ud-in shrine and mosque in 1995. A renegade faction called Al Faran took five Western hostages in July 1995 and killed one of them.[20]

Under intense pressure from the United States, the government of Pakistan banned Lashkar and four other groups in 2002. However, Lashkar simply reconstituted itself under a different name and continued operations. Its militants were later accused of the Mumbai commuter train bombings in July 2006 that killed 193 and wounded more than 700.[21]

Leadership

Kashmiris have a long history of resistance to foreign domination by Moguls, Sikhs, British and Indians. Beginning in the 1930s, Sheikh Abdullah—the so-called Lion of Kashmir—emerged as a popular leader who rejected rule by Maharajah Hari Singh and led an anti-monarchical movement allied to the Indian National Congress. Sheikh Abdullah also advanced his nationalist agenda while serving as the president of the People's Congress that included all of India's princely states. In the 1940s, Kashmiri militia groups aligned with Muhammad Ali Jinnah functioned as defense units against the forces of the Maharajah. They sought to disrupt partition negotiations by targeting communications and interrupting the flow of essential supplies from Jammu across mountain roads into the Valley. The goal was to create havoc in order to force Kashmir's accession to Pakistan.

Instead of reducing support for the militants, Kashmiris were radicalized by India's draconian policies, systematic repression, and institutionalized patronage politics benefiting the supporters of integration radicalized Kashmiris. After bogus elections in 1987, virtually the entire population of the Kashmir Valley supported independence with only a small percentage favoring unification with Pakistan.[22] The insurgency was strongest in the Valley, as well as three Muslim-majority districts in Jammu.

Maqbul Butt and Amanullah Khan co-founded the JKLF in 1965 as an off-shoot of the Plebiscite Movement led by Sheikh Abdullah who served as President of the National Conference (NC) and Chief Minister of Jammu and Kashmir. Three years later, Butt killed an Indian intelligence officer and fled into exile from where he organized the hijacking of an Indian Airlines flight in 1971. Butt was also behind the kidnapping of Ravindra Mhatre, the deputy high commissioner for India in Birmingham. Mhatre was executed when the government of India rejected proposals for a prisoner exchange.[23] Butt returned to Kashmir to recruit "boys" for armed struggle, but he was captured and hanged at the Tihar Jail in New Delhi.

Scotland Yard arrested Khan and charged him with conspiracy in the Mahtre kidnapping and murder. Khan fled to Pakistan after being served with the deportation notice. He was welcomed by President Zia Al Haq and assured that Pakistan supported independence for Kashmir. During this period, the JKLF found common cause with the ISI, which set up camps to train Kashmiri militants in guerilla warfare.[24] Highlighting operational links between the Government of Pakistan and Kashmiri militants, a major training camp was located at the farmhouse of Sheik Rashid who was Information Minister in the government of Prime Minister Nawaz Sharif.

Yasin Malik was a charismatic Kashmiri who passed through Rashid's training program. As a youth, Malik committed himself to the cause of self-determination for the people of Kashmir. He urged Kashmiris to engage in acts of civil disobedience, defy curfew restrictions, and join mass street protests. Malik was a polling agent for the Muslim United Front in 1987 but electoral fraud turned him against the political process.

Under Malik's direction, Kashmiri's launched a violent insurgency that started with the bombing of the Srinagar Central Post and Telegraph and the Amar Singh Club in July 1988.[25] The following year, JKLF cadres kidnapped Rubaya Sayeed, daughter of the Indian Home Affairs Minister who was himself a prominent Indian Muslim politician, and used her as bait to secure the release of prisoners. In January 1990, the JKLF killed five air force men in its first attack on India's armed forces.

Tensions between the ISI and JKLF surfaced at about this time when the ISI insisted that one of its intelligence officers attend all JKLF executive committee meetings as an "observer."[26] When the JKLF objected, the ISI expressed dissatisfaction with the organization's pro-independence agenda and ratcheted up the pressure. Further annoying the ISI, Malik insisted that the Gilgit-Baltistan region was part of Kashmir not Pakistan. Having made direct contact with Kashmiri militants brought to Pakistan for training, the ISI discontinued its cooperation with JKLF in 1990 focusing instead on more radical groups with a pro-Pakistan orientation.[27]

Malik was arrested by Indian police that year. Even from prison, he captured the imagination of Kashmiris by engaging in a well-publicized hunger strike and demanding that Indian security dismantle military bunkers around the Hazratbal Mosque in Srinigar. Internment gave Malik the chance to reflect on JKLF's strategy. Four days after his release from jail in May 1994, Malik declared a unilateral ceasefire and called for tripartite negotiations involving India, Pakistan and the JKLF.

Vowing to continue the struggle for independence using peaceful means, Malik's ongoing efforts focused on raising awareness of Kashmir in the media, seeking assistance through diplomatic channels, and securing a third party to mediate an end to the conflict. "We took up the gun to bring Kashmir to the world's attention," said Malik. "Once that goal had been accomplished we ceased armed struggle."[28] Setting out for Muzzafarabad, the capital of Azad Kashmir, he announced: "I'm going to explore ways to include Kashmiris in talks on Kashmir. In 1989, I crossed the Line of Control to bring the gun. Today I'm on a peace mission."[29]

Other Kashmiri leaders disdained Malik's peace overtures. Yusuf Shah was a candidate in the 1987 elections. He became so embittered by India's election rigging that he changed his name to Syed Salahuddin and assumed the leadership of Hizbul-Mujahideen, which embraced violence as the sole vehicle for political change. In response to Malik's call for negotiations, Khan retorted: "I have ideological differences with Malik as the independence he is talking about is aimed at dividing Kashmir, which is unacceptable to us."[30] As a result of differences between Malik and Khan, the JKLF into two groups both calling themselves the Jammu and Kashmir Liberation Front.

Malik's branch of the JKLF joined APHC, which is led by Mirwaiz Omar Farooq. Upon the murder of his father for initiating dialogue with India, Farooq was thrust into a leadership role as head of the Awami Action Committee at the age of 17. Farooq is a consensus builder who has tried to embrace all social, political and religious factions in Jammu and Kashmir. He has been careful not to take positions that polarize APHC members. For example, Farooq supports negotiations to resolve Kashmir's status. However, he has been studiously non-committal when it comes to staking out a position vis-à-vis Pakistan.

Some APHC members objected when Pakistani-backed militants bombed the Jammu and Kashmir state assembly in October 2001 killing thirty-seven people. Two months later, Indian authorities accused Jaish-e-Mohammed of launching an assault on India's national parliament that killed 15. APHC moderates warned that such actions would intensify repression in Kashmir and risked a broader war with Pakistan.

Financing

The JKLF receives a variety of funding streams from Kashmir, Pakistan and around the world. Voluntary contributions are solicited at the Hazratbal Mosque as well as other places of worship. However, financial support from war-weary Kashmiris has diminished dramatically since the conflict peaked in the mid-1990s. In Pakistan, "jihad contributions" are raised at collection spots on the street corners of cities Muzzafarabad and Mirpur in Azad Kashmir as well as in the Punjabi cities of Rawalpindi and Lahore.[31] With support from the government, Pakistan-based charities also provide funds to the families of "martyrs" killed in action.[32]

Significant revenues came from JKLF branches in the Gulf States of Saudi Arabia, the United Arab Emirates, Qatar, Kuwait, and Oman.[33]

Revenue was also derived through contributions from the United Kingdom where one quarter of a million Kashmiris reside. Many Kashmiris in Britain send remittances to their families in parts of Kashmir.[34] They also operated a network of charities and foundations that raised funds for the JKLF. Malik would make regular fund raising trips to the United States working closely with Pakistani-Americans. A consortium of Chicago-based physicians proved particularly generous. All money raised from international sources is transferred in violation of India's Foreign Contribution (Regulation) Act of 1976.

After 9/11, restrictions governing financial transactions made it hard to transfer funds through regular banking channels. The JKLF determined that the best way to move money was through the "hawala," an informal Islamic banking and money management system with no record or paper trail. Using the hawala, funds from Pakistan were routed to countries in the Gulf before being transferred to India and finding their way into the JKLF's coffers.[35] The police maintained, "Terror funds have a clear trail leading to Pakistan."[36]

Few funds raised in Pakistan were actually carried across the LoC. However, in a well-publicized incident that garnered support for passage of India's Prevention of Terrorism Ordinance, a woman traveling from Pakistan was found to have $100,000 stitched into her clothes. Indian police maintained that Malik was linked to the woman and arrested him in April 2002; Malik denied any connection and was soon released.

Militants also raise money via extortion payments and protection rackets. Pakistan sponsored groups and foreign fighters have been known to extort funds from local shopkeepers and exact a tax from members of Kashmir's middle class.

Elections

Democratic development in Jammu and Kashmir has lagged far behind other parts of India consistently failing to meet the expectations of Kashmiris or satisfy international standards for free and fair elections. Kashmiris did not participate in the first post-independence elections for the national assembly. Since then, they have grown increasingly resentful watching Indians exercise their voting rights while they had none. Successive Indian leaders refused to allow a legitimate ballot fearing that elections in Kashmir would institutionalize a hostile government in a sensitive border state. As a result, many Kashmiris lost confidence that their democratic aspirations could be achieved through participation in elections and integration with India. Disenfranchised and disillusioned, they rejected the political process focusing instead on violence as an outlet for their dissent.

National assembly elections of 1977 were considered to be the first credible ballot in Kashmir. The NC won 47 of 75 seats in the assembly.[37] After its resounding defeat, Congress (I) was determined to capture control of the state government in Jammu and Kashmir. In 1982, Sheikh Abdullah died and passed the mantle of NC to his young son, Farooq Abdullah, who embraced an anti-Congress and pro-autonomy platform.[38] The 1982 election was hotly contested. More than any other issue, the Re-settlement Bill proved to be a potent tool for polarizing the electorate. The Bill allowed the return of Kashmiris who had moved to Pakistan but were subjects of the state prior to 1954. The NC maintained that Kashmiris were merely exercising their right of return. Congress (I) objected asserting that resettlement was just a guise to enhance the number of Muslim voters.

Election Day was marred by violence that forced some polling stations to close. Nonetheless, 70 percent of eligible voters participated. When the votes were finally counted, the NC had won 46 seats compared to 26 by Congress (I) and three by independent candidates.[39] The NC's victory was interpreted as an endorsement of the autonomy option. With the NC's success, Farooq Abdullah had overcome claims of nepotism. According to the *Hindustan Times*, "Sheikh Abdullah's mantle has truly fallen on his son who owes no thanks to any favours from any quarter."[40]

Farooq's tenure was short-lived. In July 1984, Congress (I) and its representative in Kashmir, Governor Malhotra Jagmohan, engineered his ouster by convincing 12 members of the legislative assembly to defect from the NC and form a new government. In less than two years, however, Congress (I) withdrew its support for the NC renegade faction and reinstalled Farooq as chief minister. In return, Farooq announced that the NC and Congress had reached an agreement not to oppose one another in the upcoming state assembly election of 1987.

Secret deals and shifting alliances had the effect of undermining the participation of civil society in politics. It also fueled demands by Is-lamist groups for more transparency. The Muslim United Front (MUF) was established soon after the NC-Congress (I) deal. Positioning itself as the main opposition to the consortium, MUF helped forge common cause among Kashmir's separatist groups. Mirroring the MUF's rise, the Bhartiya Janata Party (BJP) also made inroads by appealing to Hindu nationalism and spotlighting the plight of Hindu Pandits.

Fearing a victory by the MUF, Rajiv Gandhi's Congress (I) and the NC colluded once again. Of eligible voters, 75 percent cast ballots in the 1987 state assembly election. The NC won 40 of 76 seats. Congress (I) won 26, MUF four, the BJP two, and four seats went to so-called independent parties. Though it dominated the assembly, the popular vote tally revealed shallow support for the NC-Congress (I) consortium.

India's "first past the post" electoral system favors large parties and political alliances. Though the consortium received only 53 percent of the popular vote, it was able to win 87 percent of seats in the Assembly.[41] This inevitably gave rise to charges of malfeasance and electoral fraud. The MUF was particularly aggrieved when 600 of its polling agents were arrested just prior to the election. In addition, eight senior MUF officials were arrested for "rousing religious sentiments of the people and demanding independence from the Indian Union."[42]

According to Abdul Ghani Lone, the 1987 election was a "flash point. Electoral fraud motivated the young generation to say 'to hell with the democratic process and all that this is about' and they said 'let's go for armed struggle."[43] Malik, who worked as a polling agent in 1987, also grew disillusioned. Asserting that participation in bogus elections merely acknowledged Kashmir's status as an integral part of India, he called for a boycott of national parliamentary elections in 1989. JKLF posters warned voters not to go to the polls and admonished polling officers not to show up on Election Day. As a result, about 5,000 polling officers simply did come to work. Violence was widespread; government and school buildings used as polling stations were torched. Voter turnout was as low as 2 percent in some panchayats.[44]

India pursued the same strategy in Kashmir as in Punjab. It used repression and military means to counter the insurgency while encouraging Kashmiris to participate in the political process and become stakeholders in Kashmir's political future. In 1995, India's minister for home affairs maintained, "People have now realized that, where there is a ballot, there is no place for a bullet."[45] His optimism was misplaced. Militants tried to scuttle the November 1995 state assembly elections by seizing five Western tourists as hostages. Malik also rejected India's plans. At a large rally, he vowed to burn himself to death if India went forward with fraudulent elections.

Lok Sabha elections were held again in 1996. Despite calls for a boycott, many war-weary Kashmiris decided to vote. The results were, however, discredited by widespread and well-publicized reports of Indian troops marching Kashmiris to the polls at gunpoint. The APHC cried foul, but the NC went ahead and formed a government with Farooq Abdullah as chief minister. His appointment embittered many Kashmiris who recalled his collaboration with the Congress Party in rigging the 1987 elections.

Problems with Kashmir's democratic development go beyond electoral fraud and manipulation. Institutions such as the courts the police and the electoral commission have also been corrupted. Instead of acting as a legitimate vehicle for expressing dissent, elections were seen as an effort by India to undermine Kashmir's drive for self-determination. It is a departure, the 2003 state assembly elections were largely contested on the issues. They resulted in the formation of a coalition government involving Congress (I) and Mufti Muhammad Syed's Progressive Democratic Party, provided an encouraging sign that the democratic process might be eroding support for extremism.

Autonomy

India's federal system offers a framework for addressing the democratic aspirations of Kashmiris. Kashmir's treaty of accession allocated responsibility for defense, foreign affairs, and communications, such as post, telegraph, telephones, broadcasting, railways, and air traffic control, to the central government in New Delhi. All other aspects of governance were to be controlled by autonomous self-rule structures.

By recognizing the special status of Kashmir, Article 370 of the Indian constitution affirmed the unique culture and political identity of Kashmiris. It restricted employment and property ownership to Kashmiris. It also called upon the central government to offer a generous subsidy to promote the economic development of Kashmir.[46] Article 370 was originally envisioned as a "temporary" measure binding Kashmir to the Indian Union until conditions existed for a referendum on Kashmir's status.

Penetration of Kashmir's self-determination movement by Islamist groups stirred Hindu nationalism as parties on all sides increasingly appealed to religious identity as a tool for political mobilization. Nonetheless, many Kashmiris believe that autonomy represents a system of governance capable of harmonizing competing claims. According to Sheikh Abdullah, "Our dispute with the Government of India is not about accession but it is about the quantum of autonomy."[47] Prime Minister Narasimha Rao endorsed autonomy in 1995 declaring, "Independence no, autonomy. The sky is the limit."[48] In the twilight of his life, Jawaharlal Nehru—Jammu's most prominent Hindu Pandit—took the notion of decentralization a step further. He floated the idea of a confederation between India and Kashmir as a way of addressing the Kashmir situation. He even entertained the possibility that such a confederation would pave the way for India and Pakistan to establish a confederation of their own.[49]

Those who opposed the pledge for a referendum in the treaty of accession also opposed the special status accorded to Kashmir under Article 370. They see autonomy as a pit-stop on the path to independence. Hindu reactionaries are vehemently against decentralization. Capitalizing on their strong feelings, the BJP tried to make opposition to autonomy a wedge issue, as well as a primary part of the Hindutva agenda. The BJP's 1989 platform emphasized universal human rights while rejecting special protections for India's Muslims. It embraced the demands of Hindu Pandits for full integration into the Indian state and demanded the repeal of Article 370.

The BJP sought to capitalize on rising nationalism. The concept of Kashmiriyat came under attack from both Kashmiri nationalists as well as Hindu Pandits. Spasms of violence in the early 1990s caused 150,000 Pandits to flee their homes for temporary resettlement camps in New Delhi and in the Hindu Belt of Jammu. Pandits in the border districts of Rajouri, Poonch and Doda were also targeted and displaced.[50] The government of India tried to address their plight by offering preferential job opportunities and via affirmative action in university placement. However, Hindu Pandit politicians still blame New Delhi for ignoring their suffering in order to foster antipathy against Kashmiri secessionists.

Hard-line Hindu Pandits joined the Praja Parishad Party, which has close ties with the Rashtriya Swayamsevak Sangh (RSS) and Hindu Vishva Parishad, right-wing Hindu nationalist movements. Hindu Pandits sought union territory status in order to achieve direct rule for New Delhi. They also demanded an entity of their own, which they call "Our Homeland" (*Panun Kashmir*).[51]

Kashmir's escalating violence also helped move the BJP forward. In October 1990, the party leader, L.K. Advani led agitators demanding to build a Hindu Temple on the spot of the Babri Masjid in Ayodhya. Hordes of Hindu fundamentalists wearing saffron bands with Lord Rama's name inscribed across their brow attacked the mosque with knives and pickaxes.[52] More than 3,000 Muslims were killed in subsequent spasms of sectarian strife.

Advani expected that mobilizing the Hindu masses would galvanize communalist militant organizations and, riding the wave of Hindutva, propel the BJP to a huge victory at the polls. The BJP doubled its representation in the national assembly elections of 1991. Whereas it won only 11 percent of the vote in 1989, the BJP secured 23 percent in 1991 occupying 122 of the Lok Sabha's 529 parliamentary seats, thus making it the largest opposition party.[53] However, the results fell short of expectations. Many Indians recalled that Mahatma Gandhi was assassinated for appeasing Muslims and opposing Hindu Rashtra. They were concerned that BJP orchestrated communal rioting would erode India's standing as the world's largest secular democracy capable of embracing a multitude of ethnic and religious groups.

For their part, India's 150 million Muslims refrained from taking a high-profile position on Kashmir. They feared that doing so would stir anti-Muslim feelings across the country and be used by the BJP to foment more violence such as the Gujarat riots of 2002 that claimed another 2,000 lives.

Escalation

Sure enough, India sent 700,000 troops to the LoC, including the Border Security Force and the Central Reserve Police Force.[54] Hard-liners called for a "decisive war" to deal with Pakistan once and for all.[55]

During notorious "lock-downs," neighborhoods suspected of sheltering militants were sealed by security forces that would go from house-to-house looking for weapons and hunting for militants. Shootings were common during lock-downs. So was petty theft, as well as the rape of Muslim women.[56]

India's draconian counter-insurgency operation was cloaked under the rule of law. Passed by the Legislative Assembly in September 1989, press censorship was authorized by the Jammu and Kashmir Special Powers Bill. From 1990-93, 12,950 cases were registered under the Terrorism and Disruptive Activities (Prevention) Act.[57] Institutions such as the courts, the police, and the electoral commission were also corrupted.

In addition, India's security services established, armed, trained, and financed numerous paramilitary outfits that were responsible for widespread harassment of the local population, burning of Muslim-owned properties and businesses, and the assassination of prominent Muslim leaders. Indian military intelligence made it a priority to exploit in-fighting between factions. For example, it persuaded Jamaatis to pass information on the JKLF to the Indian security services. At Pakistan's urging, Hizb targeted JKLF leaders for assassination; two JKLF members were killed by Hizb militants in July 1997.[58] India also developed an extensive network of spies and paid informants.

Taking every opportunity to exploit internal dissention, India's policy was to push militants above ground and to encourage factionalism between different groups. While opening back channels to APHC moderates via the Kashmir Committee in New Delhi, it also intensified the pressure on those who were seen as more antagonistic. India's Ministry of Home Affairs placed some APHC leaders on a watch-list. Militants were targeted for assassination. India confiscated passports in an effort to block the travel of APHC members out of the country.

Syed Geelani who leads Jamaat-e-Islam accused Farooq of being too moderate and, in September 2003, APHC split into two factions. Geelani maintained, "Our natural religious and cultural affiliation has always been with Pakistan."[59] Troubled by India's success dividing the movement, Malik and Khan argued that factionalism was undermining APHC's goal of separation from India. Malik and Khan led by example. They urged APHC members to set aside their differences and initiated discreet discussions about reunifying JKLF and adopting a common platform. At a meeting in Rawalpindi in August 2005, they agreed to establish a seven-man committee tasked with exploring ways of integrating their disparate activities.[60]

Progress

A plethora of track two civil society contacts was undertaken in the 1990s. People to people programs enabled "partition families" to make contact. Even the JKLF organized a blood drive for the victims of India's Maharashtra earthquake in 1993.[61] Civil society initiatives created a climate of goodwill that made it possible for Prime Minister Atal Bihouri Vajpayee to visit Lahore to meet his Pakistani counterpart, Nawaz Sharif, in February 1999. Soon after the Lahore Summit, however, the Kargil War cast a pall over prospects for rapprochement. It also undermined track two activities. Pakistan's military coup of October 1999 removed Sharif from power thereby nullifying the potential benefit of personal ties between the prime ministers.

Following President Bill Clinton's visit in 2000, General Pervez Musharraf offered to reduce the number of Pakistani troops along the LoC and proposed a six-month ceasefire. Hizb followed with its own conditional ceasefire proposal. However, 100 people were massacred a week later and Indian forces reprised with a large-scale military operation across southern Kashmir that involved attack aircraft, helicopter gunships, and many ground troops.[62]

After the operation, Vajpayee announced a unilateral ceasefire and the release of prisoners in November 2000. The Government of India also opened channels of communication with APHC to discuss a possible cease-fire.[63] But détente came to a standstill when a senior BJP official publicly disparaged Omar Farooq as a representative of "Islamic fundamentalism."[64] A year later Advani invited Kashmiri groups to come to New Delhi for talks. However, APHC rejected the invitation because he failed to direct the invitation to the APHC as the sole representative of the Kashmiri people. The government's unwillingness to issue passports to Kashmiri leaders for travel to Pakistan or elsewhere out of the country further poisoned relations.

After Vajpayee extended a symbolic "hand of friendship" in April 2003, India and Pakistan moved quickly to restore full diplomatic relations. They also agreed to series of summits, working-level dialogues, hotlines between senior security officials, prior notification of troop movements, and to disclose the whereabouts of nuclear facilities.

Once again the positive trend was short-lived. Progress stalled when the APHC accused the Indian government of using the ceasefire as cover for intensifying human rights abuses and the police arrested Kashmiri leaders who were outspoken in their criticism.

To regain momentum, Musharraf pledged publicly that Pakistan would not support the training of Kashmiri militants on its territory. He also entertained new approaches to the Kashmir question. Musharraf floated the idea of abandoning demands for a referendum and demilitarizing Kashmir districts on both sides of the LoC in order to establish a "condominium" between India and Pakistan.[65] Indian officials responded skeptically. They insisted that Musharraf should be judged by his actions not his words. They also criticized Musharraf for using the media rather than formal diplomatic channels to propose the initiative.

Bus service between Srinigar and Muzzafarabad was launched in April 2004. Escorted by an armed convoy, villagers threw flower petals at the marigold garlanded "caravan of peace" as it crossed the LoC. There were heart-wrenching scenes of "partition families" reunited after decades. Bus service also resumed between Lahore and Amritsar. Air links were reopened. Muslim pilgrims were allowed to visit shrines on the Indian side of the LoC.

Not everyone welcomed improved relations. Syed Geelani opposed bus service between India and Pakistan. He maintained that the need for travelers to produce passports implied that the LoC was really a permanent international border. Geelani threatened to turn the buses into "rolling coffins."[66]

Cross-border infiltration slowed dramatically in 2003 and 2004. The January 2004 summit between Singh and Musharraf led to agreement for a "composite dialogue" addressing "all bilateral issues including Jammu and Kashmir."[67] However, Indian officials renewed charges that Pakistan had failed to dismantle the "infrastructure of terrorism" after the Mumbai commuter train bombings. Both countries ordered the expulsion of each other's diplomats.[68]

Perhaps the greatest opportunity came after the Kashmir earthquake of October 2005. Azad Kashmir was hardest hit—about 73,000 people died and 3.3 million people were displaced. Thousands of homeless victims huddled on the bare hillsides of Azad Kashmir waiting for aid but the destruction of roads prevented rescue missions from reaching them.[69]

India responded immediately by sending relief supplies to Pakistan. It also offered helicopters and restored telephone communications across the LoC after fifteen years. Musharraf welcomed the helicopters but the offer was withdrawn when he refused to accept Indian pilots. Plans to open five border crossings of the LoC were almost scuttled when Pakistani militants were accused of bombings that tore through a New Delhi bus and two crowded markets in October 2005.

It was hoped that India and Pakistan would work together in the fields of disaster response and emergency preparedness similar to the earthquake diplomacy that catalyzed rapprochement between Greece and Turkey following the earthquakes of July and August 1999. Despite initial efforts to open borders and enable the free flow of relief supplies, cooperation became bogged down by bureaucratic and irredentist forces on both sides. The Kashmir quake failed to have a lasting positive impact on India-Pakistan relations.[70]

International Actors

United States

America's relations with India and Pakistan were mired in Cold War politics until the 1990s. Tilting towards Pakistan, the United States encouraged Pakistan to sign the Baghdad Pact and offered a security agreement to Pakistan in 1954-55. It also trained Pakistani Special Forces in asymmetrical warfare in order to counter threats from the Soviet Union and China.[71] India gravitated towards the Soviet camp after receiving assurances from Moscow that the Soviet Union would block any effort to review Kashmir's status in the UN Security Council.

When the Soviet Union invaded Afghanistan in 1979, the Carter and Reagan administrations worked closely with Pakistan's ISI to arm the Afghan Mujahadeen. Security sector assistance established greater parity between the militaries of India and Pakistan. It also helped Pakistan regain the sense of confidence that it had lost as a result of its resounding defeat in the 1971 war over East Pakistan.

U.S.-Pakistan relations had cooled by the mid-1980s. When information about Pakistan's covert nuclear enrichment program came to light, Senator Larry Pressler (R-SD) authored an amendment to the Foreign Assistance Act in 1985 conditioning foreign aid upon certification by the president that Pakistan did not have nuclear capability. Irking successive governments in Islamabad, the U.S. refused to deliver F-16 fighter jets for which Pakistan had already paid.[72]

With the Soviet withdrawal from Afghanistan in 1990, the United States reduced its profile in the region. However, quasi-governmental organizations like the U.S. Institute of Peace continued to facilitate track two contact between Kashmiri civil society representatives. Robert Oakley, a former U.S. ambassador to Pakistan, chaired meetings convened by USIP that created the APHC as an inclusive body positioned to represent the diverse interests of the Kashmiri people.

The United States refocused on South Asia after India and Pakistan tested nuclear devices in May 1998. Deeply concerned about a nuclear arms race on the subcontinent, Bill Clinton worked hard to improve relations between India and Pakistan after the Kargil War. He visited India and Pakistan in March 2000. Though he maintained that the United States would not seek to mediate the Kashmir dispute, he exhorted the government of Pakistan to create conditions for a dialogue with New Delhi. "When I was in New Delhi I asked India to seize the opportunity for dialogue," said Clinton. "For India and Pakistan this must be a time of restraint, for respect of the Line of Control, and renewed lines of communication.... The stark truth must be faced. There is no military solution to Kashmir. International sympathy, support and intervention cannot be won by provoking a bigger, bloodier conflict."[73]

After 9/11, both India and Pakistan aligned themselves with America's war on terror. Given Pakistan's pivotal position bordering Afghanistan, the Bush administration sought close cooperation from Musharraf in attacking the Taliban and eradicating Al Qaeda from Pakistan's northwest frontier. It waived all sanctions that were imposed after the 1998 nuclear test and the 1999 military coup. It also designated Pakistan a "major non-NATO ally" and, between FY 2002-06, provided $3.4 billion in foreign aid—almost all of it in the form of military assistance.[74] While publicly lauding Pakistan, U.S. officials privately worried about Musharraf's overthrow by Islamists or a coup by ISI hardliners sympathetic to the Taliban. Concerns grew more acute as Musharraf's tyranny intensified. Not only did he initially bar former Prime Ministers Benazir Bhutto and Nawaz Sharif from participating in the 2007 elections. Removing Chief Justice Chaudharry from the bench sparked angry protests by pro-democracy demonstrators across the country.

While embracing Musharraf, President Bush tried to maintain a balanced approach meeting India's prime minister Vajpayee soon after 9/11. Bush took important steps to enhance partnership between the United States and India. To this end, the United States and India agreed to expand security cooperation in the fields of counter-terrorism, regional security, space and scientific cooperation, joint military exercises and arms sales. The U.S. India Defense Policy Group, suspended after India's nuclear tests, was reconvened in 2001 and a U.S.-India Joint Working Group on Counterterrorism was also established. The United States and India signed a two-year defense framework agreement giving the United States permission to use India's military bases. In a dramatic move, Bush vowed to "help India become a major world power in the 21st century" and offered to assist India's civilian nuclear program in 2005.[75]

Pakistan

No issue seizes Pakistanis more than the plight of their brethren in "Indian-occupied Kashmir." Additionally, no issue is more useful to efforts by Pakistan's military and intelligence to monopolize power than continued conflict with India over Kashmir. It is said that, "Pakistan is willing to fight India to the last Kashmiri."[76]

Pakistan's domestic debate about Kashmir is dominated by the ISI, members of the security establishment, and other elites. These constituencies pay lip service to the right of self-determination while actively undermining any homegrown Kashmiri organization that does not support accession to Pakistan.

Most states have an army. In the case of Pakistan, the army has a state. Pakistan is run by a military dictatorship with theocratic tendencies. There have been four military governments since independence. Musharraf's regime is the latest. Each military ruler has suspended democratic development in the interest of stability. Yet, Pakistan is still unstable; its progress hindered by a multitude of ethnic, sectarian and resource conflicts. The conflict with India over Kashmir is used to distract Pakistanis from their own ills such as poverty, social inequality, sectarian conflict, and the lack of democratic development.

The State Department's terrorism assessment prior to 9/11 concluded that Pakistan has "increased its support to the Taliban and continued it support to militant groups active in Indian-held Kashmir, such as the Harakat ul-Mujahidin, some of which engaged in terrorism. Pakistan's military government, continued previous Pakistani government support of the Kashmir insurgency, and Kashmiri militant groups continued to operate in Pakistan, raising funds and recruiting new cadre."[77] In search of strategic depth, the ISI and military intelligence have a long history of supporting radical Muslim movements as a counter to Indian and Russian influence.

Pakistan is largely reliant upon foreign aid to support its security and development efforts. In exchange for foreign aid and debt forgiveness, Musharraf squarely aligned Pakistan with the United States in Bush's war on terror. Though Islamist elements in the ISI are accused of sheltering Osama bin Laden and Ayman Al Zawahiri in the tribal areas of northwestern Pakistan, Musharraf insisted that Pakistan was doing its utmost to apprehend or kill them. As of 2007, Pakistan has remanded about 500 Al Qaeda members into U.S. custody including Ramzi bin Al Shibh (September 2002), Khalid Sheik Mohammed (March 2003) and Abu Faraj Al Libbi (May 2005).[78] Despite the detention of these so-called big fish, Pashtun tribal loyalties defy international frontiers. Afghanistan's President Hamid Karzai has bitterly accused Pakistan of sheltering resurgent Taliban and Al Qaeda elements in order to destabilize his administration. Karzai was enraged when Pakistan's Ulama Council dignified Osama bin Laden with the honorary title "Sword of Allah."

Lacking popular support among Pakistanis, Musharraf is in a precarious political position. In 1999, Musharraf ousted the elected government and assumed the title of president. Since then, he has remained both president and army chief of staff. Musharraf is deeply unpopular as evidenced by his repudiation in parliamentary elections of February 2008. In contrast, nearly two-thirds of Pakistanis have a favorable view of Osama bin Laden.[79] Many Pakistanis condemn the deployment of Pakistan's military along the Afghan border. Occasional U.S. air strikes against targets on the Pakistan side of the border further rile the population. Musharraf lives in constant peril. Two assassination attempts nearly killed him in December 2003. All told, there have been five attempts on his life since he assumed the presidency.

Terrorism by jihadists trained in Pakistan does not stop at Pakistan's borders. Some of the London bombers who blew themselves up in the tube and on a bus in July 2005 attended terror-training camps in Pakistan. India charged that Pakistan-based militants involved in the July 2006 bombings of commuter trains in Mumbai trained at camps in Pakistan.

British citizens of Pakistani origin who plotted to blow up airlines flying from London to the United States in August 2006 also received training in Pakistan. A spokesman for India's Ministry of Home Affairs said, "People directly involved in such [terror] activities continue to occupy high positions in Pakistan. Our position remains that no effective action has been taken by Pakistan to dismantle the infrastructure of support to terrorism on a permanent basis. This is contrary to assurances given by the Pakistani leadership that Pakistan will not allow any territory within its control to be used for support to terrorism. It is our sincere hope that Pakistan will abide by its commitments."[80]

Concern about Pakistan's nuclear program spiked after India and Pakistan conducted nuclear tests in May 1998. Fears heightened when it became known that Pakistan had transferred nuclear technologies and know-how to North Korea, Libya, and Iran. Abdul Qadeer Khan, the godfather of Pakistan's nuclear industry, was implicated in the illicit transfer of technologies. Khan was detained at a minimum-security facility and then issued a presidential pardon by Musharraf.

Pakistan's corruption is rampant. Pakistan falls short of international human rights standards or norms of good governance. Indian Muslims who resettled in Pakistan after 1947 (*Muhajirs*) suffer discrimination and resent Pakistan's unitary system of governance. The government has failed to make progress on ethnic conflicts in Sindh or to develop equitable resource sharing arrangements in Baluchistan where pent-up frustration resulted in days of rioting ensued after a leading Baluchi politician was assassinated in August 2006.

Pakistan points to Azad Kashmir as a beacon for Indian Kashmir. Yet, Azad Kashmir is far from free. Its politicians and institutions are all under the control of Islamabad. Decisions affecting people at the local level are typically made by resident military and police commanders. Unless political parties sign a declaration endorsing Kashmir's accession to Pakistan, they are denied the right to function or participate in elections. Pakistan's constitution stipulates that, "No person or political party in Azad Jammu and Kashmir shall be permitted to propagate against or take part in activities prejudicial or detrimental to the ideology of the state's accession to Pakistan."[81]

China

China routed Indian troops in the border war of 1962 before declaring a unilateral ceasefire that consolidated its control over 14,000 square miles of territory. India refused to normalize relations with China for decades demanding that China withdraw from occupied territories.

In the 1960s and 1970s, tensions increased as a result of China's support for separatist and insurgent groups operating in the northeast of India. In order to neutralize India and counter the Soviet Union, China also provided Pakistan with military assistance that may have included WMD as well as "Silkworm" missile technology.[82] China and Pakistan continue to work closely together. In April 2005, Prime Minister Wen Jiaboa traveled to Pakistan and signed a series of agreements. All told, twenty-nine bilateral accords were signed in 2004-05.

Indo-China relations began improving in the early 1990s. Prime Minister Rao visited Beijing in 1993 and agreed to a troop reduction along the disputed India-China border. In April 2005, Prime Minister Wen visited New Delhi and announced expanded military and economic cooperation. During the summit, China issued a statement recognizing Indian sovereignty in Sikkim and India affirmed the position that Tibet is a part of China.[83] Though China historically supported decolonization and national liberation movements, Beijing refused to get involved in Kashmir fearing a parallel with its occupation of Tibet. Today China emphasizes good neighborly relations with both India and Pakistan.

Great Britain

Many Kashmiris blame the Great Britain for bungling the partition and thereby laying the ground for today's conflict. They still hope that the Great Britain will use its position as a permanent member of the UN Security Council to carry out the plebiscite promised following Maharaja Hari Singh's signing of the Accession Instrument with Lord Mountbatten. According to Malik, "We expect Britain to come to our rescue because [it was] in power in 1947 [and] ... left the Kashmir question unresolved."[84] Despite appeals from Kashmiris, the United Kingdom has always refused to take the lead on Kashmir in the UN Security Council and at the UN Human Rights Council in Geneva.

United Nations

The United Nations Military Observer Group in India and Pakistan (UNMOGIP) was authorized to supervise implementation of the Karachi Accord that established a cease fire between India and Pakistan in January 1949. Though India maintained that the Simla Agreement nullified UNMOGIP's mandate, Secretary General Kofi Annan determined that UNMOGIP could only be terminated through a specific resolution of the Security Council. Absent such agreement, a token force of about 45 personnel remains on the Pakistan side of the LoC. India adamantly resists internationalizing the Kashmir question insisting that third party involvement represents interference in its internal affairs.

The Way Forward

India bears the onus of leadership to resolve the Kashmir question. India's detractors use the ongoing Kashmir dispute to argue that India will not fully emerge as a leader on the world stage or have hopes for gaining a seat on the UN Security Council unless it resolves the Kashmir question and stabilizes its relations with Pakistan. For its part, Pakistan must shut down its terrorist infrastructure, stop supporting militant groups, and seal its side of the LoC in order to block the transfer of arms.

The Kashmir question will not be resolved all at once. India and Pakistan should focus initially on confidence-building measures and interim solutions. To reduce the current climate of fear, India should instruct its troops to remain in their barracks and take steps to gradually reduce their overall number in Kashmir. It should also dismantle military bunkers, barricades, checkpoints, and watchtowers in civilian areas. Kashmiris imprisoned for their political views should be released.

The appointment of a credible special envoy to coordinate policy and act as the interlocutor for Kashmiris would show that India is serious about negotiations. Kashmiri groups that demand independence or are engaged in armed struggle must be involved if talks are to have any chance of success.

India can help forge consensus among Kashmiris by encouraging dialogue between Kashmiri leaders on both sides of the LoC and allowing them to travel abroad without hindrance. The APHC leadership should undertake a systematic intra-Kashmiri dialogue. All of Kashmir's residents—Muslims, Hindus, Sikhs, Dogras, and Buddhists—must ultimately be involved. Kashmir is a mosaic of groups, each with their own interests. A final settlement must take into account their different aspirations and tailor solutions that meet the needs of the region's disparate peoples. Until that time, conflict management rather than resolution will remain the goal.

Pressure from the United States is needed on both India and Pakistan. However, U.S. officials must act discreetly. Their interference could, for example, cause unrest in Pakistan strengthening either the Islamists or emboldening the military. Despite legitimate concerns about Pakistan post-Musharraf, the United States cannot turn a blind eye to repression that denies democracy and fuels fundamentalism. Musharraf was given a blank check for far too long. The U.S. Congress should condition payments to Pakistan's military for operations against the Taliban and Al Qaeda with tangible results and counterterrorism milestones. If the Bush administration is true to its word about supporting democracy, it will have to forge cooperative relations with all of Pakistan's political parties, especially those supported by the voters.

Track two activities have been successful in the past. They should continue with special emphasis on the younger generation. Today's third generation has not experienced any of the major wars between India and Pakistan. They are more pragmatic and forward looking. Communication, contact and cooperation—especially in business and areas of commercial endeavor—may contribute to an improved atmosphere for India-Pakistan bilateral relations.

Free and fair elections, monitored by international and independent domestic observers, will make Kashmiris stakeholders in Kashmir's political future. Given the track record, India must prove its commitment to a transparent and accountable ballot. Appointing a regional election commissioner to assist the State Election Commission's work in Kashmir would be a good first step.[85]

Most Kashmiris are weary of violence and have come to believe that decentralization is the best way to advance their democratic aspirations. India can accommodate the demands of Kashmiris by reordering Indian federalism through customized arrangements to address the expectations of different groups and states. Currently the Indian constitution stipulates that the governor of Kashmir will be appointed by the president of India. As a result, the governor is seen as a partisan instrument of New Delhi's policies rather than as a genuine public servant of Kashmiri constituents. Article 155 of the constitution should be amended so that the governor would be elected by the state assembly. Alternatively, the state assembly could submit a panel of candidates for consideration by the president.[86] Used prior to 1965, traditional terms of honor—"head of state" (*Sadar-I-Riyasat*) and "prime minister" (*Wazir-e-Azam*)—should be restored given their symbolic value to Kashmiris.

To promote economic well-being, India should increase investment in Kashmir and improve transport infrastructure enabling the delivery of goods to and from the Valley. Demonstrating to Kashmiris the benefits to being a part of the one of the world's fastest growing and most dynamic economies could be very compelling. Pakistan should not stand in the way. It should allow expanded trade across the LoC. The South Asia Association for Regional Cooperation (SAARC) has made proposals to create a common economic space with free movement of goods, capital and services that are worth pursuing. Economic cooperation can help create conditions that are conducive to progress and must not wait until Kashmir's status is fully and finally settled. Job creation for Kashmiris can be achieved through affirmative action employment policies targeting the Indian Administrative Service and Indian Forest Service. Increasing the number of Kashmiris in the Indian Police Service and deploying security personnel to areas where they have tribal or family affiliations has multiple benefits.

The goals of justice, truth and reconciliation can be advanced by arresting members of the security services and paramilitaries suspected of human rights abuses and trying them before an independent tribunal. Reconciliation can also be achieved by creating conditions for the return of Hindu Pandits to their homes. Pandits should be compensated for lost or damaged property. They must not be used to stir Indian public opinion or as pawns in India's struggle with Kashmiri militants. The justice, truth, and reconciliation process could also focus on the manipulation of past elections.

NGOs have sought to address the Kashmir question by formulating confidence, building measures between Indian and Pakistani civil society and prescribing innovative strategies to harmonize competing claims. Perhaps the most innovative of such proposals draws on the Triest and Andorra models whereby the same territory is shared by two states or a nominally sovereign territory is linked to other states.[87] This approach may not be tenable when it comes to Kashmir. It is, however, important to think outside of the box when it comes to intractable conflicts.

In December 1998, members of the Kashmir Study Group together with Indians, Pakistanis and Kashmiris from both side of the LoC developed the Livingston proposal recommending that portions of the former state of Jammu and Kashmir be reconstituted as five self-governing sovereign entities with all the trappings of a state but without international personality. Each of the entities would have its own democratic constitution, as well as its own citizenship, legislature, flag, and anthem. While India and Pakistan would be responsible for defense and foreign affairs, each entity would establish its own police force to maintain internal law and order. Both India and Pakistan would demilitarize the area.

The proposal envisioned that the LoC would remain until India and Pakistan decided otherwise. The borders of India and Pakistan would be open allowing the free transit of people, goods, and services. Residents would have the option of using either Indian or Pakistani passports, or passports from the entities where they reside.[88] Residents of Kashmir, Jammu, and Ladakh on the territory currently administered by India and Azad Kashmir and the Northern Areas on territories currently administered by Pakistan would enjoy free access to one another and to and from both India and Pakistan. Kashmir, Jammu, and Ladakh would form a body to coordinate issues of mutual concern as would Azad Kashmir and the Northern Areas. An All-Kashmir body, made up of representatives from the five entities as well as from India and Pakistan, would coordinate broader regional interests such as trade, tourism, environment and water resource management.

The Livingston proposal evoked considerable controversy. Its critics claimed that it would cause social disruption and polarization of India's Muslim population. In addition, it would establish a dangerous precedent for communal relations in other parts of India where Nagas, Sikhs, and Mizos reside. It embodies, however, important and innovative ideas that go a long way to meeting the needs of Kashmiris and thereby resolving the principal issue that risks the escalation of conflict between India and Pakistan.

Notes

1.   http://daga.dhs.org/justpeace/urgent/kashmir/divideveil.html.
2.   1991 Census of India.
3.   *Kashmir: A Way Forward.* February 2005.
4.   John Gershman. *Foreign Policy in Focus.* "Overview of Self-Determination Issues in Kashmir." The Interhemispheric Resource Center and the Institute for Policy Studies.
5.   Sumit Ganguly. "Explaining the Kashmir Insurgency: Political Mobilization and Institutional Decay." *International Security.* Vol. 21. No. 2. Fall 1996.
6.   Stephen Philip Cohen. "India, Pakistan, and Kashmir." *Journal of Strategic Studies.* Routledge Press. Vol. 25. No. 4. December 2002. p. 47.
7.   According to the Henry L. Stinson Center, 474 Indian soldiers were killed and 1,109 wounded in the Kargil War. The Center does not provide any data on the number of Pakistani soldiers killed citing Pakistan's position that it was not involved in the conflict.
8.   K. Alan Kronstadt. "Pakistan-U.S. Relations." *Congressional Research Service Issue Brief for Congress.* The Library of Congress. July 26, 2005.
9.   Includes text from http://shell.comsats.net.pk/jklf/index.html.
10.   http://www.thehindu.com/2003/07/19/stories.
11.   *The Indian Express.* Hurriyat: A crowded house, a divided house. May 23, 2002.
12.   Reeta Chowdhari Tremblay. "Nation, Identity and the Intervening Role of the State: A Study of the Secessionist Movement in Kashmir." *Pacific Affairs*, Vol. 69, No. 4 (1996-1997). p. 480.
13.   Navitna Chadha Behera. *Asia Times.* Chasing a Mirage in Kashmir. January 23, 2003.
14.   U.S. State Department. Patterns of Global Terrorism 1994. Washington, D.C. 1995. p. 4.

15. http://www.kashmirherald.com/profiles/hurriyat.html
16. Amitabh Mattoo. "India's 'Potential' Endgame in Kashmir." *India Review*. Special Issue on the Kashmir Question. Editor: Sumit Ganguly. p. 18.
17. *Ibid*.
18. Sten Widmalm. "The Rise and Fall of Democracy in Kashmir." *Asian Survey*. Vol. 37, No. 11. November 1997. p. 1028.
19. Reeta Chowdhari Tremblay. "Nation, Identity and the Intervening Role of the State: A Study of the Secessionist Movement in Kashmir." *Pacific Affairs*, Vol. 69, No. 4 (1996-1997). pp. 471-497.
20. *Ibid*.
21. Salman Masood. *The New York Times*. "Founder of Pakistani Militant Group Is Placed under House Arrest. July 11, 2006. p. 3.
22. Reeta Chowdhari Tremblay. "Nation, Identity and the Intervening Role of the State: A Study of the Secessionist Movement in Kashmir." *Pacific Affairs*, Vol. 69, No. 4 (1996-1997). p. 471-497.
23. http://www.satp.org/satporgtp/countries/india/states/jandk/terrorist_outfits/jammu_&kashmir_liberation_front.htm.
24. *Ibid*.
25. http://www.flonnet.com/fl2214/stories/20050715001104900.htm.
26. *Ibid*.
27. http:///www.dawn.com/2005/06/18/nat3.htm.
28. Jonah Blank."Kashmir: Fundamentalism Takes Root." *Foreign Affairs*. Vo. 78. No. 6. November/December 1999. p. 41.
29. *Hindustan Times*. Hurriyat leaders set off on historic Pakistan trip. June 2, 2005.
30. http://news.indiainfo.com/2004/11/27/2711jklf.html.
31. Sultan Shahin. *Asia Times*. Across the Divide—Part 1: Lifting the Veil. December 16, 2004.
32. Ramesh Vinayak. "Jammu & Kashmir: Money Games." *India Today*. April 8, 2002. p.. 37.
33. http://www.kashmirherald.com/profiles/hurriyat.html
34. Sultan Shahin. *Asia Times*. Across the Divide—Part 1: Lifting the Veil. December 16, 2004.
35. Ramesh Vinayak. "Jammu & Kashmir: Money Games." *India Today*. April 8, 2002. p. 37.
36. *Ibid*.
37. Sten Widmalm. "The Rise and Fall of Democracy in Kashmir." *Asian Survey*. Vol. 37, No. 11. November 1997. p. 1007.
38. Atul Kohli. "Can Democracies Accommodate Ethnic Nationalism? Rise and Decline of Self-Determination Movements in India." *The Journal of Asian Studies*. Vol. 56, No. 2. May 1997. p. 340.
39. Sten Widmalm. "The Rise and Fall of Democracy in Kashmir." *Asian Survey*. Vol. 37, No. 11. November 1997. p. 1011.
40. Brij Bhardwaj. "Protest Against Poll Rigging in J&K." *Hindustan Times*. June 11, 1983.
41. Sten Widmalm. "The Rise and Fall of Democracy in Kashmir." *Asian Survey*. Vol. 37, No. 11. November 1997. p. 1021.
42. Inderjit Badhwar. "A Tarnished Triumph." *India Today*. April 15, 1987.
43. Sten Widmalm. "The Rise and Fall of Democracy in Kashmir." *Asian Survey*. Vol. 37, No. 11. November 1997. p. 1022.
44. Reeta Chowdhari Tremblay. "Nation, Identity, and the Intervening Role of the State: A Study of the Secessionist Movement in Kashmir." *Pacific Affairs*, Vol. 69, No. 4 (1996-1997). p. 492.

45.   *Agence France Presse*. "Kashmir leader threatens self-immolation to foil polls."
      March 31, 1995.
46.   Atul Kohli. "Can Democracies Accommodate Ethnic Nationalism? Rise and De-
      cline of Self-Determination Movements in India." *The Journal of Asian Studies*.
      Vol. 56, No. 2. May 1997. p. 339.
47.   Peter Hezelhurst. *The London Times*. March 10, 1972.
48.   Mubashir Hasan. "Settling the Kashmir Issue." The Henry L. Stimson Center.
49.   S. Gopal. *Nehru*. Oxford University Press, Vol. 3. 1980.
50.   Ashutosh Varshney. "India, Pakistan, and Kashmir: Anatomies of Nationalism."
      Asian Survey. Vol. 31. No. 11. November 1991. p. 1017.
51.   Amitabh Mattoo. "India's Potential 'Endgame' in Kashmir." *India Review: The
      Kashmir Question*. Editor: Sumit Ganguly. 2003.
52.   Lloyd I. Rudolph and Suzanne Hoeber Rudolph. "Unholy Rao." *The New Republic*.
      February 14, 1994. p. 16
53.   *Ibid.*
54.   K. Shankar Bajpai. Untangling India and Pakistan." *Foreign Affairs*. Vol. 82. No.
      3. May/June 2003. p. 113.
55.   K. Alan Kronstadt. "India-U.S. Relations." *Congressional Research Service Issue
      Brief for Congress*. The Library of Congress. July 15, 2005. p. 3.
56.   Interviews by the author. Srinigar. May 1994.
57.   Reeta Chowdhari Tremblay. "Nation, Identity and the Intervening Role of the
      State: A Study of the Secessionist Movement in Kashmir." *Pacific Affairs*, Vol.
      69, No. 4 (1996-1997). p. 471-497.
58.   Ramesh Vinayak. "Jammu & Kashmir: Money Games. *India Today*. April 8, 2002.
      p. 37.
59.   Jonah Blank. "AS High Stakes Kind of Peace." *U.S. News and World Report*. July
      19, 1999.
60.   "JKLF Factions Unite." *Dawn*. August 2, 2005.
61.   http://www.rediff.com///news/2005/jan/06jklf.htm.
62.   *Newsline*. Vol. 17, Issue 19. Sept. 16-29, 2000.
63.   Ramesh Vinayak, Harinder Baweja and Rory McCarthy. "Can Kashmir's Bloody
      Puzzle be Solved?" *India Today*. August 14, 2000. p. 28
64.   *Newsline*. Vol. 17, Issue 19. Sept. 16-29, 2000.
65.   "Commando Diplomacy." *The Economist*. October 30, 2004.
66.   Zahid Hussain. Kashmir's Berlin Wall." *Newsweek*. April 9, 2005.
67.   K. Alan Kronstadt. "Pakistan-U.S. Relations." *Congressional Research Service
      Issue Brief for Congress*. The Library of Congress. July 26, 2005.
68.   K. Alan Kronstadt. "Pakistan-U.S. Relations." *Congressional Research Service
      Issue Brief for Congress*. The Library of Congress. July 26, 2005. p. 6.
69.   *Scotland on Sunday*. "Failure in Pakistan." October 23, 2005, p. 14
70.   Randeep Ramesh. "Police arrest 20 in search for New Delhi bombers." *The Guard-
      ian (London)*. October 31, 2005. p. 17
71.   Interview with Barnett R. Rubin. New York University's Center for International
      Cooperation. October 25, 2006.
72.   K. Alan Kronstadt. "Pakistan-U.S. Relations." *Congressional Research Service
      Issue Brief for Congress*. The Library of Congress. July 26, 2005.
73.   Quoted in footnote no. 23. Amitabh Mattoo. "India's 'Potential' Endgame in
      Kashmir." *India Review*. Special Issue on the Kashmir Question. Editor: Sumit
      Ganguly. p. 18.
74.   K. Alan Kronstadt. "Pakistan-U.S. Relations." *Congressional Research Service
      Issue Brief for Congress*. The Library of Congress. July 26, 2005.

75. K. Alan Kronstadt. "India-U.S. Relations." *Congressional Research Service Issue Brief for Congress.* The Library of Congress. July 15, 2005. p. 3.

76. Stephen Philip Cohen. "India, Pakistan, and Kashmir." *Journal of Strategic Studies.* Routledge Press. Vol. 25. No. 4. December 2002. p. 57.

77. *U.S. Department of State.* Patterns of Global Terrorism, 2000 (Washington, D.C., 2001).

78. K. Alan Kronstadt. "Pakistan-U.S. Relations." *Congressional Research Service Issue Brief for Congress.* The Library of Congress. July 26, 2005. p. 5.

79. K. Alan Kronstadt. "Pakistan-U.S. Relations." *Congressional Research Service Issue Brief for Congress.* The Library of Congress. July 26, 2005.

80. http:///www.indiaexpress.com/full_story.php?content_id+72644

81. Sultan Shahin. *Asia Times.* Across the Divide—Part 2: Lifting the Veil. December 17, 2004.

82. Stephen Philip Cohen. "India, Pakistan, and Kashmir." *Journal of Strategic Studies.* Routledge Press. Vol. 25. No. 4. December 2002. p. 44.

83. K. Alan Kronstadt. "India-U.S. Relations." *Congressional Research Service Issue Brief for Congress.* The Library of Congress. July 15, 2005. p. 5.

84. http://www.geocities.com/capitolhill/lobby/8125/fpage.html. July 19, 2001.

85. See Article 32(4) of the Indian constitution.

86. Amitabh Mattoo. "India's 'Potential' Endgame in Kashmir." *India Review.* Special Issue on the Kashmir Question. Editor: Sumit Ganguly. p. 18.

87. Stephen Philip Cohen. "India, Pakistan, and Kashmir." *Journal of Strategic Studies.* Routledge Press. Vol. 25. No. 4. December 2002. p. 42.

88. Includes text from *Kashmir: A Way Forward.* February 2005.

7

Lessons Learned

For extremist Muslim movements to transition from violence to politics, they must come to understand that their interests are better served through a political process rather than via terror and violence. Rather than a strategic decision, this is more likely to occur as an evolutionary process. The United States has an interest in encouraging this process to go forward. Military action and diplomacy backed by the threat of force are options.[1] However, President George W. Bush's global war on terror has imparted a simple lesson: it is not possible to kill every adversary. Some combination of confrontation, coercion, and cooperation is required.

Extremist organizations can generally be categorized as (1) groups with illegitimate goals that use illegitimate means; (2) groups with legitimate goals that use illegitimate means; and, (3) groups with legitimate goals that use legitimate means. In the first category are foreign terrorist organizations (FTOs) that exist for the sole purpose of spreading chaos and destruction. They use violence indiscriminately including against civilians. In the second category are groups that respond to the denial of their rights by targeting both government assets and civilians. In the third category are democratic, self-determination and national liberation movements who suffer tyrannical rule and, lacking the political space to express their democratic aspirations, focus operations on abusive security forces and symbols of the regime.

The template of case studies in this book can be used to identify trends and develop strategies aimed at influencing the conduct of violent Muslim movements as well as the regimes that harbor or support them. Each situation is unique. Distinctions are not ironclad. Groups may often fit into more than one category or, as part of their transition, may be evolving from one category to another. Regardless of such trends, an effective strategy addressing groups that use the Qur'an to justify sensational violence must be based on a thorough understanding of Islam's influence.

A Religion of the Sword?

Murder in God's name both perplexes and deeply disturbs Western-ers. What are the roots of Muslim rage? What motivates fanatics to kill innocent civilians? Why do groups opt out of the political process to pursue their goals through sensational violence?

A debate is currently underway within Islam. Islamist proponents of violence are on one side. On the other are those who believe that ter-ror committed in the name of God contradicts the traditions and noble values of Islam. Like any religion, there is no absolute interpretation of religious doctrine.

It would be wrong to conclude that Islam condones violence. It would also be naïve to assume that Islamists are all persons of peace committed to propagating Islamic values of tolerance and charity. Plenty of evidence exists to the contrary, including many accounts of terrorists slaughter-ing civilians in Islam's name. It is a fact that many of today's terrorist organizations are comprised of Muslim fanatics who embrace religion as justification for violence and commit atrocities in the name of God.

That being said, it would also be wrong to assume that violence is endemic in Islam or that all Islamists are prone to violence or condone terrorism. The term "Islamist" can be used to characterize both peace-loving and militant Muslims. It describes an orthodox Muslim who is devoted to Islamic studies and an Islamic way of life. The term can also be ascribed to a fanatic who uses Islamic religious precepts to justify violence in service of a political ideology based on the conviction that the Qur'an should govern all legal, economic and social aspects of society and the state.[2]

Violence in Islam can be traced back to the Kharijites in the seventh century. It was also practiced by a sect called the Assassins in the Middle Ages. Ibn Taymiyya (1268-1328) was the first Muslim theologian to promulgate a radical ideology. Five hundred years later, Muhammad ibn Al Wahhab launched a period of Islamic revivalism (1703-1791). In the twentieth century, political Islam—"Islamism"—was formally introduced by "neo-fundamentalists [who] reinterpreted Islamic sources in response to challenges of the modern world."[3]

To neo-fundamentalists, Islam was always a religion of the sword. They believe that Islam condones violence when Muslims are denied the ability to practice their faith, when believers are forcibly subjugated, or when lands are seized.[4] According to the Qur'an, "Whoever transgresses against you, respond in kind."[5] Islam is the "conqueror of all religions"[6] and it is a sacred duty to "Slay [aggressors] wherever you find them."[7]

To mobilize the Muslim masses, Islamists equate suffering and injustice with lack of faith. They maintain that Islam is in decline because of irreverence and the reliance of Muslims on the West. Only a return to religious life will restore sanctity in this world and ensure heavenly rewards. Some Islamists successfully exploit feelings of anger to justify extremism and use oppression as an excuse for violence.

Such feelings are also exploited by Islamists who believe that it is the religious duty of all Muslims to finance jihad. They maintain that those that cannot engage directly in jihad are expected to provide financial to those who do. The Qur'an instructs believers to "Fight with your possessions and your souls in the way of Allah."[8]

Islamists reject innovation (*Bida*). They believe that any Muslim who deviates from Shari'a is impure (*Takfir*) and should be excommunicated. They promise that piety will bring about an end to corruption and misrule. In so doing, they reject constitutional democracy as the basis for secular government, which empowers human rulers over the word of God. Democracy is viewed as an innovation that ignores the laws of Islam by enshrining a belief system that transcends divine instruction. To them, Islam is the only alternative to ineffective, corrupt or authoritarian governments. "Give the people Islam, for Islam is the school of jihad, the religion of struggle; let them amend themselves and transform themselves into a powerful force, so that they may overthrow tyrannical regimes and set up an Islamic government."[9]

Al Qaeda goes one step further; Osama bin Laden espouses war with the "far enemy." He believes that killing Americans and their allies, whether civilian or military, is an obligation of every Muslim"[10] He endorses a "Third World War...between infidelity and Islam.[11] According to bin Laden, infidelity takes many forms. He also calls for jihad against the "near enemy" that includes secular Arab leaders who collaborate with the West particularly in the plunder of natural resources, as well as Muslim Shi'a whom he castigates for rebelling against the Sunni hierarchy.

Iran's President Mahmoud Ahmedinejad is also the proponent of a radical political theology, which maintains that that Islam and democracy are fundamentally incompatible. In an open letter to Bush (May 2006), he declared: "Liberalism and Western-style democracy have not been able to realize the ideals of humanity. Today, these two concepts have failed. Those with insight can already hear the sounds of the shattering and fall of the ideology and thoughts of liberal democratic systems.... Whether we like it or not, the world is gravitating towards faith in the Almighty [Allah] and justice and the will of God will prevail over all things."

Not all Muslims agree that Islam and democracy are incompatible or that Islam is a religion of the sword. Many Islamists reject fanaticism citing traditions of pluralism, cosmopolitanism, and open-mindedness within Islam. They affirm the religion's peaceful nature and reject the justification of violence using its teachings.

After Chechen terrorists massacred hundreds of innocent South Ossetian school children in 2004, Abdel Rahman Al Rashed, the managing editor of *Al Arabiya*, wrote: "It is a certain fact that not all Muslims are terrorists, but it is equally certain, and exceptionally painful that almost all terrorists are Muslims." Calling terrorism "shameful and degrading," he asked: "Does this tell us anything about ourselves, our societies and our culture?"[12] Al Rashed is as indignant about attacks on non-believers as he is about suicide bombers who attack Shi'a mosques in Iraq or wedding parties in Jordan.

Muslim clerics have also weighed in on the debate—many on the side of moderation. They note that Qur'an opens with an invocation of God's mercy and repeatedly urges Muslims to practice patience, compassion and kindness.[13] Meeting in Mecca a few months after 9/11, the World Muslim Council rejected the link between Islam and terrorism. Its declaration underscored that the word Islam is derived from the Arabic word for peace (*Salam*) and the Qur'an portrays God as merciful and compassionate. "God does not love those who do wrong."[14]

The Qur'an states, "Islam prohibits terrorism, forbids aggression, and affirms the meaning of justice, tolerance and the importance of dialogue and communication between people."[15] "Fight in the way of God with those who fight you, but aggress not: God loves not aggressors."[16] It forbids murder and suicide: "Nor take life, which Allah has made sacred, except for just cause."[17] "Do not kill yourselves."[18] The Qur'an also encourages Muslims to treat others with justice, securing for them safety in Muslim territories and imposing a blood payment on anyone who violates their rights. "O mankind! We created you from a single pair of a male and a female, and made you into nations and tribes, that you may know each other."[19]

Many Islamists claim that jihad has nothing to do with violence. They assert that jihad is really a struggle to extend the boundaries of peace, purify Islam, and create a just social order. They distinguish between "Greater Jihad," which is the personal struggle of each individual to suppress sins and live a righteous life inspired by the teachings of Mohammed, and "Lesser Jihad," which is warfare.

Dealing with Islamists requires an understanding of Islam's nuances. Effective strategies must be based on in-depth knowledge encompassing historical and cultural circumstances. Calibrating the right balance between confrontation, coercion, and cooperation is essential to convincing Muslim extremists that their goals are better served via the political process than through sensational violence. Both hard and soft power are needed.

Confrontation

Preemptive action, preventive war, and targeted killings are the primary tools of confrontation. Though international law opines on each, policymakers do not make decisions based solely on conformity with international law. First and foremost, U.S. leaders are committed to America's security. They adopt policies that advance the national interest.

Preemptive Action

Every U.S. president has had the option—indeed the responsibility—to use all necessary means for preempting an attack against the United States. No president would hesitate to use America's unparalleled military might in response to an imminent threat. Nor would any president hesitate to strike a sovereign state harboring a non-state actor that posed a threat either because of its conventional weapons or WMD capabilities.

Nine days after the heinous attacks of 9/11, Bush addressed the U.S. Congress affirming that the United States would no longer proceed reactively given the magnitude of potential harm that could result from the intersection of terrorism and technology. Bush threw down the gauntlet, declaring:

> We must adapt the concept of imminent threat to the capabilities and objectives of today's adversaries. Rogue states and terrorists do not seek to attack us using conventional means. They know such attacks would fail. Instead, they rely on acts of terror and, potentially, the use of weapons of mass destruction—weapons that can be easily concealed, delivered covertly, and used without warning.[20]

Bush asserted that the right to self-defense was enshrined in international law. Published in September 2002, Bush's National Security Strategy included the Doctrine of Preemption affirming America's right to destroy its adversaries before they could attack. "We do not create terrorism by fighting the terrorists," explained Bush. "We invite terrorism by ignoring them. And we will defeat the terrorists by capturing and killing them abroad [and] removing their safe havens."[21] Bush maintained that a formal doctrine of preemption was more effective than deterrence. His remarks put both terrorists and countries that harbor them on notice: the United States would take action.

Citing the UN Charter, which establishes "the inherent right to self-defense of states," Bush insisted that it was both legally correct and morally justified for the United States to attack Afghanistan and dislodge the Taliban. Furthermore, he maintained that the United States would be justified in using military action when its territory risked attack, its interests were threatened, or when its citizens were at-risk. However, the case for preemption is not so clear. Ambiguities in international law cast doubt on the core tenet of Bush's National Security Strategy.

Prior to 9/11, the commonly held opinion was that the right to self-defense does not justify a preemptive strike absent an immediate threat. However, noting that customary law also includes the intent to establish new rules (*opinio juris*), the Bush administration argued that the attack on Afghanistan itself brought about a change in international law due to the widespread support it received from other states. This is, at best, debatable. For a specific state action to change international law, the action must be universally approved. Such was not the case when the United States attacked Afghanistan as both Iran and Syria objected.

Pronouncing the Doctrine of Preemption with such fanfare also galvanized detractors of the United States. Bush's focus on necessity while ignoring proportionality alarmed America's allies who were already concerned by his avowed preference for unilateralism without the legitimacy that comes from an international coalition or sanction by international law. They also worried that other countries might take a page from Bush's playbook to justify a crackdown against internal dissent or to legitimize acts of aggression against neighboring states where opposition groups reside. They warned that trumpeting the Doctrine of Preemption ran the risk of undermining its strategic benefits by causing countries to initiate measures aimed at protecting their assets from preemptive attack.

Preventive War

Conflating preemption with preventive war further exacerbated concerns. Bush maintained that gathering threats posed special risks, especially when rogue regimes have WMD or when terror groups seek to acquire the world's deadliest weapons. He justified preventive war to keep such gathering threats from increasing over time. However, Bush ignored an essential distinction. Preemption is justifiable when a state is actually threatened, whereas preventive war involves the use of force when there is no imminent threat.

The 2002 National Security Strategy acknowledged the distinction between preemptive action and preventive war declaring:

> The United States will always proceed deliberately, weighing the consequences of our actions. To support preemptive options, we will (i) build better, more integrated intelligence capabilities to provide timely, accurate information on threats, wherever they may emerge; (ii) coordinate closely with allies to form a common assessment of the most dangerous threats, and; (iii) continue to transform our military forces to ensure our ability to conduct rapid and precise operations to achieve decisive results. The purpose of our actions will always be to eliminate a specific threat to the United States or our allies and friends. The reasons for our actions will be clear, the force measured, and the cause just....In keeping with our heritage and principles, we do not use strength to press for unilateral advantage. We seek instead to create a balance of power that favors human freedom.[22]

The Iraq debacle cast doubt on this assertion. Bush violated his administration's own guidelines by confusing an actual threat with the perception that Iraq represented a growing danger. The fact that no WMDs were found underscored that invading Iraq was a choice and not a necessity. Going to war was based on assumptions that turned out to be wrong. It confirmed that Iraq was a preventive war rather than a preemptive action. It also contradicted relevant international law embodied in the UN Charter, which stipulates: "All Members shall refrain in their international relations from the threat or use of force against the territorial integrity or political independence of any State."[23]

Blurring the lines between preemption and preventive war is a grave risk to international peace and security, especially when the proponent enjoys unparalleled military superiority. It also casts doubt on the justification for humanitarian intervention to prevent atrocities and genocide, as affirmed in the UN Doctrine on "The Responsibility To Protect" Ignoring the distinction between preemption and prevention risks war without end.

Targeted Killings

Targeted killings are distinct from the extra-judicial execution of an individual who is under administrative or criminal detention. Targeted killings are also different from assassination of an individual for his or her political beliefs. However, targeted killings and assassinations share the common feature that they ignore the possibility of arrest as well as other forms of law enforcement.

Both extra-judicial execution and political assassination are forbidden under international law; U.S. statutes also forbid them. Not only are extra-judicial execution and assassination wrong, both are counterproductive. While extra-judicial execution or assassination may eliminate an individual, they rarely neutralize the cause that the individual championed. To the contrary, they lead to intensified zealotry, fervor, and commitment to the cause. Others almost always stand ready to replace those who have fallen.

The Fourth Geneva Convention and the 1977 First Additional Protocol allow targeted killings when all reasonable alternatives have been exhausted. The Convention and Protocol supposed the argument that targeted killings fall into a separate legal category when they are used for self-defense or to prevent the killing of civilians. Moreover, the Laws of War legitimize targeted killings when there is no other chance to prevent attack by, for example, arresting the perpetrator. Both in law and practice, targeted killings are different from a policy of random violence whose goal is to inspire fear and intimidation among non-combatants. Every effort must be made to avoid collateral damage or, make it proportional to the harm intended.[24]

The distinction between "armed combatants" and "civilians" is also relevant when applying the Laws of War. Armed combatants are legitimate military targets because they take part in hostilities. When, for example, a civilian suicide bomber dons an explosive vest, he or she becomes an armed combatant and, as such, a legitimate target. Individuals who provide infrastructure, expertise, coordination or otherwise enable the terrorist's attack are also legitimate targets. When civilians exhort for violence, they also lose their protected status and become legitimate targets for as long as they exhort or take part in hostilities.

The definition of "international armed conflict" and "organized armed groups" also has bearing. According to the International Committee of the Red Cross, an international armed conflict exists when organized armed groups possess several characteristics including: a military force under responsible command, possession over part of the national territory, and the characteristics of a state including authority over persons within the territory.[25] The targeted killing of an individual involved in an international armed conflict and belonging to an organized armed group is a legitimate act of self-defense.

Factors that influence the decision to conduct a targeted killing go well beyond international law. Decision-makers must consider whether its short-term benefits enhance overall security or whether they are counter-productive by fueling a cycle of violence and revenge. Targeted killings run the risk of exacerbating insecurity when harm to innocent civilians is excessive or when killings, undertaken as a deliberate state policy, inspire new recruits to fill the shoes of those who have been killed. Targeted killings may deal with the immediate threat, but they also increase the number of one's enemies and their desire to do harm.

Whereas targeted killings are an option during armed conflict or when confronting armed groups they must not become habit or state policy. The practice should be used rarely and only under dire circumstances when no other option exists and when there is a clear evidence that the targeted killing will successfully prevent an attack. To do otherwise increases insecurity and is counter-productive.

Coercion

Coercive tactics are intended to ratchet up the pressure in order to induce a change in behavior. Coercion can take many forms by targeting an organization's leadership, financing, or communications. Coercion may also focus on countries that aid and abet violent groups or harbor terrorist organizations.

Sanctions

Comprehensive sanctions are a blunt instrument. They have little impact on rogue states that simply do not care when sanctions are imposed. Moreover, they rarely achieve the desired result. Comprehensive sanctions are never airtight. Entrenched elites often enrich themselves while civil society goes without. Though sanctions often cause unnecessary hardship to civilians, they can actually strengthen the regime by motivating the affected polity to rally around political leaders that the sanctions are intended to undermine.

Alternatively, "smart sanctions" target individuals while seeking to minimize hardship to the society as a whole. By holding individuals accountable, smart sanctions tend to be more effective in achieving the desired result while minimizing the unintended consequences of a more sweeping approach. Sometimes the threat of smart sanctions can be more effective in modifying an individual's behavior than actually imposing them.

Sanctions targeting an individual or corporation typically include a travel ban as well as the freezing of assets in overseas banks. Smart sanctions are not only imposed on the individual of concern. They are most effective when the individual's family members, business partners and inner circle are treated similarly.

Banning the sale of luxury goods, such as high-end automobiles, alcohol, perfume and caviar can also have impact on the government and its inner circle. While embargoing imports potentially impacts consumers nationwide, a ban on luxury goods usually affects only that portion of the population with the means to afford them.

Individuals should not be sanctioned willy-nilly. It is important to first conduct research that identifies their passport numbers and other data such as information on their corporations so that, when sanctions are imposed, they target the right individual and the right enterprise. This problem can be especially vexing when sanctioning individuals from the Middle East where many persons have the same or similar names.

In addition to sanctions on individuals and corporations under their control, other steps can ratchet up the pressure. Commercial banks should suspend operations in countries that sponsor terror. In order to increase the government's isolation by squeezing its access to credit. Sanctions targeting foreign companies that do business with state sponsors of terror also have an impact. Disallowing a presidential waiver would eliminate an important loophole.

Smart sanctions may also be effective by promoting factionalism that can lead to the splintering of organizations or regimes. Factions within an organization usually arise between generations, as well as between ideologues and pragmatists. Factions may also arise between in-country leaders and those in exile. Not only do those living outside the country tend to be more hardline. They also have a propensity to monopolize assets by collecting taxes from the field and then using those funds to support their government in exile or subsidize personal lifestyles.

Multilateral approaches always make sanctions more effective. When the United States imposes bilateral sanctions on its own, other countries are quick to take advantage and fill the breach. Multilateral measures require cooperation to monitor the movements, contacts, and financial activities of a suspect individual or group. Interpol, the International Organization for Migration, the World Customs Organization, the International Civil Aviation Organization, and the International Maritime Organization are indispensible when it comes to monitoring and enforcement.

Though multilateral sanctions are better, they are far from perfect. Sanctions-busting typically takes place. It is also difficult to maintain multilateral sanctions over a long period of time. Weaknesses of the international system and limits to international cooperation become more glaring the longer that sanctions are in place.

Financing

Financial intelligence can be used to choke off financial flows, disrupt hawala banking, and curtail fund raising at its source by targeting foundations and individuals who raise money to support violence and terror. Post-9/11, the Bush administration sought financial information from central banks and members of the global banking industry, which sponsor the Society for Interbank Financial Telecommunication (Swift). The United States saw Swift, which handles 2.5 billion financial messages annually between banks, brokerages, stock exchanges, and other institutions, as an essential resource for mapping terrorist webs and conducting link analysis on individuals and organizations of concern.[26]

A firestorm of controversy erupted when it was reported that the Bush administration was monitoring private transactions without individual court-approved warrants or subpoenas. Revelations about Swift struck a raw nerve; they ensued after disclosures that the National Security Agency was invoking its "state secrets" privilege to amass domestic phone records and eavesdrop without warrants. Civil rights and privacy advocates invoked the Fourth Amendment and the 1978 Right to Financial Privacy Act to point out that link analysis can implicate innocent persons who inadvertently deal with a terrorist.

Using Swift was especially controversial in Europe. Privacy advocates charged that use of the program violated the European Union's privacy rules. Revelations came after reports that the CIA was operating secret detention facilities in Eastern Europe and kidnapping suspects in European countries for rendition to countries that use torture as an interrogation method.

U.S. officials defended the practice of mining data from Swift citing previous experience with administrative subpoenas under the 1977 International Emergency Economic Powers Act. As a messaging service not a financial institution, they maintained that Swift was not protected by U.S. laws restricting government access to individual financial records. They pointed out that accessing Swift enabled them to secure invaluable information while abiding by traditional safeguards against abuse and privacy intrusions. Moreover, the Justice Department insisted that individuals suspected of being foreign terrorists were exempt from privacy laws.

Though financial intelligence is an essential tool in countering terrorism, measures are needed to mitigate the potential for abuse. To this end, searches must be based on credible information derived through variety of sources such as telephone chatter and email intercepts that result from an ongoing investigation. As agreed with the European Union, the program should be used only for counterterrorism and data will be retained for a prescribed period.

In addition, the U.S. Treasury Department needs to work with the Congress to develop new rules governing data mining for U.S.-based banks and their overseas affiliates. Authorizing legislation would be more effective than relying on a national security letter to exploit the grey areas of existing law. Given the concern of European privacy advocates, central banks should also be kept informed so that they can exercise effective oversight.

Adopted several weeks after 9/11, UN Security Council Resolution 1373 put forward multilateral approaches to gathering financial intelligence. UNSC Res. 1373 set-up the Counter-Terrorism Committee (CTC) to coordinate assistance to states striving to fulfill their obligations but lacking the capacity to meet international best practices, codes and standards. The CTC was also mandated to evaluate the extent to which states have implemented their international commitments.

The CTC's performance has fallen far short of expectations. To enhance its impact, the CTC needs to undertake more proactive outreach through its global information network and intensify its dialogue with states aimed at strengthening the facilitation of technical assistance. The CTC could expand its roster of experts and make them available to conduct needs assessments. Experts could help draft model legislation in the fields of financial law, customs, immigration, and extradition law incorporating both the principles and body of international law in countering terrorism.

Assistance should also be expanded to strengthen the executive machinery of states needed to prevent recruitment, movement, and the establishment of safe havens. Police, law enforcement, and intelligence agencies need training and capacity building. Customs, immigration, and border control agencies should also be bolstered. In addition, the CTC should work with states to raise awareness and build political support towards the goal of ensuring that they adopt the twelve international conventions and protocols related to terrorism.[27]

The CTC conducts regular evaluations of states using compliance and capacity as the primary benchmarks. In the spirit of transparency, the CTC's evaluation should be made public and countries "outed" that fail to meet reporting requirements or that lag far behind with implementation. Opprobrium is not enough. Non-compliance warrants some penalty. Temporary suspension of membership in the UN General Assembly as well as Bretton-Woods institutions could here be considered.[28]

The United States should take the lead in publishing a "watch list" of international charities involved in fund raising, recruitment, or assisting violent groups. Terror takes money. Therefore, prohibiting financial transfers can be an effective counterterrorism tool. When an organization is labeled an FTO by the Treasury Department or an individual is identified as a person of concern, formal channels for transferring funds to and from the United States are denied. When formal channels are closed, the FTO is drained of resources or forced to move its money using slower and more risky methods involving couriers carrying cash across borders.

Banking cooperation should extend to financial institutions worldwide. The United States can cooperate with like-minded countries by encouraging them to adopt national legislation requiring the closure of charities and banning the transfer of funds to groups on the watch-list. Cracking down on such groups could include arresting their officials, seizing their assets, and closing their offices. Follow-up measures are needed to prevent charities from simply shutting down their operations and reconstituting under a different name with the same leadership and agenda.

Foundations as well as suspect individuals and corporations require scrutiny. However, action should be taken only against those with verifiable links to terrorist financing. It is easy for a charity to make a mistake and get listed. Getting off the list is much more difficult.

Hawala poses a unique challenge as an informal, grass-roots financial system widespread in the Arab and Muslim world. Mobilizing local law enforcement is the only way to restrict hawala transactions. Particularly in the Gulf States and South Asia where hawala banking is widespread, the United States should encourage the adoption of legislation to restrict unregistered financial transactions for which there is no record or control.

Local clerics use their pulpits to raise funds for educational and humanitarian activities (*Zakat*). Some clerics also collect funds under the pretense of humanitarian action, that are actually used to support militant activities and as payment to the families of martyrs. They also use their pulpits to incite hatred and intolerance. In the event that such clerics are based in Western countries, they should be prosecuted or expelled. When they are based in their country of origin, local law enforcement should prosecute them or extradite them to stand trial in countries where their funds were used to pay for terrorist attacks.

Communications

The first amendment right of free speech is at the core of America's open society and democratic governance. Consistent with American values, U.S. counter-terrorism efforts must not abridge basic freedoms enshrined in the U.S. Constitution or international covenants. A dilemma arises when the instruments of free speech—such as the World Wide Web—are used by anti-democratic groups to further their extremist agendas and murderous goals. It would be hypocritical and wrong to disable websites simply because their content is undesirable. However, there is a red line that—when crossed—requires actions against websites that are used to inspire or coordinate violence.

The Web has become a vital part of the communications strategy for Muslim extremists. Online forums and chat rooms have more than propaganda value. By disseminating on-line libraries of sacred texts, they have also become the intellectual foundation for the worldwide jihadist movement. Extremist groups use Web-based audio and video messages to incite hatred, raise funds, and for recruitment. Encrypted messages may also be embedded in websites to facilitate the command and control necessary for coordinating terror operations.

It is appropriate to block access, subvert, or disable FTO websites when they are used for nefarious purposes. Unleashing viruses, computer worms, and other rogue programs on suspect computers can help address security risks. A "Denial of Service Attack" is one of the most effective ways to shut down a website. In this case, the host servers are subjected to tens or hundreds of thousands of simultaneous hits rendering it impossible for the site to respond to other requests. The critical mass can be reached by taking over computers via "Trojan horse" software surreptitiously installed on remote computers for the purpose of attacking the targeted server. Tampering with the domain name server record is another way to "force-redirect traffic" to another site. It is also possible to break into the target site's servers in order to change or deface the content of a website. This can be done by launching a brute force password assault wherein the target is hit with thousands of successive login attempts until the right combination is realized. It is also possible to "keylog" software in order to capture the keystrokes and passwords of the site administrator.

Disabling or corrupting a website is not as easy as it sounds. Webmasters can command computers from a distance or route their activities through off-site machines anywhere in the world making it extremely difficult to pinpoint cyber risks.

After 9/11, the Federal Bureau of Investigation (FBI) expanded its cooperation with other domestic law enforcement agencies by forming Cyber Action Teams (CATs)—including agents, computer forensic experts, and computer code specialists associated with the FBI's science and technology branch. CATs work closely with international partners by providing training, technical and investigative assistance, and equipment to cyber crime units within the national police of partner countries. Posting CATs and other computer crime experts at U.S. embassies and consulates around the world would enhance relations with local cyber law enforcement. Experts could also assist drafting legislation allowing for the seizure and spontaneous inspection of hard drives when there is need for urgent action.

Some European countries take a more pro-active approach to cyber terror than the United States. However, British courts convict people merely for possessing militant or terror-related materials on their hard drives, prosecuting online terrorism is far more difficult in the United States. Though prosecutors may bring charges in U.S. courts under statutes governing criminal solicitation, they are far more likely to succeed if specific plans to commit violence can be documented. It is hard to get a conviction unless there is a plan for attack or evidence that the cyber terrorist is under the direction or control of an FTO.

Cooperation

Confrontation and coercion are necessary options when dealing with the world's most dangerous groups. The United States cannot, however, kill all its adversaries. Nor should it try. A useful approach includes co-opting groups that have a nascent interest in the democratic process assisting the or democratization of regimes on whose territory they reside.

Decades of successful democracy assistance as well as recent experiences yield some guiding principles. They proceed from the recognition that America's role in democracy assistance should always be to stand behind, not in front of democracy movements. The United States should not seek to "lead" democratic revolutions or "teach" about democracy. The United States can make an effective contribution by acting as a catalyst for and supporter of change.

- *Be Patient:* Democratization is a process, not an event. It is based on evolutionary rather than revolutionary change and cannot be achieved over a short period of time or on a timetable.

- *Maintain Modesty:* There are limits to the ability of the United States to influence events; democracy assistance efforts should proceed accordingly. Pro-democracy activists risk being discredited within their countries if it appears that they are acting as agents of the U.S.

- *Tread Softly:* External actors can help create an environment of change, but domestic factors ultimately drive the democratization process in ways that are consistent with local conditions, history, and culture.

- *Localize Leadership:* Democratic reforms are driven by societal demand. The participation of local stakeholders is critical to the sustenance and legitimacy of democratic institutions.

- *Recognize the Limits of Military Intervention*: Initiating armed conflict creates difficult conditions for implementing effective democracy assistance, undermines US credibility, and raises suspicion about all forms of intervention. Although the military has contributed to democratization, the goal of democracy must not be used as a post-facto justification for armed conflict.[29]

Whereas free and fair elections are essential to the transition from violence to politics, elections are merely part of a process to convince groups that their interests can be served through the political process. To be effective, democracy assistance must take a long-term approach that emphasizes building democratic institutions, such as an independent judiciary and a freely elected legislature, strengthening civil society, including an independent media, and creating a self-reliant and entrepreneurial middle class.

Elections

Elections are about the peaceful transfer of power, enabling citizens to determine the policy direction of their government. However, they are not a panacea. Nor are they the litmus test of a country's democratic development. For countries emerging from authoritarian rule, premature elections may have the negative affect of strengthening hardliners and institutionalizing illiberal governance. There is also the potential for abuse when controlling authorities use their resources to manipulate the Electoral Management Body and pre-determine the outcome.

That being said, elections are an important milestone in the democratization process. There are few more thrilling sights than voters waiting to cast their ballot after suffering decades of repression. For example, the first election in South Africa after the end of apartheid was a truly celebratory moment. The resolve of Iraqi voters to overcome threats and intimidation was an inspiration to freedom loving people the world over.

No elections are, however, better than bogus or rigged elections. Unless voters are convinced that elections are free and fair, the ballot can spark widespread protest that those in power that to justify a crackdown and stymie democratic development. Voters who feel cheated and disenfranchised become radicalized. Such was the case in 1987 when India's manipulation of elections drove Kashmiris into the embrace of militant groups. Leaders who come to power in tainted elections lack the credibility and popular support to implement real reforms.

Universal suffrage for both voters and candidates is the most important measure of credible elections in a representative democracy. Freedom of speech and equal access to independent media is essential. So is an election commission that operates without interference from the government. Staffing local branches of the national election commission with community representatives who have a reputation for honesty and impartiality enhances the credibility of results.

Several elements must be in place for elections to function smoothly. To ensure an election's integrity, local and international election monitors should be allowed to work without hindrance. Their mere presence can guard against election fraud, ensure transparent ballot counting, and help verify the accuracy of results. In addition to electoral laws, regulations are needed governing the formation and operations of political parties. Democracy would be strengthened in countries such as Turkey by reducing the threshold requirement for smaller political parties to assume seats in the national parliament. Proportional representation, as opposed to a system of party lists, is desirable as it allows smaller or regional parties to have a greater voice in the political process.

Beyond elections, checks and balances that distribute and regulate the use of power are essential to good governance. Meaningful checks and balances on the executive can be achieved through term limits, as well as through statutes providing for expanded parliamentary oversight of government bodies and political figures. Measures are also needed to prevent the co-mingling of authority between the state and the ruling political party. Effective governance obviates the possibility of a state within a state, which, as evidenced in Lebanon, leads to factionalism, instability, and conflict.

A dilemma arises when Islamists try to use the democratic political process to accumulate power and then impose laws that are fundamentally undemocratic. Democracy's advocates must be careful not to have a knee-jerk reaction against Islamic parties. There is a critical distinction between Islamists, who seek to impose their extremist views on others, and parties with an Islamic orientation that respect the difference between governance and spiritual guidance. Islamists should not be barred from political participation just because of their religious beliefs. Nor should parties with an Islamic orientation be excluded from the political process. It is possible to embody Muslim values without adopting extremist interpretations of Islamic law. For example, the leaders of the Justice and Development Party in Turkey have an Islamic orientation but they have done more to democratize Turkey and bring the country into compliance with standards of the European Union than its predecessor parties have over decades. Political participation is a boon for transparency as it requires Islamic parties to go beyond slogans. Publishing their platforms on Shari'a, women's rights, and economic development reveal where they stand on the issues.

In response to those who maintain that democracy and Islam are incompatible, Muslim theologians at leading institutions, such as Al Azhar University in Egypt, should raise their voices to affirm the compatibility of Islam and constitutional democracy. Rather than use the mosque to propagate extremism, local clerics should disseminate the teachings of moderate scholars. Civil society groups can also play a key role spreading a message of tolerance, pluralism and diversity. The Islamic process of consultation is entirely consistent with democratic debate.

The United States faces a real conundrum. It wants to support democratization but confronts a dilemma when non-democratic and unfriendly candidates win free and fair elections. In several instances, the United States lost credibility by advocating elections and then refusing to deal with the winner. Pressing the Palestinian Authority to hold elections but refusing to recognize Hamas did little to burnish the Bush administration's credentials as a champion of democracy or as a mediator of Middle East peace. It convinced many Palestinians that Bush's democracy agenda was based on expediency rather than principle.

A debate has emerged in the United States between the proponents of stability and the supporters of democracy assistance. The former believe that democracy assistance distracts the United States from its core strategic interests: fighting terrorism, enhancing economic growth, and securing reliable energy supplies (even when they come from anti-democratic regimes). The latter maintain that there is no trade-off between a policy that emphasizes democracy assistance and the promotion of U.S. security and economic interests. Claims of maintaining stability are too often the last refuge for despots desperate to maintain power. While there is often genuine tension between maintaining stability and promoting democracy, particularly in the short term, ultimately these two goals are intertwined and interdependent.[30] Supporting autocratic rulers—such as Mubarak or Musharraf—convinces the affected polity that the United States places a higher priority on stability than on democracy. U.S. efforts worldwide would be more credible if they focused on the rule of law to advance human rights and realize local aspirations—not America's agenda.

The Rule of Law

The rule of law is a shorthand term used to characterize constitutional and statutory measures that ensure the fundamental social, political, and economic rights of individuals. It is essential to preserving and promoting the right of people to freely determine their own destiny. It guarantees freedom of expression, belief, and association, free and competitive elections, respect for the inalienable rights of individuals and minorities, and free communications media.[31] Its cornerstone is an independent judiciary with the power, authority, and resources to hold officials accountable. In democratic societies, the rule of law is more than the judiciary. It includes the entire justice system from law enforcement through prosecution and detention.

In addition, the rule of law provides a legal framework governing economic development, trade, and foreign investment. It is also essential for combating corruption that, left unchecked, disillusions civil society and has a corrosive affect on democracy. Anti-corruption laws hold police, judges, and elected officials accountable. More than legal recourse, combating corruption can be advanced through administrative measures such as shrinking the bureaucracy and downsizing the public sector. Providing adequate salaries and benefits to security personnel also helps discourage plunder and corruption.

The Bush administration's war on terror raised doubt about the commitment of the United States to the rule of law. To be sure, the United States is entitled to defend itself by rooting out terrorists before they attack. However, its use of state security courts and the rendition of persons to countries that practice torture invite criticism that the United States violates norms of due process in service of its counter-terrorism goals. Cutting corners also sets a bad example for new democracies that are trying to balance stability requirements with the goal of fostering meaningful long-term reform. Sacrificing rights in service of security also has the unintended consequence of fueling anti-Americanism and undermining security by encouraging a new generation of antagonists wanting to harm the United States.

To walk its talk, the United States must close state security courts and allow observers at every stage of the proceedings when prosecuting individuals for terrorism. Holding terror suspects as enemy combatants at Guantanamo exacerbates the view of the Muslim world as well as of many U.S. allies that the United States practices a double standard when it comes to enforcing the rule of law. Only complete transparency and adherence to international norms can ensure that the juridical process of the United States sets a standard to be emulated worldwide.

Truth, Justice, and Reconciliation

International humanitarian and human rights law evolved over the twentieth century. The Hague Convention (1907), the Nuremberg Tribunal Charter (1945), the United Nations Convention on the Prevention and Punishment of the Crime of Genocide (1948), and the four Geneva Conventions have come to define state obligations when it comes to investigating and providing redress to victims of human rights abuse, atrocities, or genocide.

As political transition unfolds following a period of violence or repression, a society is often confronted with the difficult legacy of human rights abuse. In attempting to come to terms with past crimes, government officials and non-government advocates are likely to consider both judicial and non-judicial accountability mechanisms, and are increasingly employing a combination of both. A society in political transition often confronts difficult challenges addressing its past—whether it is seeking to prosecute individual perpetrators, make reparations to victims of state sponsored violence, convene truth commissions, implement institutional reforms or remove human rights abusers from positions of power.[32]

Truth-telling is the starting point. Not only does truth-telling acknowledge individual suffering. It also has a healing affect on the teller. Shining a light on past events helps prevent them from happening again and breaks the cycle of violence that typically afflicts war-torn societies: "Reconciliation as encounter suggests that space for acknowledging the past and envisioning the future is the necessary ingredient for reframing the present. For this to happen, people must find ways to encounter themselves and their enemies, their hopes and their fears."[33] Truth-telling does not, however, derogate the need for justice and institutional redress. Unless there is transparency and accountability, victims are condemned to a perpetual state of victimization. The truth and reconciliation process is not a substitute for accountability through trials. Reconciliation is delayed when justice is deferred.

Since 1973, more than twenty truth and reconciliation commissions (TRCs) have been established around the world. Most were created by governments and authorized by national parliaments. Some were established by international organizations and a few by NGOs. Different countries have tried to balance amnesty and accountability in different ways. TRCs emphasizing amnesty use confessions to construct a narrative of the truth. Alternatively, TRCs that prefer prosecution over amnesty emphasize that justice is the best deterrent to prevent victimizers from committing future crimes. Unless individuals are held accountable, the tendency exists to hold an entire society or system responsible.

Harmonizing the balance between amnesty and accountability varies from case to case. The right balance requires multi-stakeholder dialogue—involving former combatants, civil society, local politicians, and national figures—that gives everyone the opportunity to present their views and assume ownership of the outcome. Civil society can serve as the watchdog of reform and the guardian of political progress by playing a central role at every stage of the TRC's design, development, and implementation.[34]

Every post-conflict country needs a strategy to disarm, demobilize, and reintegrate (DDR) former combatants or groups that have abandoned violence to pursue their goals through politics. Disarmament strategies include choking off the supply of small arms via measures that prevent weapons sales by indigenous security personnel who often play a double game. Regional consortia can help control arms trafficking. Regional cooperation also extends to shutting down training camps and other guerilla infrastructure based in neighboring countries. Weapons buy-back programs and assigning individuals, not units or cells, into formal security structures are essential components of DDR.

DDR also applies to state-sponsored paramilitaries and death squads that will only disband when they see that their official sponsors are serious about terminating them. Committing abuses in the government's name, paramilitaries have used tactics such as assassinating political opposition leaders and burning businesses owned by persons suspected of supporting regime opponents. Police should protect merchants from extortion by both paramilitaries as well as armed insurgent groups. It is better to focus on ceasefires and truces that include disarmament procedures than comprehensive peace agreements that are more difficult to negotiate and even harder to implement when both paramilitaries and insurgents are involved.

During the difficult and tumultuous transition to democracy, outgoing regimes fear that their successor will bring them to account for past abuses. Post-authoritarian governments must not be deterred. Their failure to address past violations risks undermining the rule of law as well as the legitimacy of new democratic institutions. The TRC can be an essential instrument to consolidate political progress and democratic reform.

Minority Rights

Conflict can often be attributed to ethnic or religious groups that turns to violence when they lack recourse through the political system. Addressing their grievances can put them on the political track. For this to occur, they must be convinced that political participation can enable their aspirations and that effective institutions exist to safeguard their interests.

The best way to advance minority rights is through a comprehensive bill of rights that benefits all citizens. The two over-riding issues under international law are equality and non-discrimination. Translated into juridical standards, they are part and parcel of all of the major human rights treaties.[35] When it comes to minority ethnic and religious groups, both protection and promotion are required.

The International Covenant on Economic, Social and Cultural Rights holds: "In those states in which ethnic, religious or linguistic minorities exist, persons belonging to such minorities shall not be denied the right, in community with the other members of their group, to enjoy their own culture, to profess and practice their own religion, or to use their own language."[36] According to the UN Human Rights Commission, "Individual rights ... depend on the ability of the minority group to maintain its culture, language or religion. Positive measures may be necessary to protect the identity of a minority and the rights of its members to enjoy and develop their culture and language and to practice their religion, in community with the other members of the group."[37] The 1992 UN General Assembly Declaration on Minority Rights requires that states recognize minority rights in their national laws and policies;[38] adopt legislative and financial measures to ensure the effective implementation and enforcement;[39] and undertake regular evaluations, planning, and oversight to ensure accountability and provide effective remedies when minority rights are violated.[40]

Minorities often assert their right to self-determination when the state fails to advance their interests. Enshrined in international law, the principle of self-determination appears in the UN Charter (1946) and the Declaration of Universal Human Rights (1948). During the decolonization period, self-determination evolved from a "principle" to a "right." The Declaration on Colonial Countries (1960) states, "All peoples have the right to self-determination. By virtue of that right, they freely determine their political status and freely pursue their economic, social and cultural development." The Declaration on Friendly States (1970) says, "Every State has the duty to promote self-determination in order to bring about a speedy end to colonialism. The International Covenant on Economic, Social and Cultural Rights (1966) stipulates that, "(All peoples) should determine their political status and pursue economic, social and cultural development."

While the right of peoples to self-determination is embodied in both treaties and customary international law, this right is by no means unequivocal. In numerous instances, the right to self-determination is asserted by a people but goes unrecognized by states that are first and foremost committed to stability and defense against threats to their sovereignty.

Short of breaking up the state or establishing a state within a state, minority rights can be achieved through a variety of constitutional remedies that promote meaningful self-governance by decentralizing power to regional or local authorities. A growing body of autonomy precedents provides guidance to minority groups with historical ties to a specific territory and a history of self-governance.[41] In a federal or confederal arrangement, states retain powers not specifically granted to the central government.[42] Other models invest all powers in the central government unless specifically allocated to federal states.[43] Chapter XI of the UN Charter stipulates that non-self-governing territories "can achieve the full measure of self government" as a sovereign state or through free association with and/or integration with an independent state "on the basis of complete equality."[44] Each arrangement seeks to enhance stakeholder participation and thereby reduce the possibility of conflict escalation.

Security Reform

A stable society is a harmonious one that welcomes diversity and the unfettered expression of different views. Autocrats may believe that repressive measures enhance stability. They are wrong. Stability is ill-served by repression.

Heavy-handed tactics may create the appearance of stability in the short-term, but they almost always backfire.

Accountable for their conduct, organs of the security sector are established to protect civil liberties, uphold human dignity, and serve the public good. They are entitled to intervene in the private lives of citizens only under specific circumstances. The security services in democracies are subordinate to civilian authority. A clear delineation of responsibilities between security branches helps to promote professionalism and prevent their politicization. Power is not arbitrary. It must be exercised proportional to risk with punishment extended only after an impartial judicial process determines guilt.

Of course, extraordinary circumstances require extraordinary means. Martial law may be necessary when violence spirals out of control. However, the decision to declare a state of emergency must never be taken lightly. It should always be a last resort. When declaring a state of emergency, it is best to target well-defined conflict zones rather than whole regions. At checkpoints, security personnel should avoid gratuitous confrontation that causes humiliation. Lock-downs and collective punishment antagonize civilians and are to be avoided. So are provocative security practices, such as outlawing the call to prayer or blocking access of worshipers to holy sites and shrines.

Human rights training of security personnel guards against abuses by helping them distinguish between legitimate law enforcement activities and human rights offenses. Instruction on the norms that govern arrest, detention, and the use of force is also beneficial. Truncheons, stunguns, rubber bullets, and live ammunition should only be used under special circumstances and never on peaceful pro-democracy demonstrators. Judges also need the training and know-how to enforce laws and regulations so that every citizen can enjoy equal protection under the law.

A comprehensive security strategy involves more than preventive and punitive measures. It should also include confidence building to help calm incendiary situatios. Releasing political prisoners, especially women and children, is an important gesture of good will. Lowering the profile of troops by keeping them in their barracks and decreasing the frequency of patrols has a salutary affect. Dismantling bunkers, barricades, check posts and watchtowers in civilian areas also reduces tensions by eliminating the symbols of repression.

Conflict escalation can also be mitigated by reducing the number of troops, especially those that are not organic to the region. Community-based policing is another confidence building technique that helps calm tensions by emphasizing a decentralized structure immersing law enforcement representatives in the community they serve. Prevention is central to their mandate. As problem-solvers, they seek input from the community before disputes escalate into violence. Hiring local residents as local security and deploying them to areas where they have family or tribal affiliations is a facet of community policing. Engagement of affected communities can also obviate the need for corporations to pay the costs of official security services or engage private security firms for site protection, which often creates a culture of impunity with mercenaries acting as though they are above the law.

Civil Society

Civil society—a term for non-governmental organizations (NGOs) including youth groups, student unions, women's associations, trade syndicates, and independent media—can play a pivotal role encouraging moderation as stewards of reform. Civil society groups are is essential bulwark against extremism.

As such, they should be allowed to freely associate and aggregate their interests, which is intrinsic to political mobilization.

In some cases, NGOs evolve into political movements or political parties. This evolution is a healthy indication that the polity is taking responsibility for its future and its country's well-being. It should be welcomed. When governments ban opposition rallies or adopt anti-terror legislation that restricts the space for democratic participation, populations become radicalized and may seek redress outside the political process.

NGOs also promote good governance by holding governments accountable. They liaise with public administrators to influence government decision-making.[45] It is important for government to create conditions conducive to a more active civil society. To this end, legislatures should enact clear procedures for granting identity and enabling financial support to NGOs and not-for-profit organizations. In addition to provisions for tax-deductible contributions, as practiced in the United States, NGOs would also benefit from discounts, refunds, or exemptions from other tariffs, such as customs duties or a value-added tax. Procedures for accepting contributions from non-country residents and foreign governments also require clarity.

NGOs need access to policymakers, but they should not get too close. It is best to maintain independence so they can freely and publicly dissent.

Education

Education is vital if civil society is to act as an antidote to extremism. Not only is education essential for human development. It makes good citizens and functions as a counter-balance to intolerance and hatred. Education for children in their formative years instills self-respect and respect for others. A curriculum emphasizing math and science in primary and secondary schools cultivates critical thinking and protects against intolerance.

Global education goals emphasize access to universal primary education and better-quality education. Education for all can be achieved by reducing the costs of education to poor and working families. A national education system needs adequate infrastructure, trained teachers, and a curriculum that meets UNESCO standards. Access and quality are interdependent. One way to increase attendance is via a community-based development approach that offers incentives encouraging parents to send their children to school.

Schools and teachers are the key. Donors should resource the construction and equipping of schools while making sure that pupils have adequate learning materials and textbooks. Funds are needed improve the status, compensation, working conditions, and professional development for teachers who should be held accountable for their performance. Students also need a responsive learning environment and a teacher-pupil ratio that enhances quality instruction. Investing in the formal educational sector, including information and communications technology, develops an alternative to madrassas and other forms of alternative education that are used to propagandize youth.

Knowledge is not only derived in the classroom. A free and independent media helps inform an active civil society. New communications tools—television, radio, the Internet, satellite communications, cell phones, and text messaging—have dramatically increased the availability of information while mobilizing civic action and political participation. Free speech using new media technologies needs protection. In countries with state-sponsored media, steps should be taken to privatize the media or transform media into public service outlets.

Upholding the principle of free speech does not, however, legitimize hate mongering or use of the media to incite violence. Independent media is expected to lead the struggle against press-censorship and other anti-democratic practices. Its efforts are strengthened by voluntary codes of conduct that promulgate responsible journalistic expression. Procedures are needed for penalizing and potentially closing media outlets when they cross the line and become detrimental to the goals of an open society.

Women and girls are an often-neglected sector of civil society. Their voices need to be heard and tangible steps taken to expand their leadership role and decision-making authority at all levels of society. Education should benefit boys and girls equally. Gender-sensitive education encompassing curricula, teaching methods, and learning environments not only promotes gender equity, it enhances the potential of women in the workforce as well as the political arena. In many Muslim countries, marginalized women still struggle for equal protection under the law. They cannot inherit land, challenge divorce, or exercise their right to political suffrage. Expanding women's economic, political, and civic participation would contribute to the secularization of society and, by improving social harmony, harness the potential of women to stabilize societies that are prone to extremism.

Economic Development

Poverty causes more than human suffering. It is also a source of instability creating potential breeding grounds for violent political expression, extremism, and terrorism. At least half the world's population survives on less than $2 each day. Globalization has lifted millions of people from poverty by integrating them into the world economy. It has also spurred unprecedented volumes of trade that fuel entrepreneurship creating wealth, driving innovation, developing technology, and raising living standards. Since globalization also contributes to inequities and disrupts social cohesion, the challenge is to make globalization fair and equitable.

In accordance with the Monterrey Consensus, developed countries have been called upon to increase levels of foreign aid. More than aid, developing countries emphasize international trade. To expand trade and aid, they must reform their economies, eliminate corruption, reduce tariffs, and adopt transparency. Cross-border trade can be enhanced by working with regional bodies to create a common economic space. Reducing tariffs and providing preferential treatment to goods originating in conflict zones also stimulates production.

More than trade and aid, poor countries need debt relief. National debt forces governments to divert resources to debt service instead of spending money on poverty reduction and other critical needs. Donor financing mechanisms should concentrate on grants rather than loans. Resources must also be delivered faster and more reliably, while respecting the dignity of beneficiaries.

Regardless of donor support, governments must take it on themselves to foster sustainable economic development through investments in transportation, utility, and water systems. In addition to infrastructure and macro-economic reforms, state-sponsored development schemes can maximize benefits by linking investments to "social action plans" that are designed in consultation with affected populations.

Massive regional development schemes, like GAP in Turkey, should be avoided. Investments are more productive when they focus on smaller scale community development. Micro-credit is a boon to small business, especially women-run enterprises. Small-scale quick impact projects, such as land mine clearance, generate employment and promote rural reconstruction in the economies of countries emerging from conflict. Local government is best placed to liaise with the community in order to develop projects that maximize grass-roots benefits.

Local government should have the authority to approve foreign investment, issue import and export regulations, and promulgate rules on maritime and aviation activities. Policies to promote local employment, including hiring preferences for local residents or affirmative action are also desirable. So are hiring preferences for local residents and the employment of civil servants proportional to resident groups.

Regulations on property and land ownership can also help safeguard local populations against exploitation. Mechanisms for collaborative decision-making and revenue sharing between central and local governments help prevent exploitation of natural resources that deprives local residents of economic opportunity and limits the tax base for local government.

Indonesia's National Autonomy Law (NAD) is a useful model. NAD stipulates that resource-rich regions retain a percentage of earnings from extractive industries. To maximize shared benefits, resource developers should publish what they pay so there is a transparent process to calculate the return of revenues. Multinational corporations should also commit a percentage of their gross income for reinvestment in education, health and other social welfare projects. Affected populations, not only local elites with ties to the government, should have input into reinvestment plans in order to ensure that projects are responsive to local needs.

Hardship and resulting extremism can be mitigated by providing a social safety net focusing on the health sector. Though access to health is a fundamental human right, dramatic health disparities exist between developed and developing countries. Nearly all infant deaths occur in the developing world. Millions die each year from malnutrition and preventable waterborne diseases linked to inadequate sanitation and lack of access to clean drinking water. With a gap in life expectancy between developed and developing countries of more than 30 years, the global health system is unprepared to deal with existing problems no less emerging pandemics such as HIV/AIDS, malaria and tuberculosis. Women are especially vulnerable.

A genuine partnership is needed between donors and beneficiaries with the goal of reducing infant and maternal mortality rates, reversing the spread of HIV/AIDS, and eliminating gender disparities. Practical measures include immunization, breast-feeding, rehydration for diarrhea, anti-malarial drugs, bed nets, lower pricesfor and enhanced access to drugs. These measures, however, are likely to have little effect without steps to improve access to health care. Official development assistance and private philanthropy can help develop community and national health systems by expanding infrastructure, training, and professional development.

Humanitarian Assistance

The same principle of decentralization applies to humanitarian assistance, which is most effective when it bypasses the central government and gets channeled through local governments and NGOs. A decentralized approach also helps build NGO capacity thereby equipping civil society with the tools to oversee good governance and encourage stakeholder participation.

Giving food and housing allowances directly to community organizations not only addresses their immediate requirements. It also circumvents government officials who might steal contributions from donors or manipulate contributions for political purposes. Shielding donors from political manipulation can also be accomplished by setting up private grass-roots social service organizations directly linking donors with service providers.

In the event that assistance is suspended for political reasons, loopholes can be carved out so that humanitarian projects still receive support. Direct assistance to beneficiaries was effective in Palestine where, after Hamas took control of the PA, donors issued family stipends and worked with independent NGOs rather than provide grants to the Hamas-led government. It is important to sustain humanitarian assistance lest affected populations become reliant on Islamist charities. Controls are needed for humanitarian agencies affiliated with sectarian movements, be they Islamic or other, in order to separate proselytizing from their life-saving work.

Return and resettlement are key components of humanitarian assistance for persons displaced by conflict. More than food and shelter, displaced persons look to the international community to create conditions enabling their safe return home and eliminate conditions giving rise to conflict in the first place. As seen in Kashmir, reuniting "partition families" is part and parcel of this effort. Other components include a property claims and compensation process for homes, businesses, or agricultural lands that have been lost or destroyed. So that beneficiaries can restore normalcy and dignity to their lives, resettlement strategies should also incorporate plans for job creation and strategies for transitioning from relief to development.

Though refugee flows usually involve those fleeing conflict, population transfers may also include persons whom the government moves into a conflict zone in order to change the ethnic balance of a region with the goal of advancing its political objective. For example, Javanese transmigrants were relocated to Aceh in order to shift the province's demography and thereby dilute demands for independence. This practice should be avoided. It fuels conflict and inevitably leads to reprisals by the indigenous population against the transmigrant group.

After the 2004 tsunami, more than $13 billion was provided for reconstruction to Acehnese and other tsunami-affected areas. Several lessons were learned from the recovery effort. Assistance agencies should rely on local partners at every stage of design and implementation. Emergency assistance can be an important tool for peacebuilding if it engages former adversaries in collaborative efforts. Humanitarian assistance can also used to consolidate peace agreements. Accords typically include a peace dividend aimed at demonstrating immediate benefits and thus creating conditions for sustainable peace. It is important to minimize the considerable lag that arises between signing of an accord, convening a donor's conference, collecting and then delivering pledges.

Donor countries, such as the United States, should contribute towards a post-conflict stabilization fund making resources available in timely fashion. The recently established United Nations Peacebuilding Commission initially focused on two target countries in Africa. Norway, which is a primary sponsor of the Commission, and other supporters should finance an emergency stand-by fund for other war-torn countries in different geographic regions.

Humanitarian assistance does not occur in a vacuum. Viewing humanitarian assistance through a conflict prevention lens fulfills the dual purpose of addressing basic needs and promoting political goals such as stabilization, which is a necessary condition for breaking the cycle of violence and countering extremism.

Multilateralism vs. Unilateralism

To lead a team, you must know how to be a team player. To inspire people or nations to follow you, you must have a reputation for moral uprightness, wisdom, and veracity. To retain authority, you must demonstrate the capacity to reward as well as to punish, and you have to track up a record of success. To sustain the loyalty of followers, you must be loyal to them, and considerate of their views and interests as well as your own. To hold other peoples or nations to rules, you must be prepared to follow them too. We all know these things. Why don't we act accordingly?[46]

Ambassador Chas W. Freeman (USFS, Ret.)—January 6, 2007

Engaging multilateral partners in cooperation is always preferable but, when coercion or confrontation is necessary, the United States must not hestitate or shy away from acting on its own. Some goals are, however, more realizable when the United States acts in concert with other countries. For example, partnerships can more effectively restrict financial transfers, limit arms flows, track weapons of mass destruction, and seal borders to preventing holy warriors from reaching the battlefield.

Multilateralism relies on diplomacy and compromise is the core of diplomacy. Concessions are not made solely for the sake of generating goodwill. Nor are favors and perks extended to countries just so they do America's bidding. Diplomacy is about convincing countries that they have something to gain from collaborative efforts.

Should United States ever refuse contact with another country? On one side of the debate are those who insist that the United States should place equal importance on engaging with its adversaries as its friends. They point out that even during the most bitter days of the Cold War, the United States maintained diplomatic relations with the Soviet Union and interacted with Soviet officials.

Those on the other side point out that the United States is at war and should not engage incorrigible and irredeemable adversaries. They believe it is counter-intuitive to collaborate with rogue regimes, or extremist groups especially when it comes to spreading democracy and free markets. In any case steely eyed realism is necessary.

Theory to Practice

This theoretical debate played out in real time during deliberations by the Bush administration on whether to engage with Syria and Iran. Proponents of engagement—such as the Baker-Hamilton Commission—argued that, precisely because of their nefarious role, Syria and Iran have the capacity to make a positive contribution in Iraq and elsewhere (e.g., Lebanon and Palestine). Talking to them is the only way to explore areas where respective national interests overlap.

Detractors in the Bush administration advocate regime change over policies aimed at behavioral change. Averse to rewarding Syria and Iran in exchange for their cooperation, they maintain that steadfast foes would never voluntarily help advance U.S. goals in the Middle East, much less marginalize Hezbollah and Hamas. They are deeply skeptical about diplomacy insisting that military action is the only way to conform rogue regimes like Syria and Iran to international agreements and norms.

After Rafik Hariri's assassination in 2005, Bush withdrew the U.S. ambassador to Damascus and the United States was subsequently represented by a *chargé d'affaires*. The decision to downgrade diplomatic representation was also a protest of Syria's failure to restrict the flow of arms, money, and foreign fighters into Iraq. However, isolating Syria only aggravated problems. As Syria's centrally planned economy struggled to recover from years of neglect, Iran made strategic and significant investments in auto and cement plants, as well as refineries and electricity projects in Syria. The decision to isolate Syria economically deepened ties between Iran and Syria thereby increasing Iran's influence in the region. Syria also turned to North Korea for assistance developing a nuclear processing program.

Rather than isolation, a more effective approach would be to recognize that Syria and Iran are very different countries with different interests. Syrians are 80 percent Arab Sunni. Bashar Al Assed is Alawite, a small Shi'a sect. He is wary of antagonizing Syria's Sunni majority by appearing too close to Iran, a country whose population is Persian and Shi'a. In this light, the goal of the United States should be to drive a wedge between Iran and Syria, which is more pragmatic than ideological approach. Flipping Syria could potentially stop its support for insurgents in Iraq, reduce tensions in Lebanon, and encourage Syria to use its influence with Hamas.

Bashar Al Assad will not be helpful out of the goodness of his heart. Syria will want something for its cooperation. It is likely to demand that the U.S. leverage its relations with Israel to promote a comprehensive Middle East peace that would include return of the Golan Heights. Rather than continue a policy of isolating Syria, that has proven ineffective, US officials would be well advised to talk with their Syrian counterparts in order to explore the benefits and costs of engagement.

Outreach to Syria can also be done through third parties and messages sent via conduits. Turkey has recently played a helpful mediation role. Many Arab leaders share the dismay of the United States over Syria's ties to Iran and its role in Lebanon. Saudi Arabia in particular has championed putting pressure on Syria. Arab states would normally have complained when the United States sent warships near to Lebanese waters, but they welcomed the strong signal the flotilla sent to Damascus. In an extraordinary move, Egypt, Jordan, and Saudi Arabia intimated that they might stay away from the 2008 Arab League Summit to protest Syria's efforts to create a power vacuum in Lebanon.

Engaging Iran is more problematic. Iran has been an iconic foe of the United States since the 1979 seizure of U.S. embassy personnel in Tehran. Repeated opportunities for rapprochement have been missed by both sides. The climate of U.S.-Iran relations shifted after 9/11. Iran turned a blind eye when U.S. warplanes accessed its air space in operations against the Taliban. Iranian leaders suggested they would allow search and rescue missions for American pilots downed on Iranian territory. The United States sponsored the overland transport of supplies by the World Food Program through Iran to Afghanistan. Iran and the United States worked together through the Bonn process that established post-Taliban governance in Afghanistan.

During the run-up to the war in Iraq, the United States and Iran also shared common goals. Both were adamant about preserving Iraq's territorial integrity. Both opposed vigilantism and revenge-taking. And both wanted to ensure that Iraq's ethnic and religious groups, disenfranchised for decades under the Ba'ath Party, secured their political and cultural rights in a post-Saddam era. Iran's leaders were delighted that U.S. troops and treasure were used to eliminate their chief regional rivals—Mullah Omar in Afghanistan and Saddam Hussein in Iraq.

Any chance to overcome deep and historic enmities between the United States and Iran was lost when Bush included Iran in his axis of evil. In the months after his January 2003 State of the Union address, Bush administration officials repeatedly accused Iran of harboring Al Qaeda leaders. U.S. officials also accused Iran of sponsoring the Riyadh bombing of May 11, 2003. Mahmoud Ahmedinejad, a relative unknown, rose to the presidency of Iran by castigating America's hegemonic ambitions in the region and by rallying popular support against Israel.

No greater threat to global peace and security exists than Iran under Ahmedinejad. He crossed the line by ignoring concerns of the international community and pursuing an enrichment program to develop Iran's nuclear capabilities. Ahmedinejad maintains that there was no Holocaust but threatens that there will be one. Iran remains an active state sponsor of terror supporting Hamas and Islamic Jihad in Palestine, Hezbollah in Lebanon, and Shi'a groups in Iraq.

By late 2006, Ahmedinejad appeared to have over-reached. Iranians proved to be more interested in economic development than Ahmedinejad's relentless pursuit of nuclear technology. Investors grew hesitant in light of Iran's worsening nuclear dispute with the International Atomic Energy Agency. Angered by the purge of professors and diminished academic freedoms, university students protested Ahmedinejad's visits to campus. Signaling popular discontent, Ahmedinejad's candidates were swamped in municipal elections.

When Iran refused to compromise on its nuclear program, the UN Security Council adopted Resolution 1737 (December 23, 2006). As of this writing, the UNSC has adopted three sanctions resolutions. The most recent urges states to inspect Iranian cargo ships and aircraft if they are suspected of bearing nuclear-related materials and equipment.

The United States implemented a variety of diplomatic strategies designed to ratchet up pressure on Ahmedinejad. In addition to UN-backed sanctions, the United States pressured governments and businesses to abandon contact with individuals and organizations involved in Iran's missile and nuclear programs. The U.S. Treasury Department imposed financial penalties on international banks doing business with targeted individuals and organizations. Extraordinary persuasion was used to convince banks from Europe and Asia to take steps against Iran outside of those required by the Security Council.

Barring U.S. financial institutions from conducting dollar-denominated transactions with Melli, Sepah, and Saderat, state-owned Iranian banks, had a chilling affect worldwide. UBS and Credit Suisse suspended transactions with Iran, and the Japan Bank for International Cooperation froze its lending program pending progress on nuclear negotiations. The United States also encouraged governments and businesses to break off contact with bodies it accused of involvement in terror, such as the Iranian Revolutionary Guard Corps (IRGC), which operates a vast network of telecommunications, construction, and energy firms. The U.S. Congress overwhelmingly passed a resolution identifying the IRGC as a terrorist organization.

When Vice President Dick Cheney visited Riyadh in January 2006, he discussed with King Abdullah a plan to vastly increase the Kingdom's oil production. The plan sought to create a controlled slide in oil prices that would wreak havoc on Iran's economy, which relies heavily on oil revenues. Despite increases in the Kingdom's crude production, oil prices have continued to spiral.

Iran is at a fork in the road. The Iranian leadership should be presented with a clear strategic choice: it can abide by international norms or entrench Iran's status as an international pariah. Verifiable steps towards the former should be rewarded; the latter would meet ever more stringent sanctions. Hawks in the Bush administration disparaged diplomacy with Iran, maintaining that military action leading to regime change was the only way to compel a behavioral change in the regime. This view was echoed by Israel. officials with Ehud Olmert taking an increasingly hardline as his political and legal problems worsened.

U.S. policies towards Iran cannot be static. They must be allowed to evolve giving space for discussion that advances the possibility of collaboration when national interests converge. The United States should never pursue a policy of engagement with Iran or any other rogue state solely for engagement's sake. However, the United States should explore finite arrangements that advance America's interests when U.S. and Iranian interests overlap. This can be done by sending a high-level envoy to Iran to convey benchmarks for progress linked to diplomatic and economic rewards. When interests do not overlap or when Iran acts outside the boundary of international norms, the United States should work multilaterally so that Iran pays a steep price for ignoring the will of the international community.

Notes

1. In Fiscal year 2006, the United States defense budget was $441.5 billion, 3.6 percent of the U.S. economy and, according to Amb. Chas W. Freeman (USFS, Ret.), more than the combined military expenditures of all other 192 countries in the world. U.S. national security expenditures are $729 billion, 5.7 percent of GDP when factoring in Homeland Security, intelligence, and other security-related costs.
2. en.wikipedia.org/wiki/Islamist
3. John L. Esposito. *Unholy War.* Oxford University Press. 2002. p. 51.
4. Statement of the Sixteenth Islamic Fiqh Council of the World Muslim League. Mecca. January 10, 2002.
5. Qur'an (2:294).
6. Qur'an (61:9).
7. Qur'an (2:191).
8. The Qur'an. Surah 9, Verse 41 (Al-Tawbah).
9. John L. Esposito. *Unholy War.* Oxford University Press. 2002. p. 61.IRA
10. *CNN Profile*: People in the News. Ayman Al Zawahiri. August 30, 2005.
11. Christopher M. Blanchard. Al Qaeda: Statements and Evolving Ideology. *The Congressional Research Service.* June 20, 2005.

12.   John Kifner. "Russian school siege brings soul-searching and denunciations in the Muslim world." *The International Herald Tribune*. September 10, 2004. p. 3.

13.   Emram Qureshi. *The New York Times* (editorial). "The Islam the Riots Drowned Out." February 12, 2006. p. 15.

14.   *Qur'an* (42:40).

15.   Statement of the Sixteenth Islamic Fiqh Council of the World Muslim League. Mecca. January 10, 2002.

16.   *Qur'an* (2:190).

17.   *Qur'an* (17:33).

18.   *Qur'an* (4:29).

19.   *Qur'an* (49:13).

20.   U.S. National Security Strategy. September 2002. p. 15.

21.   George W. Bush. Remarks to the Nation. December 9, 2005.

22.   National Security Strategy. September 2002. p. 16.

23.   Charter of the United Nations. Article 2. Item 4.

24.   Amos Guiora. "Terrorism on trial: Targeted Killings as an Act of Self-Defense." Presented at the War Crimes Research Symposium at Case Western Reserve University School of Law, sponsored by the Frederick K. Cox International Law Center. October 8, 2004.

25.   ICRC commentary on the First Geneva Convention.

26.   Josh Meyer and Greg Miller. *The Los Angeles Times*. "U.S. Secretly Tracks Global Bank Data." June 23, 2006. p. 1.

27.   In September 2001, fewer than a dozen States were parties to all 12 international conventions and protocols (Letter of 15 July 2003 - S/2003/710).

28.   Before enacting punitive measures, it is important to distinguish between countries that make a good faith to meet requirements but fail because they lack capacity and countries that fall short because they fundamentally oppose the CTC's mandate.

29.   Lincoln A. Mitchell and David L. Phillips. "Enhancing Democracy Assistance." The National Committee on American Foreign Policy, the Atlantic Council of the United States and the Arnold A. Saltzman Institute of War and Peace Studies at Columbia University. January 2008.

30.   Lincoln A. Mitchell and David L. Phillips. "Enhancing Democracy Assistance." The National Committee on American Foreign Policy, the Atlantic Council of the United States and the Arnold A. Saltzman Institute of War and Peace Studies at Columbia University. January 2008.

31.   Draws from the Founding Statement of Principles and Objectives of the National Endowment for Democracy.

32.   International Center for Transitional Justice. Annual Report. 2002.

33.   John Paul Lederach. *Building Peace: Sustainable Reconciliation in Divided Societies*. U.S. Institute of Peace Press. 1997.

34.   This section draws from *Unsilencing the Past* by David L. Phillips. Berghahn Books. 2005.pp. 91-99.

35.   Such as the UN Charter, the International Covenant on Civil and Political Rights (CCPR), the International Covenant on Economic, Social and Cultural Rights (CESCR), and the International Convention on the Elimination of all Forms of Racial Discrimination (CERD).

36.   Article 27.

37.   HRC, General Comment 23, (1994) (GC#23), Para 3.

38.   CCPR, Article 2.2, CESCR, Article 1.2 Minority Rights Declaration.

39.   CERD Article 2.

40.   CCPR Article 2.3.

41.   See generally, Geoff Gilbert, "Autonomy and Minority Groups: A Right in International Law" *35 Cornell Int'l L.J.* 307 (2002); Philip Alston "Peoples' Rights: Their Rise and Fall" in (P. Alston ed.) *Peoples' Rights* (2001).

42.   Examples are Greenland, Hong Kong, Mindanao, and South Tyrol.

43.   For example, India.

44.   UN General Assembly Resolution 1541 (1960).

45.   This section draws on *Balkans 2010*. The Council on Foreign Relations. 2002. The author was a task force member and prepared the section on civil society.

46.   Remarks by Amb. Chas W. Freeman (USFS Ret.). Williamsburg, Virginia. January 6, 2007.

Index